D1320513

AN OUTLINE

of

THE LAW OF PRODUCT LIABILITY

and

CONSUMER PROTECTION

BY

RONALD IRVING

SBN 0 85992 166 2

Published by
BARRY ROSE (Publishers) Ltd
Chichester, West Sussex
Printed by
Adams & Sons (Printers) Ltd
East Street, Hereford

AN OUTLINE

OF

THE LAW AND PRODUCT LIABILITY

AND

CONSUMER PROTECTION

by

RONALD IRVING

CONTENTS

CHAPTER VII — BUYING AT AUCTION

CHAPTER XXII — TAKING THE TRADER TO COURT

CHAPTER I

THE CONSUMER TRANSACTION

The Civil Law. A customer who has a complaint against a shop or manufacturer is amply protected both by the civil and the criminal courts. To bring a civil claim it is for the consumer to go to the county court and issue a summons. He simply writes out the details of his complaint on a printed form called "particulars of claim". Once he has filled in the form and paid the appropriate fee, the court will issue a summons against the trader.

The disadvantage of a civil claim is the trouble and expense. Going to court is very much a last resort and is seldom worthwhile unless a considerable sum is involved. Even after the court has given judgment in his favour the consumer may still not get his money. For example, the trader may go out of business.

To meet this kind of situation the Consumer Credit Act, 1974, Section 75, makes the organisation which provides the consumer with credit liable for the trader who defaults. Thus lenders such as credit card companies must now compensate the consumer in respect of any retailer on their list who fails to supply satisfactory goods or services. (see page 240).

A consumer who is of limited means may be eligible for low-cost or even completely free legal aid. Application forms for legal aid are available at advice centres and solicitors' offices. There will usually be a delay of some weeks while the local Legal Aid Area Committee considers his application. They will appoint a solicitor to handle the claim on the consumer's behalf, if he does not know one.

Prior to 1975 a consumer was deterred from pursuing a court claim against a trader because of the risk that if he lost the case he might have to pay heavy legal costs. Now a consumer risks nothing except the original court fee if he loses his case. No legal costs can be awarded against him, provided he limits his claim to £200.

Compensation through the Criminal Law

A more important development has been the extension of the criminal law to provide consumer protection, eg The Weights and Measures Act 1963. The advantage to the individual consumer is that, where a trader infringes the criminal law, it is the State and not the consumer himself which has the task and expense of initiating legal proceedings.

Thus where a supplier gives misleading information, the local Trading Standards Officer may prosecute him in the magistrates' court under the Trade Descriptions Act 1968, provided the consumer lodges a complaint promptly. Normally the Trading Standards Officer has one year in which to institute a prosecution where misleading information is contained in a document but this is cut to six months if it is merely spoken, eg where the consumer is told something misleading in the shop or on the telephone.

Prosecution is also possible for various offences under the Consumer Credit Act 1974. Sometimes too, the supplier may be prosecuted for breach of an order made under the Fair Trading Act 1973, prohibiting an unfair trade practice.

"No Refunds"

One example is the order which prohibits shops displaying notices which purport to take away consumers' legal rights under the Sale of Goods Act. Thus it is a criminal offence for a shop to display a notice saying, eg "No refunds in any circumstances" because this implies that no refund can be claimed where the article bought is defective.

Powers of Criminal Courts

The chief object of a prosecution is to impose a penalty, either a fine or imprisonment, on the offender. Now, in addition, the Powers of Criminal Courts Act 1973, Section 35, enables a criminal court to award up to £400 compensation to any individual loser. Thus, when a trader is convicted, the court can order him also to pay compensation to any person who has suffered loss as a result of the offence.

It is significant that this Act specifically authorises the court to award compensation although the amount awarded **might not be recoverable as damages in a civil action.** The result is that many statutes whose primary object is punishing the trader can now give the consumer a financial benefit.

Where the court takes into consideration additional offences in determining sentence, it can allow compensation in respect of those offences too, to all customers who have suffered loss, eg where a tour operator has attracted holiday-makers by means of a misleading description in his brochure.

These powers are likely to be of increasing importance to consumers whose loss is too small to be worth pursuing by civil action in the county court. Indirectly, prosecution by the Trading Standards Officer thus provides a quick and easy remedy for the consumer.

The advantages are that:
- (a) the threat of prosecution may persuade the supplier to offer compensation;
- (b) if the Trading Standards Officer prosecutes the supplier, this will not involve the consumer in any expense;
- (c) the magistrates' court can, as well as fining the supplier, order compensation to be paid to the consumer.

The moral is that a disappointed consumer should complain in the first place to the Trading Standards Officer at the local town hall. Even if this officer does not think the supplier has broken the criminal law, he will be able to advise on the best course of action.

Contractual Nature of a Consumer Transaction

Every consumer transaction involves a legal contract. A contract is an agreement whereby each party undertakes to do something for the benefit of the other. In the case of a sale, the customer who asks for or orders an article is making an offer to buy it at the price marked. The retailer, by accepting this offer, clinches the contract. Such an agreement is binding and imposes important legal obligations on both supplier and consumer.

It may be noted an agreement need not be in writing to impose legal obligations on both consumer and trader. Thus I can agree over the telephone to buy a Rolls Royce for £20,000. Once I have promised to buy and the seller has promised to sell at an agreed price, our agreement constitutes a legally enforceable contract, although made by word of mouth only. However, if a credit transaction is envisaged, writing would generally be necessary.

When a Contract is binding

The commercial world is made up of myriads of agreements, each called "a contract". In the course of a normal day the ordinary person will readily enter into half-a-dozen contracts. Shopping, traveling by bus or train (provided we remember to pay), or having lunch in a restaurant are all transactions involving a binding contract which is legally enforceable. In each it is assumed that those agreeing intend to enter into a legal relationship which cannot be altered by a change of mind or for some frivolous reason, although there are certain exceptions, such as doorstep selling, where the householder is protected by a statutory, cooling-off period.

24

Subject to Contract

Another important exception arises where two people come to a provisional agreement but do not intend it to have legal effect until a formal or final contract is drawn up and signed. A person who wishes to preserve his right to withdraw should make it clear that he is agreeing "subect to contract".

By using these words he leaves himself an escape route. For example, he may wish to take the advice of a lawyer or other experts before finally clinching the deal. This is commonly the case where someone wishes to buy a house or land. Here a signed letter can constitute a binding contract unless the person signing specifically states that the terms agreed are "subject to contract". Without these words there is a basic presumption in every commercial transaction that those agreeing intend to establish a binding legal relationship.

Unfair Terms

Once you have made a contract you cannot alter any of the terms agreed without the consent of the other party. What if some of the terms are unfair? In the case of exemption clauses a consumer may be able to claim the protection of the Unfair Contract Terms Act 1977. This Act gives a judge the power to strike out of the agreement exemption clauses which are loaded in favour of the trader against the consumer. Accordingly the judge can disregard any term which unfairly restricts the trader's liability. But this Act does not permit a judge to reopen a contract merely on the ground that it contains "unfair terms", unless those terms seek to exempt the trader from liability. On the other hand, extortionate credit terms, for example, can be set aside by the judge under the Consumer Credit Act 1974.

Special Terms

A contract of sale may incorporate special terms or

conditions. For example, the following notice may be displayed in a shop:

"If you can buy more cheaply elsewhere anything you
have just bought from us we will refund the difference."

Such a notice will govern all items sold in the shop. A consumer who sees an article he has just bought offered more cheaply elsewhere is entitled to sue for the amount over-paid.

The general rules of sale can be altered by special agreement. Thus the normal rule is that it is not the seller's obligation to deliver goods to the buyer's home. Normally it is the buyer's duty to collect what he has bought (Sale of Goods Act 1979, Section 29(2)). Only if the seller has expressly agreed to do so, or it is his standard trade practice will he be obliged to transport the goods to his customer's address.

Similarly a sign declaring: "Money back if not completely satisfied" will entitle a consumer to return an article which he does not like. Normally the right to a refund would be limited to articles which are actually defective.

Guarantees

Guarantees given by retailers are examples of special terms. Such terms cannot diminish the rights given to consumers given by the Sale of Goods Act (discussed in Chapter II.) They can only add to them. For example a shop which sells "indestructible" rubber toys may guarantee them for 10 years. An expert might say that such items will have an average life expectancy with normal wear and tear of two years. Even so, the shopkeeper would be obliged to refund a proportionate part of the price if the article lasted only three years, although this **exceeds** his liability under the Sale of Goods Act.

Many car retailers offer a guarantee or warranty (or "mechanical breakdown insurance") for, say, one year, usually at an extra charge. If so, this will be additional

to their legal guarantees under this Act (see p 36).
(As to manufacturers' guarantees see page 83)

Contracts which are not binding in Law

Agreements "binding in honour only" can present a trap
for the unwary. Oddly enough, every day millions of people
enter into "honour" contracts in which their legal rights are
specifically excluded. Take promoters of the football pools.
Over the years a long line of punters have come to grief on
this rock of "honour", when trying to sue pool promoters,
usually for losing their winning coupon. So far, the
promoters have always won, relying on their "honour
clause" which gives them the right to dishonour any coupon
at choice.

As one judge put it "He (the punter) has got to trust the
defendants and if something goes wrong, it is his funeral,
not theirs".

Certainly there are many arrangements made in daily life
which are not intended to have any legal effect at all. An
invitation to dinner cancelled at the last moment may cause
great inconvenience. It may even have caused the person
invited to decline an important business opportunity.
Again, a man may travel many miles to attend an auction
or a charitable garden party which the organisers have
failed to tell him they were calling off. No one would
imagine for a moment that these situations would have
legal consequences.

Offer and Acceptance in a Self-service Shop

For a contract to exist in law, there must be an "offer"
and an acceptance of that offer. In a self-service shop
the customer selects those articles he wants from the
shelves and puts them in his wire basket which he then
carries to the cash desk. The cashier scrutinises the articles,

adds up their total price and asks the customer for payment. The law is that by presenting the articles to the cashier the customer makes an offer to buy each at the price marked. The cashier accepts his offer to buy and the sale is finalised when the cashier receives his cheque, credit card or money. Upon payment the buyer becomes their owner.

Suppose one of the articles on display is marked at a mistakenly low price. Even if the customer appreciates this, the sale is still valid once the shop has accepted his offer to buy it at the price marked. (See further page 285)

Legal Nature of a Sale

Most consumer transactions involve a sale, ie a transfer of ownership of goods either for cash or on credit. However, consumers often take articles on a rental basis only, eg tv rental where ownership is never transferred. Where the trader provides only a service, eg repairs, no sale will generally be involved.

Strictly, a hire-purchase agreement is not a sale because although the hirer has an option to buy at the end of the hiring period the hirer is not **obliged** to buy. Moreover, if the hirer defaults, the finance company becomes entitled to have the goods back. Contrast a **credit sale** where the buyer gets ownership from the outset and only payment is deferred.

Transfer of Ownership

A sale is "a contract whereby the seller transfers or agrees to transfer . . . goods to the buyer (consumer) for a . . . price". The transfer of ownership is usually immediate as in the case of a sale of a specific article over the shop counter where the exchange of money for goods is simultaneous. Ownership usually passes to the buyer and the sale is legally binding despite the fact that:

   (i) delivery of the item is postponed;

   (ii) payment is postponed;

   (iii) both payment and delivery are postponed.

28

Should a thief run into the shop and steal the article purchased just as the customer is waiting for change, it would be the customer's loss not the shop's, although it was still lying on the cash desk and had not been placed in the customer's bag. Similarly, articles left in the care of the shop after purchase are the responsibility of the buyer.

NOTE: ON A SALE OWNERSHIP IS TRANSFERRED IMMEDIATELY AND SO IS THE RISK OF DAMAGE.

Responsibility of buyer where goods are damaged after agreement for sale
Once a person agrees to buy, say, a second-hand car, it becomes that person's property at once although naturally the dealer is entitled to retain possession of it until the price is paid.

Suppose that before the buyer can collect the car it is burnt out in a fire. The loss would be the buyer's because the ownership has been transferred, although it has not yet been paid for. Of course, if the fire started or the car is damaged owing to the carelessness of an employee of the shop, then the shop will have to stand the loss.

The moral of this situation is that the buyer should take out insurance at once, even though a deposit has not been paid for the car. Again, the buyer may be allowed to take the car before his cheque is cleared or payment made and while parked outside the shop it is struck by an unknown vehicle. Here too, the loss would fall on the buyer.

Storage by the seller
A person who has agreed to buy, say, a quantity of wine, could lose out should the shopkeeper go bankrupt while storing it. The customer should, before leaving the shop, insist on seeing that the crates, etc, are put on one side and clearly marked with the buyer's name; otherwise

ownership will not pass to the customer. In practice, leaving goods bought with the seller for any length of time after purchase is unwise.

Articles on Display
The display of an article in a shop window is not an offer to sell it. Even though the price is clearly stated, the customer cannot in law insist on buying it.

For example, a building society may display a variety of goods to catch the eye. A prospective customer could not object to being referred to the original supplier.

Suppose someone sees an attractive fur coat at a very reasonable price in a furrier's window. Upon inquiring, the prospective buyer is told the coat has already been sold. Can the would-be purchaser insist on having an identical coat at the same price? He cannot.

Nevertheless by displaying the coat, the furrier may have committed an offence under the Trade Descriptions Act 1968, if he demands a higher price than shown in the window. "A person exposing goods for supply shall be deemed to offer to supply them." (Section 6). "If any person offering to supply any goods gives any indication that the goods are being offered at a price less than that at which they are in fact being offered, such person shall be guilty of an offence." (Section 11(2)).

If satisfied that the shop has committed an offence under the Act, the Court could order it to pay the thwarted customer compensation.

Consumer Choice
Is the seller within his rights in preventing a customer selecting or insisting on having the best food on display? Obviously as a shopper I cannot compel the barrow boy to deal with me at all. He can just ignore me and leave me standing there if he chooses. But if he refuses to serve a shopper on request with fruit or vegetables of the same

30

quality as those displayed at the price marked up, he will be committing an offence.

A disgruntled shopper should notify the Trading Standards Office at the local town hall and the likelihood is that the stall-holder will be prosecuted. What he has done constitutes a false indication as to price and is contrary to Section 11 of the Trade Descriptions Act.

This prevents shopkeepers offering to supply goods by displaying them at a certain price and then refusing to let the customer have them at that price. So if he refuses to sell to a housewife apples or pears as good as those on display at the price indicated, he commits an offence.

All market stall-holders and street traders must display their prices. If they do not, the maximum fine is £400 at the local magistrates' court.

In Wellingborough some years ago housewives saw an advertisement in the local paper offering tomatoes at 10p a pound but when they got to the shop they found it was asking 12p a pound. The local Trading Standards Officer was informed and the shopkeeper was told that he had to sell them at the price advertised or risk a fine.

Quality

What quality is the housewife entitled to when she goes shopping for fruit and vegetables? Supposing she asks for two pounds of apples and the shopkeeper serves her, not from the front where the best fruit is displayed, but from the back where she cannot see what he is putting into the bag. The law protects the housewife by clearly stating that every apple he puts into the bag for her must be sound and of reasonable quality.

The Sale of Goods Act 1979 says that an item is of "merchantable" quality only if it is as **fit for its purpose** (in this case to be eaten!) as is reasonable to expect, having regard to all the circumstances. So a housewife has the right to reject every item which is not up to standard. She need not accept any apple, part of which is so bruised that it has to be cut away before it can be eaten. Sellers are **not** entitled to say "You must take the good with the bad".

Examination
Is the housewife obliged in law to examine the contents of the paper bag when it is handed to her before she leaves the shop? If she **does** look inside to see the quality of what she has been given and makes no complaint before leaving, she is stuck with those items which she can see are obviously bruised or over-ripe. However, where she does not look into the bag until she gets home because she trusts the shopkeeper, she is entitled to bring back any substandard item. Of course anyone buying a melon would be wise to examine it before leaving the shop. If it seems over-ripe (or even under-ripe) we may reject it then and there.

Exchanging Goods
Since contracts to buy are binding, it follows that once an article has been purchased the customer has no automatic right to exchange it or return it. He can demand his money back only in the following cases:
(a) the item turns out to be defective, ie unfit for its purpose or otherwise not up to standard;
(b) the retailer expressly states that the customer may exchange or return the item purchased or this is contained in a notice as the declared policy of the shop.
Where the sales assistant assures the buyer that any item may be exchanged or returned, eg if it does not fit, this right will then become a term of the contract of sale. The article must be returned within the time fixed or within a reasonable time. In the meantime it is the buyer's responsibility if it is lost or damaged.

Credit Notes
The shop cannot insist on the consumer accepting a credit

note for a faulty item instead of a refund and a wise customer will insist on cash. Reputable shops often have a special refund department. A consumer who accepts a credit note instead of a cash refund will have to use it in the same shop. There may be difficulty in getting them to cash it but there is nothing in law to prevent the customer later insisting on cash in exchange for the credit note.

Sales "On approval"

English law regards "Delivery on sale or return" or "on trial" or "on approval" as having the same meaning.

Where one of these phrases is used the person who orders the article has an open **option** to buy or not at the stated price.

The buyer becomes the owner:

(i) when he signifies his approval or acceptance to the seller;

(ii) if he does any other act adopting the transaction, eg uses the article excessively;

(iii) if a time has been fixed for its return, on the expiration of such time;

(iv) if no time has been fixed for its return and the buyer does not state he rejects it, after the expiration of a reasonable time. What is a reasonable time is a question of fact and depends upon the circumstances.

During the trial period the **buyer is not responsible** for loss or damage to the article save where this is due to his fault. In *Elphick v. Barnes* (1880) a horse was taken on trial for eight days. It died on the third day through no fault of the buyer. The court held that it was at the seller's risk so that he could not claim payment from the buyer.

The buyer will not have the risk of accidental loss or damage unless the seller expressly stipulates this.

Where an article taken on approval is returned damaged through the **buyer's fault** he must pay the cost of repair. Once

33

the prospective buyer decides not to exercise his option to buy he must return the goods. If he fails to do so he will be liable for any loss howsoever caused.

Goods mistakenly delivered

"If I order from a wine merchant 12 bottles of whisky at so much a bottle and he sends me 10 bottles of whisky and two of brandy and I accept them, I must pay a reasonable price for the brandy." (Lord Atkin.)

In these circumstances the law implies a contract to buy the articles in question. On the other hand a consumer cannot be compelled to pay for something he has not ordered and does not want. (See Inertia Selling, p 65)

CHAPTER II

LIABILITY OF SELLER FOR DEFECTS

The responsibility for any defect in an article sold always lies with the seller (retailer). Although the original fault is generally the manufacturer's, the retailer has to put it right.

This liability of the retailer to the consumer arises under the Sale of Goods Act. It is a strict liability. This means that it will be no excuse for the retailer to show that he has exercised all reasonable care to prevent the defect.

The consumer does not have to establish that the seller was negligent or in any way at fault. He need only satisfy the judge there is a defect in the article and will be awarded compensation. He does not have to show, for example, that the seller ought to have known about the defect.

The distinction between the liability of the seller and that of the manufacturer is illustrated by the case of a doctor whose 18-month-old car broke down after it was out of guarantee. The garage did the necessary repairs and sent him a bill for over £200, explaining that the breakdown was due to a fault in manufacture. A small part had accidentally fallen into the engine during assembly and in due course found its way into the oil pump which was consequently damaged.

Although the car was no longer under guarantee the manufacturers admitted a manufacturing fault and agreed to pay 75% of the cost of repairs. But in law it was the retailer who had sold the doctor the car who was responsible under the Sale of Goods Act to put right the defect. The doctor was advised to sue the retailer, whereupon he received the full cost of the repairs.

The retailer's "obligation without fault" under the Sale

35

of Goods Act is the subject of this chapter. How the manufacturer may also be liable under a document of guarantee is discussed in Chapter IV. So too when the manufacturer can be responsible should the consumer be injured owing to a fault in the product.

Retailer is strictly liable for Defective Goods

Every shop, whether it sells for cash, on hire purchase or credit, is deemed in law to guarantee what it sells. This guarantee is not in writing but implied by the Sale of Goods Act 1979, ss. 13, 14 & 15. Where the retailer gives a written guarantee it cannot in any way reduce the guarantee implied by the Act: it can only add to the protection the consumer already gets under the Act.

The Sale of Goods Act guarantee covers:
1. the quality of the article sold
2. its fitness for any particular purpose
3. the correctness of its description
4. its conformity with any sample given or shown.

The Unfair Contract Terms Act 1977 prevents the seller avoiding this implied guarantee towards consumers. (Whether an exclusion clause in a sale agreement can deprive a **business** customer of this guarantee depends on the test of reasonableness (see Chapter VIII).)

It is the duty of the retailer himself to replace or repair any defective article he sells. He is not entitled to wash his hands of the article by referring the buyer to the manufacturer. No consumer should let himself be fobbed off by shop staff who try to insist that faulty goods are the manufacturer's responsibility.

Samples and Descriptions

The relevance of any description applied to second-hand and sale goods is discussed at the end of this Chapter. Misdescriptions generally are dealt with in Chapter V.

A consumer who buys anything on the basis of a sample he has been shown is guaranteed that what is delivered:

(a) will correspond to the sample in quality

(b) will be free from any defect rendering it unmerchantable unless such defect is **apparent** on a reasonable examination of the sample. Basically this means the item must satisfy the test of merchantable quality discussed below.

If the goods do not correspond with the sample the buyer can reject them even though by a simple process the goods can be made to do so.

In one case buyers were shown two samples of smooth rubber sheeting suitable for shoe-making. Unlike the samples, the rolls finally delivered were hard and crinkly. It was argued that this could be corrected by the simple process of warming the rubber and pressing out the crinkles but the judge held that the rolls were not up to sample.

Merchantable Quality

Where a retailer sells goods (but not a private seller) there is an implied condition that the goods supplied are of merchantable quality.

The law in fact talks not of "fair" or "reasonable" but of "merchantable" quality. Merchantable is an archaic legal term meaning "saleable".

The statutory definition of "merchantable" which applies to both new and second-hand articles alike is that:

Goods **of any kind** are of merchantable quality . . . if they are as **fit for the purpose** or purposes for which goods of that kind are commonly bought as **is reasonable to expect** having regard to . . .

* any **description** applied to them;
* the **price** (if relevant);
* and all other relevant circumstances.

Judges have explained "merchantable" in various

cases. Generally the article should be of such quality and in such condition that a reasonable person would, after a full examination, accept it.

Merchantable quality requires that the article should be in such an actual state that a buyer who is fully acquainted with the facts and knowing what hidden defects exist, would buy it without abatement of price. The acid test is "Would the average person have bought the article if he had known its true condition?" If not, then the buyer has the right to claim. Whether or not the goods are of merchantable quality is essentially a question of fact.

The seller is under a **strict duty** to ensure that every article he sells is "merchantable" and it is no defence for him to prove that all possible care was taken to prevent any defect if the article turns out to be defective.

In practice, the meaning of the legal phrase "merchantable quality" is often difficult to formulate and apply with precision in a given situation and there are numerous court decisions. Woollen undergarments which contain an excess of chemical sulphites are not of merchantable quality since they are unfit to wear next to the skin. "Merchantable", said Lord Wright, "does not mean that the thing is saleable in the market simply because it looks right. It is not merchantable if it has defects unfitting it for its proper use but not apparent on ordinary examination."

Basically, the shop or supplier is responsible for selling an article which has a hidden defect which renders it unfit for the purpose for which it is normally used, even though that defect cannot be discovered by reasonable examination.

The following are instances where the consumer has been awarded damages:

Articles sold as new but delivered dented and scratched, owing to bad packing.

A plastic catapault which broke after a few days use, injuring child's eye.

38

Contaminated beer (although the chemical present could be detected only by scientific examination).

Onions which are sprouting.

A bun containing a stone.

A ton of coalite containing a piece of explosive which blew up and damaged the buyer's room.

A bottle of ginger wine which when being uncorked broke at the neck and cut the buyer's hand. This means that the container must be sound and safe, as well as the contents. The seller's duty to furnish a safe and suitable container applies equally where the container provided is returnable or stipulated as the property of the seller.

Where perishable goods are to be sent to the buyer by post or carrier, it is reasonable to expect the goods to be of such quality as to be able to withstand a normal journey. They should also be properly packed.

However, a pork chop which proved poisonous when undercooked was not unmerchantable because it would not have caused any ill effects had it been properly cooked.

Rejection of defective article

A new article is still in law unmerchantable even though its defects can easily be remedied or put right at very little cost. The customer is under no obligation to expend time and money putting right an article sold as new. A buyer need not accept a new washing machine which is badly chipped, even though it works adequately. However, if it is sold as second-hand the buyer must expect that minor repairs may be necessary. (As to acceptance, see s. 35, Sale of Goods Act.) If he keeps the item he can claim compensation for its defects and any financial loss as well. If he rejects it, he is entitled to be repaid the purchase price and also any additional financial loss but he is not entitled to hang on to the item until he gets his money back. Nor can he reject it after using it, unless its defect renders it unusable.

In order to reject it he must at once notify the seller who, if he wants it, can come and collect it. The buyer is not obliged to transport the item back to the seller but he can do so if he wishes.

The buyer must act promptly. If he retains it for more than a reasonable length of time without informing the seller that he rejects it he will be taken to have accepted it. Unless he acts promptly his right of rejection will be lost and he will have to keep the item but can claim full compensation for all his financial loss, eg repairs, loss of use, and other expenses (see p 98). Thus once a buyer has taken delivery of a complex machine such as a motor car he may not reject it on account of a mechanical fault which later comes to light **after some period of use** (unless it is a very serious defect).

Product life and durability
After what period of use can a seller wash his hands of the article if it develops a fault? With normal daily use a tape-recorder or radio could reasonably be expected to work trouble-free for at least a year. Many such articles treated with reasonable care will last for a number of years. On the other hand if mal-treated or exposed to the attacks of small children, even a well-made article may give trouble.

In the case of products such as cars or furniture, the amount of use an article receives is obviously relevant to its probable life expectancy. On the other hand articles like watches or refrigerators should be made to function continuously without giving trouble for a number of years. An expensive watch should be sufficiently well designed to last a lifetime with proper treatment and servicing. On the other hand, a cheap watch might not be expected to last more than a year or two. Yet we have all known of cheap watches which have lasted many years without even being serviced and expensive articles which have given trouble within a short time of purchase.

Although no specific rules can be laid down as to life expectancy, price is an important consideration. On the other hand with certain articles, the price paid may be largely irrelevant to the question of durability. Cheap stainless steel cutlery may well last as long or longer than silver-plated. The more complicated a piece of equipment, the more likely it is to go wrong.

If the transmission or gear-box of a car has to be renewed after 18 months and only moderate mileage, the vehicle could be regarded as defective. The retailer would have to remedy it or pay compensation even though the period of guarantee had expired. To prove his case the consumer would need to call an expert engineer to tell the court that the normal life expectancy of that piece of mechanism is, say, five years.

It is in this situation that the Codes of Practice laid down by the various trade associations with the encouragement of the Office of Fair Trading can clarify the consumer's rights.

As an indication of the durability of electrical products the Association of Manufacturers of Domestic Electrical Appliances gives the following table for availability of functional parts after the date on which the production of an appliance ceases:

small appliances	5–8 years
cleaners, refrigerators, spin dryers and heaters	8 years
cookers, dish-washers, washing machines	10 years
thermal storage radiators	15 years

Most electronic equipment can be expected to last about seven years and in certain cases this period may be longer.

The RETRA Code of Practice for the selling and servicing of electrical and electronic appliances recommends that the retailer should **guarantee** new goods for both parts and labour for a period of not less than **12 months** from the date of purchase and this should apply even if the manufacturer's **guarantee** is for a shorter period. It excludes damage caused by customer misuse, negligence or failure to adhere to instructions for use.

In some instances a manufacturer will specifically advertise that his product has a minimum life expectancy. For example, "double-life" light bulbs are advertised to give a minimum of 2,000 hours of use. Such a declaration will not give a consumer a direct right to sue the manufacturer if his light bulb expires before this period. But it will indicate the quality and durability the consumer can expect from the product and so give him a right to have it replaced by the **retailer.**

Where buyer examines article for defects before purchase

Although an article is not of merchantable quality or is unfit for its purpose, the seller is not responsible for defects in two specific situations:

(a) as regards defects specifically drawn to the buyer's attention before the contract is made; or

(b) if the buyer examines the goods before the contract is made, as regards defects which that examination ought to reveal.

Where a defect is specifically drawn to the attention of the buyer before buying, as where a salesman points out that a carpet is discoloured in one patch, no liability attaches to the seller. However, should defects such as holes or weak fibres, which were not pointed out, be found later, the seller will be liable.

Thorough examination by buyer bars later claim

Where the buyer examines the article before buying he cannot complain of any defects found later which that examination ought to have revealed. The presence of arsenic in beer or the defective manufacture of a catapult are defects which a prior examination would **not** reveal.

Accordingly prior inspection by the buyer will not release the seller from liability for such hidden defects.

The buyer of a second-hand car who inspects it **externally only,** cannot complain later of dents or a buckled wing which any ordinary person ought to have seen but he can complain of internal defects, even though he would have seen them had he troubled to lift the bonnet.

The legal moral is that a buyer may be better off not making an on-the-spot inspection himself. If he makes an inspection he may lose his right to complain of defects which he missed but **ought** to have noticed.

His wisest course is simply to ask the seller for a positive asurance (preferably in writing, see p 104) that the article is in good working order. Once he receives this assurance he can take it away, retaining the right to sue for breach of contract or misrepresentation if defects are discovered sabsequently. If so an unskilled buyer may have better legal protection where he does not himself examine the article for defects but waits until he gets it home where he can examine it at leisure and with the help of an expert if necessary.

Where buyer relies on seller's advice

The consumer will often seek guidance from the sales staff in choosing what to buy, eg "What cement do I need to waterproof the swimming pool I am building?" Should they give him the wrong advice or guidance the customer can claim compensation. This responsibility applies only to a shop or business, not where a private seller gives advice.

"Where the seller sells goods in the course of a business and the buyer, expressly or by implication, makes known to the seller **any particular purpose** for which the goods are being bought, there is an implied condition that the goods supplied under the contract are reasonably fit for that purpose, whether or not that is a purpose for which such goods are commonly supplied, except where the circumstances show that the buyer does not rely, or that it is unreasonable for him to rely, on the seller's skill or judgment." (Sale of Goods Act 1979, Section 14 (3)).

For the seller to be liable the buyer must make known for what particular purpose the article is needed. Alternatively, the seller may be aware of it by implication. If so, the article must be reasonably fit for that purpose. Even though such articles are not usually intended for the kind of use the buyer has intimated, the seller is responsible if it proves unsuitable for such use.

The seller can escape responsibility by proving:
- that under the circumstances the buyer did **not** rely on the shop assistant's advice in selecting the item.
- that it was **unreasonable** for the buyer to rely on the assistant's skill and judgment.

A shopper may ask for an article to perform a particular task, say, glue to mend a broken china ornament. The glue supplied must serve that specific function.

Even where the buyer orders an article to be made to his specification, certain matters may be left to the discretion, ie skill and judgment, of the seller. Cammell Laird ordered two ship's propellers to be made to their own design. One of the propellers was cast too thick and was very noisy in use. This defect was the responsibility of the seller because the thickness of the blades was left to the seller's expertise. (*Cammell Laird v. Manganese Bronze & Brass Co Ltd*, 1934).

Special requirements
A consumer who has special requirements for an article must make this clear to the seller. Someone prone to dermatitis may seek the seller's advice regarding a type of cosmetic suitable for her skin condition. In some circumstances it may be unreasonable for the consumer to seek advice in a shop since anyone with a medical condition might normally be expected to seek expert medical advice.

Again a consumer may ask advice regarding a garment

she is proposing to buy. Will the material affect her unusually sensitive skin? In these circumstances she might be justified in relying on the retailer's advice.

Mrs Griffiths had unusually sensitive skin. She bought a tweed coat and as a result of wearing it she suffered a skin complaint. She claimed compensation on the ground that the coat was not fit for its usual purpose, that is, for wearing.

The court held that nothing in the tweed coat would have harmed the skin of a normal person. Mrs Griffiths did not tell the shop assistant that she had abnormally sensitive skin, ie that she required the coat for a special purpose. Unless she made this plain she could expect the to be **reasonably fit** only for the purpose of being worn by a normal person. (*Griffiths v. Peter Conway Ltd*, 1939).

"Reasonably fit for its purpose"

Generally the purpose for which the consumer buys an article will be obvious, eg milk must be fit to be drunk, food to be consumed, clothing to be worn. It must be "reasonably fit" for that purpose. It need not however be **"perfectly"** fit. Nevertheless if the article sold is not reasonably fit, it is no defence for the seller to prove that he took all proper precautions to ensure reasonable fitness.

Thus tinned food must be fit for consumption. If it makes the buyer ill, the seller cannot excuse himself from paying compensation on the ground that he could not possibly have detected that it was contaminated.

Illustration

The consumer's wife died after drinking milk contaminated with typhoid. Such infection was not apparent on any reasonable inspection. It was found as a fact that no amount of care taken by the dairy could have prevented it. Nevertheless it was held that the liability of the dairy under the Sales of Goods Act is strict. (*Frost V. Aylesbury Dairy Co* (1905)).

Foodstuffs

All foodstuffs, whether bought in a shop or consumed in a restaurant, must be fit for human consumption. It is no defence that sellers have taken all reasonable precautions as to hygiene.

However, the legal guarantee that food is fit for human consumption applies only where you pay for it. For example, if you go as a guest to a free reception and the lobster makes you ill, there is no automatic right to compensation. For your claim to succeed you must establish that your host was negligent in preparing the food or perhaps storing it too long or at the wrong temperature.

For the same reason, a paying patient in a hospital or nursing home will have an automatic claim if the food makes him ill. If he goes in as a non-paying patient on ordinary admission, there is, ironically, no guarantee that the food he is given is fit for human consumption. He will have a claim only if he can prove the hospital was negligent in the storage, handling or preparation of the food.

Food Poisoning in a Restaurant

The proprietor is responsible for the quality of all food served. Should a customer suffer food poisoning he is entitled not only to a refund of the price of the meal but also compensation for pain and suffering for the period of his illness. He can also claim for any time away from work or business.

In the case of seriously contaminated food or drink, compensation may be extremely high. £43,000 was awarded to a girl aged 10 who was served caustic soda solution in a Kent restaurant when she asked for lemonade. Her brother was also served with a glass of the same solution but luckily spat it out and suffered only mild injuries. He was only awarded £200 but the girl's throat was seriously injured and she had become a semi-invalid.

Payment was ordered to be made both by the restaurant

and by the firm which was responsible for servicing bar equipment at the premises and which had left a lemonade bottle containing the caustic soda solution in the restaurant. (*Studer v. The Kashmir Restaurant and Carlsberg Distributors Ltd* (1977)).

Quality of food in restaurants

Anyone eating in a restaurant is entitled to be served with wholesome food prepared to a reasonable standard. If it is tasteless, cold or overcooked or soggy, you can refuse to eat it. In the event of the restaurant declining to replace it with something eatable you are entitled to give your name and address and decline to pay. If they think they are entitled to payment they can sue you for a civil debt in the county court. They cannot charge you with the crime of deception since you have not sought to avoid payment dishonestly. If the restaurant threatens to call the police you should if possible wait until they arrive and give your reasons for refusing to pay.

If you suspect the restaurant is unhygienic you can report it to your local Environmental Health Officer. He can close down dirty premises within three days if he thinks there is an imminent risk to health. The Food & Drugs (Control of Premises) Act 1976 gives him this power. Detailed Regulations made under powers contained in the Food & Drugs Act 1955 lay down specific hygiene requirements relating to the design and maintenance of restaurants (as well as food shops, food factories, dairies and so on). Other regulations cover people involved in the handling of food. They must not smoke while handling food. They must cover cuts with waterproof dressings. In some cases protective clothing must be worn.

Prosecution for Sale of Unwholesome Food

Consumers have always been protected against the sale

of deleterious food. A retailer who knowingly sells food which is not fit for consumption is guilty of an offence at common law.

Today prosecutions for having on sale food or drink which is unfit for consumption are generally brought under the provisions of the Food & Drugs Act 1955 which imposes strict liability on the seller. Government regulations and orders relating to labelling and additives to foodstuffs, etc are also enforced under the Act.

This Act also makes it an offence to sell to the prejudice of the buyer any food or drug which is not of the "nature, substance or quality" demanded by the purchaser. For example, where penicillin is found in milk it is no defence to say that the milk is in the same state as it came from the cow because that constituent has no business being in milk.

The statutory test is whether the food is **injurious to health.** It need not be injurious to the health of **everyone.** It is an offence if it is injurious to certain people such as children or invalids.

The prosecution does not have to prove guilty knowledge on the part of the seller. He is guilty of an offence simply because the purchaser has not received the quality or type he asked for or could reasonably expect. The presence of virtually any extraneous matter in food is an offence where it is likely to be of prejudice to the buyer. It is not necessary to show that the food has actually caused injury, only that it is likely to do so if consumed. Some examples are:

a piece of metal in a chocolate cream bun;

a piece of string in a loaf of bread;

a fly or a piece of glass in a bottle of milk.

Local authorities have the duty of enforcing the law through their inspectors who deal with complaints and make test purchases. Suspect samples are sent to the public analyst for the area. A consumer may himself send a suspected food sample direct to the public analyst for examination, but as a ratepayer he is entitled to have his problem investigated by the public health or trading standards officer at public expense.

Controls under the Food and Drugs Act

This vast statute contains a number of other sections. It controls the way food and drugs are labelled and advertised. In law, date-marking by manufacturers is not compulsory, except for egg boxes which must also be marked with their source and quality. Hence it is not an offence to sell pre-packed bacon after the date stamp on the packet has expired, unless it is unfit to eat. The "sell by" stamp on foodstuffs is merely advisory to let shops know roughly how long to store them. Labels on some foodstuffs must give detailed information about ingredients, particularly if they contain flavoured substitutes such as vegetable protein. Unless actual amounts are stated (which in any case will be mostly meaningless to the ordinary consumer) ingredients of certain foodstuffs must be listed in strict order of amount, starting with the largest quantity.

Complex regulations lay down what additives are permitted by law, although control of colouring and preservatives is not yet as strict as in some parts of the EEC. They also tell us how much meat should be in a beef sausage (50%) – pork sausages at least 65%. Again a bottle of orange squash must contain 25% or more pure orange juice. Orange crush, which is drunk undiluted, need contain only 5% orange juice and so on. In the event of doubt your local Environmental Officer will examine and test it.

Second-hand, Shop-soiled or Imperfect Goods

Provided you buy from a shop or dealer (not from a private individual) a second-hand article must by law be of "merchantable" quality at the time of sale. The test is whether it is "as fit for the purpose or purposes for which goods of that kind are commonly bought as it is reasonable to expect." We can apply three criteria to determine whether the article satisfies this test:

1. The Description applied to the Article

A second-hand car may be described as "one-owner". More is to be expected from a vehicle so advertised than one which has passed through many hands. Where an article is described as "imperfect" or "sub-standard" the buyer is entitled to assume that any imperfection relates to ornament or finish, not to a latent defect which will render it unusable.

Also he is entitled to ask and to be told the exact nature of the imperfection. Naturally anyone who examines a second-hand article before buying is assumed to have seen those defects which his examination ought to have revealed.

However, the buyer is entitled to be warned of any hidden defects which the article may have. A china tea pot bought in a sale must not crack when used. An electric kettle must not leak. The article must still be usable although "imperfect" or second-hand. Unfortunately Parliament has not specified how long it must remain usable. One judge has said that a second-hand article must remain usable for a "reasonable time". There is no easy answer to this question. What is a reasonable length of time will depend partly on the price paid and partly on the nature of the article.

2. Relevance of price to quality

The price paid can be an important indication of the quality the buyer is entitled to expect. For example, a carpet which is discoloured is not fit for its normal purpose. However it might suit a buyer who wants it for a playroom. He may readily put up with the particular defect if the price asked is well below what he would have to pay for a perfect carpet of that type.

If the price is drastically reduced –say to a quarter of the normal price for articles of that kind – then the consumer should expect a corresponding diminution in quality, unless the shop gives some other explanation for the reduction in price, eg "shopsoiled". This does not imply that it is "sub-standard". Where an article is bought, say, in a 'clearance sale' the consumer is entitled to assume the article is as good as new, the reduction in price relating only to the shopkeeper's desire to clear old stock.

3. All other relevant circumstances

In the case of a second-hand article, its age will be relevant in determining the quality and period of useful life the buyer can expect. Obviously a ten-year-old car cannot be expected to last as long as a two-year-old car. It will probably require to be repaired sooner. It may also require more extensive repairs. But it must still go as a car for a reasonable time.

The nature of the article bought is relevant. Thus a relatively simple article such as a tool or piece of furniture should be trouble-free even though second-hand for a longer period than something more complex such as a tv receiver or automatic washing machine.

What the dealer says about a second-hand article is relevant, eg that a machine has recently been overhauled or fitted with a reconditioned motor or that a car has been regularly serviced.

Again the amount of previous use is a relevant indication as to probable life-expectancy. Here the buyer is entitled to rely on the accuracy of the mileage clock.

How the Judge decides

In a dispute over a defective second-hand article the judge will assess whether the buyer got a fair deal by balancing its defects against its description and price. If the defects are greater than one should expect in view of the price paid or the description given, the buyer will be entitled to compensation proportionately.

Second-hand Cars

The fact that a second-hand car requires more expensive repairs than was thought at the time of sale does not necessarily mean that it is not of "merchantable quality".

However, a second-hand car with the gearbox and differential split and requiring major repairs was held not of merchantable quality. (*Frank v. Grosvenor Ltd* (1960)).

When Mr Bartlett agreed to buy a Jaguar car for £950 the salesman pointed out that the clutch was not operating properly but could be put right by a minor repair. After driving it for a month Mr Bartlett's own garage told him the clutch would have to be renewed at a cost of £84, of which £50 was due to dismantling the engine to do so. The Court of Appeal found that the car was roadworthy since it was fit to be driven in safety. This was the most that the buyer of a second-hand car could require unless he was given an express guarantee as to its condition. "A second-hand car is "merchantable" if it is in a usable condition even though not perfect." (*Bartlett v. Marcus Ltd* (1965)).

By contrast, a Mr Crowther bought a 1964 Jaguar car for £390 in 1972. It had 82,000 miles on the clock and had passed its M.O.T. test. He drove it over 2,000 miles in three weeks. Then the engine seized up on the motorway and had to be replaced with a reconditioned engine. The Court of Appeal approved an award of £460 in his favour. The evidence was that the engine was "clapped-out", although the dealer had told him the car was "in very good condition for its age."

Judgment was given under Section 14 of the Sale of Goods Act on the ground the buyer had relied on the seller's skill and judgment and that the car was not reasonably fit for the purpose for which it was required,

52

namely for use on the roads. (*Crowther v. Shannon Motor Co* (1975)).

Sale of Unroadworthy Vehicles

A private individual as well as a trader commits an offence under the Road Traffic Act 1972, if he sells a vehicle in an unroadworthy condition. This covers brakes, steering, lights and tyres.

To avoid conviction, the seller would have to prove that he had good reason to believe that the car would not be used in that condition. He should write out a list of defects, get the buyer to sign it and insist on his written undertaking not to use the car until those defects are repaired.

Sales not in the course of business

Anyone advertising an article for sale must make it clear if he is selling in the course of business. Since the Business Advertisements (Disclosure) Order (1977) it is an offence for a trader to pretend he sells as a private individual, eg suggesting that he has an unwanted present or is going abroad, when in fact the seller is a trader seeking to avoid his obligations under the Sale of Goods Act. This is because the Act guarantees merchantable quality only if you buy from someone who sells in **the course of any business** (see below). Under the Act a private seller guarantees only that the article is correctly described eg a car described as "one-owner" must not be third-hand. The private seller is also liable for misrepresentations.

Buying from a private seller

In theory a private seller might avoid even this implied condition as to description. It can be excluded by appropriate words of exemption brought to the buyer's attention before the contract of sale is completed. Moreover such an exemption need not satisfy the test of reasonableness unless it relates to misrepresentations. (See Chapter VIII).

Needless to say one would be most unwise to deal with any seller who seeks to exclude such liability.

Since the Sale of Goods Act gives the buyer no legal guarantee of merchantable quality when he buys from a private seller, the old maxim "let the buyer beware" (*caveat emptor*) still applies. As he does not sell in the course of business, a private seller is deemed to give no assurance as to quality, condition, fitness or otherwise.

The exception is where a private seller sells through an agent (who is selling in the course of business) and the buyer is unaware that the seller is a private person.

Where a private individual sells **through an agent**, the condition as to merchantable quality will operate if the agent sells in the course of business unless the private seller has taken reasonable steps to notify the buyer that the sale is a private one, or the buyer is otherwise aware of this.

CHAPTER III

UNFAIR TRADING

Fair Trading Act 1973

This Act protects consumers in a general way. It establishes the Office of Fair Trading and gives wide-ranging powers to the Director-General of Fair Trading. Unlike other consumer legislation it does not give individual consumers specific rights. Thus Section 26 specifically states that "A contract for the supply of goods or services shall not be void or unenforceable by reason only of a contravention of an order made under . . . the Act . . . which shall not be construed as conferring a right of action in any civil proceedings."

Functions of the Director-General of Fair Trading

Much of the Act is concerned with monopolies and mergers in respect of which the Director-General has important functions.

The Director-General also has an overall responsibility for the implementation of the Consumer Credit Act 1974 and overseeing the working and enforcement of its provisions. He has the not inconsiderable task of administering that Act's credit licensing system. He is obliged to hear representations from any licensee before withdrawing, suspending or varying a licence granted to cover moneylending, giving credit or credit brokerage. He is responsible for keeping under review and advising the Secretary of State about social and commercial developments relating to credit and hiring.

The general functions of the Director-General are contained in Section 2 of the Fair Trading Act, viz:

(a) to keep under review commercial activities and in particular practices which may adversely affect the economic interests of consumers; and

(b) to keep a dossier on such activities as evidence of practices which may adversely affect the interests of consumers.

A consumer trade practice is widely defined under Section 13. The Director-General can ask the Advisory Committee to examine any trade practice to see whether it adversely affects the economic interests of consumers. This Committee, whose full title is the Consumer Protection Advisory Committee, reports on the practice and considers any proposals of the Director-General for regulating it.

Breach of Order is a criminal offence

Once the Advisory Committee approves the proposal as made, or modified by them, the Secretary of State can give effect to it by making an order to regulate the trade practice. After this order has been approved by resolution of each House of Parliament its contravention becomes a criminal offence. Prosecution of offenders is the duty of local Trading Standards Officers.

The penalty for breach of any requirement imposed by such an order is, on summary conviction, a fine not exceeding £400. In the case of a serious offence brought before the Crown Court, the fine is unlimited. Also imprisonment for a term not exceeding two years is possible apart from, or in addition to, any fine.

Specific defences are allowed by Section 25 as follows:

(a) that the commission of the offence was due to a mistake;

(b) or to reliance on information supplied;

(c) or to the act or default of another person, an accident or some other cause beyond his control.

In addition to establishing any of the above defences the accused must also prove he took all reasonable precautions and exercised all due diligence to avoid commission of such an offence by himself or any person under his control.

Despite the impressive machinery set up by the Act for curbing adverse trade practices, it has been seldom used. Orders have been made:

(1) To outlaw notices which purport to take away a buyer's rights under the Sale of Goods Act, eg "No refunds in any circumstances on sale goods".

(2) To compel mail order advertisements, circulars and catalogues to carry the name and address of the advertiser.

Civil Proceedings to curb unfair trade practices

Traders who persistently ignore their obligations under civil law or who deliberately flout the criminal law can be brought before the Restrictive Practices Court or the county court. Sections 34 to 43 of the Fair Trading Act give the Director-General power to take action against traders who persist in practices which are detrimental to the interests of consumers.

Initially the Director-General will ask the trader to give a written assurance to abandon the practice in question. If he fails to give such an assurance, or breaks an assurance once given, civil court action can be taken against him.

Regulation by Voluntary Codes of Practice

These codes are of far greater practical benefit to consumers generally, particularly in the service industries, than many of the Director-General's specific powers of action. The codes are an area of growing importance. So far about a dozen have been introduced. The Director-General has a duty under the Fair Trading Act, Section 124, to invite trade associations "to prepare codes of practice for guidance in safeguarding and **promoting** the interests of consumers". Although these codes have no legal force as such they are effective because:

(a) The trade association can enforce the code itself, police its own members under the code and look into complaints promptly.

(b) The sanction for breach can be expulsion from the association (or sometimes a financial penalty).

(c) As the code is deemed to set reasonable standards of conduct for the entire trade, a judge when hearing a court action would tend to regard non-compliance with the code as evidence that the trader had acted unfairly.

(d) Each code is tailored to meet the specific problems of its own particular trade, eg by laying down regulations about service calls, repairs and availability of spare parts. It can pronounce upon the life expectancy of trade products. These are matters all too often beyond the reach of legislation as such.

(e) The codes provide for conciliation of complaints at no expense to the consumer.

(f) Arbitration of disputes is usually referred to the Institute of Arbitrators, should a consumer prefer not to go to court.

(g) Trade associations can arrange facilities for the testing of defective products.

The Codes of Practice in Operation

Codes are being introduced for trades as varied as furniture and funeral directors. They set out guidelines which determine what is good trading practice. Thus the furniture code has provisions regarding delivery dates and transport costs. It stipulates that staff must quote "realistic" delivery dates. When a deposit is taken the delivery date should be quoted in writing on the receipt. Otherwise it is assumed delivery will be made within one month. The customer must be advised immediately it becomes apparent that the date quoted is not likely to be met. If he is not prepared to accept a later delivery date his deposit must be refunded on request. Where a repair is the responsibility of the retailer (or manufacturer) the retailer must meet transport costs.

The furniture code also lays down a glossary of terms which must be strictly observed. Thus the term **antique** denotes that the piece of furniture is at least 100 years old and has not been essentially changed since it was made. If a certain period is specified, eg Regency, the piece must have been **made** during that period. "Replica" and "facsimile" mean the piece is an **exact** copy of an antique piece.

Reproduction and traditional denote only that the piece clearly displays the form of the period or style stated, although modern techniques and materials may have been used in its design and manufacture. Solid wood denotes that the constructional material is nothing but wood. It excludes the use of plywood, hardboard or chipboard. "Fully sprung" signifies that the whole seat, including the front edge, is supported by springs.

Extract from Code of Practice for the Motor Industry

Dealers must ensure that all used cars are subjected to a pre-sales inspection in accordance with a standard form, a copy of which should be available to the consumer.

Copies of relevant written information provided by previous owners regarding the history of the car should be passed to the consumer. This may include service records, repair invoices, inspection reports, handbooks and copy warranty.

Any warranty document should notify the consumer that the warranty given is **in addition to** his statutory and common law rights.

If a printed warranty or guarantee form is not used, then any specific promises which the dealer is willing to make in relation to the used car should be set out in writing.

Reasonable steps should be taken to verify the recorded

mileage of a used car. Unless the seller is satisfied that the quoted mileage of a used car is accurate, such mileage should not be quoted in advertisements, discussions or negotiations or in any documents related to the supply of the used car.

Dealers should pass on any known facts about a previous odometer reading to a prospective customer, and if a disclaimer is used it should be in the following form: "We do not guarantee the accuracy of the recorded mileage. To the best of our knowledge and belief, however, the reading is correct/incorrect."

Resale price maintenance

Statute now affirms the common law freedom of a seller to sell at any price he pleases. In order to encourage free competition in the interests of the consumer, manufacturers are prohibited from stipulating that the retailer shall not resell below a specified price.

Under the Resale Prices Act 1976 price fixing is abolished and any condition as to resale price maintenance is void where this is attached to a sale by a supplier to a dealer. One exception is where the article is to be resold outside the United Kingdom. Certain goods such as books and medicaments are also exempt, since price fixing is considered in these two cases to be in the public interest.

The operation of these exceptions however is limited by Article 85 of the Treaty of Rome which applies to all agreements which may prevent or distort competition within the Common Market. Generally speaking, an agreement which fixes purchase prices or selling prices is unenforceable. However, manufacturers are still at liberty to **recommend** prices.

Under the Resale Prices Act 1976 manufacturers and wholesalers who attempt to fix retail minimum prices can have a civil action brought against them in the Restrictive Practices Court by the Director-General of

Fair Trading. Retailers and members of the public can also sue if they have been prejudiced by price fixing. In practice individual consumers should report price fixing to their local Trading Standards Officer.

Pressure can be put on a retailer in various ways to keep to a minimum price. Sometimes a retailer is threatened that his supplies will be cut off if he sells below the recommended price. Consequently withholding supplies as a means of enforcing his observance of the minimum price is unlawful. The wholesaler must treat all retailers the same whether they retail at cut prices or not. The object of the law is to encourage retailers to sell at any price they see fit. The wholesaler or manufacturer is not allowed to offer unfavourable terms of supply to an individual discount retailer as a means of discouraging price cutting.

Discounts and loss leaders

What is the wholesaler to do if other traders start to put pressure on him to discontinue supplies to a discounter whose competition is ruining their business? The Resale Prices Act gives the wholesaler a let-out, where he has reasonable cause to believe any of his goods are being sold as "loss leaders".

A loss leader means a sale not for the purpose of making a profit. The object of a loss leader is to attract customers who are likely to buy other items. A loss leader may also serve to advertise his business generally. Genuine clearance sales are not loss leaders.

In order to demand continuance of supplies the retailer may have to prove he actually makes a profit on the item in question. The law is silent so far about what a "profit" means. The layman might think that any resale at a higher price however small amounts to a profit. On the other hand "profit" may mean a price which, taking into account all his overheads, is within the profitability margins of the business as a whole.

Trading stamps

As a method of attracting custom the issuing of trading stamps is now virtually an industry in itself. In essence it is a simple way of giving customers a discount. To control the promoters of such schemes, the Trading Stamps Act 1964 allows them to be carried on **only** by a company subject to the requirements of the Companies Acts (ie as to annual returns) or by an industrial and provident society. In particular the Act gives consumers the right to exchange their stamps for cash.

As a result of the Supply of Goods (Implied Terms) Act 1973 quality guarantees now apply to all goods exchanged for stamps. They must be exactly as described in the catalogue. They must be of merchantable quality and fit for the purpose for which they are to be used, just as if the consumer had paid cash for them.

Right to cash stamps at face value

Every stamp issued must bear on its face in clear and legible characters a **value** expressed in current coin of the realm. It must also show the name of the society or company issuing it or their registered business name. The stamp company must redeem stamps for their face value. Every consumer has the right to turn his stamps into **cash** (minimum 25p). He may do this by presenting the stamps personally at the promoter's registered office or by sending the stamps by post to that office with a request for cash, or in any other manner offered by the promoter.

Trading stamp schemes which are carried on as a business, ie for profit, must observe the following regulations:

(i)   All catalogues published by the scheme and all stamp books must state the promoter's registered office in prominent letters.

(ii)   The Act prohibits advertisements referring to the value of trading stamps in a way which is misleading or exaggerated, eg by suggesting that the stamps' cash value is related to what the consumer must spend to obtain them.

(iii) Every shop where a trading stamp scheme is operated must display a notice stating the cash value of the trading stamps issued.

(iv)   This notice must give such particulars as will enable customers readily to ascertain the number of trading stamps they are entitled to on any purchase.

(v)   The shop must have a catalogue available for consultation by customers.

Unit-pricing and standard packaging

In order to shop selectively the shopper must be able to decide instantly whether he or she is getting value for money, particularly on basic commodities in the local supermarket.

Is the $10\frac{1}{2}$-oz pack at Xp better value than the 12-oz pack at Zp next door? To work it out a consumer needs a pocket computer. Such non-standard packaging is often a clever method of masking higher profit margins. It not only causes confusion but is a source of real unfairness to the ordinary consumer.

Unit pricing means stating the actual price **per pound** of a piece of cheese, as well as pricing the pack itself. It ensures the shopper can see the basic price of the commodity and can compare it with what it is priced at in other shops.

Under the Prices Act 1974 orders can be made requiring the price of certain commodities such as meat and cheese to be displayed in this way. Under the Price Commission Act 1977 similar orders can be made with regard to the pricing of **services**. Failure to comply with an order means the trader is in breach of the criminal law so that the Trading Standards Officer can prosecute him in the magistrates' court.

As part of the government's programme to cut back inflation, prices of basic foods, butter, loaves of bread and cheese can be fixed by an order under the Prices Act.

The Weights and Measures Act 1963 (as amended in 1976)
As is well known, this Act makes it a criminal offence to sell short weight. Even unintentional errors are punishable whether or not there was any intent to cheat the customer. The Act also gives the government power to make unit-pricing compulsory. Section 21 gives the Secretary of State power to regulate the sale of commodities:
- by specified weights;
- in specified quantities;
- with appropriate marking of the weight or volume on the container.

Thus the long-overdue move towards standardised packaging is slowly progressing. Pre-packed basic commodities like sugar, flour, jam and fat, can now only be sold in prescribed weights with the weight duly marked on the package. The Department of Trade makes orders requiring pre-packed goods to be sold only in packets or containers of specified sizes.

Unit-pricing and standard packaging go hand in hand. Once an order is made stipulating standard sizes of containers, the shopper can see at a glance which shop gives best value and whether one is really making a saving by buying the larger size.

Inertia selling

Prior to 1971 mail-order firms often sent householders articles without order or request. The senders would then demand payment by means of a barrage of intimidating letters. This technique is known as inertia selling. It is **not** a sale on approval since the article sent is unsolicited.

Firms who send goods to householders without being asked and subsequently demand payment may be liable to penalties under the Unsolicited Goods and Services Act 1971.

. An offence is committed where the senders demand payment or assert that they are entitled to payment for an unsolicited article. They can also be fined if they attempt to get payment by threatening legal proceedings or debt collection. Threatening to put the recipient on a list of defaulters is also an offence. These are all matters which should be reported to the local Trading Standards Officer for appropriate action to be taken.

However, *actually* bringing legal proceedings is **not** an offence because it is up to the judge to decide if the Act has been contravened.

Moreover, the recipient of an unsolicited article can in certain circumstances acquire it without payment. For example, after a lapse of six months he can keep it.

The Act applies provided the recipient never agreed to acquire the article or to return it, ie it was not delivered on approval but arrived completely unsought. Secondly, the recipient must have no reasonable cause to believe it was sent with a view to being acquired for the purpose of a trade or business.

Under the Act he can **acquire ownership** in one of two ways:

1 He need do nothing but wait for six months. If within this time the senders do not come to collect it, it will then belong to him. Of course, the recipient must not

unreasonably refuse to let them take possession of the article or in any way hinder the senders collecting it.

2 Alternatively, the recipient can shorten the six months waiting period to 30 days by simply writing to the senders concerned and telling them:

(a) that he did not order the article sent;

(b) his name and address so they can come to pick it up.

(Proof of posting this letter is desirable, eg recorded delivery.)

If the firm fails to come to collect it within 30 days of his posting this letter the article will belong to him.

In either case, whether the 30 days' notice is given or the six months' period is allowed to tick away in silence, any right of the senders in the article sent is extinguished by law at the termination of the relevant period. In the meantime he must not sell it, damage it or throw it away. Thereafter he can deal with it or dispose of it as if it were an unconditional gift to him.

Monopolies and Mergers

Monopolies stifle free competition. Without competition a monopoly can fix its own standards of quality and efficiency of service. The consumer has no choice but to accept what is offered and to pay the price demanded. A monopoly situation is where 25 per cent of a particular market is supplied by one supplier or one group of companies.

Members of the Monopolies and Mergers Commission are appointed by the Secretary of State for Prices and Consumer Protection up to a maxium of 25. Under the Fair Trading Act 1973 the Commission has two purposes:

1 To investigate the existence of a monopoly situation.

2 To investigate whether or not certain mergers between business organisations are in the public interest.

After investigating the facts the Commission has a duty to

report on the extent to which the monopoly or merger is likely to affect adversely the public interest.

Under the Fair Trading Act a company with a large share of the market may be required:

1 To reduce its prices;
2 To abandon uncompetitive trading practices.

Restrictive Trade Practices Act 1956

An agreement between traders to restrict competition among themselves is a restrictive trade practice. Similarly an agreement to charge the same prices is restrictive of free competition. So is an agreement to divide up a particular market by limiting the quantities or kinds of goods each supplier sells. An agreement by traders to employ the same terms of supply or conditions of sale is also a restrictive practice.

Agreements containing restrictive trade practices must be registered with the Office of Fair Trading. The Director-General can bring civil proceedings in the Restrictive Practices Court against a trader who operates a restrictive agreement which has not been registered. Any member of the public can also sue personally if he has been affected by such an agreement.

The Director-General can ask the Restrictive Practices Court to decide whether an arrangement is in the public interest or not. If the restrictions it contains are found not to be in the public interest, an order can be made to stop it being operated. It follows that such an arrangement is legally unenforceable as between the parties.

The Fair Trading Act extends the rules against restrictive trade practices to cover agreements concerning **services** as well as goods. However, professional services such as law and medicine are not affected.

Pyramid Selling

Pyramid marketing schemes are based on obtaining

payments from those joining who are promised they will receive commission for introducing other participants. In fact, the statutory restrictions on pyramid selling operate to protect prospective suppliers rather than actual consumers.

These schemes offer individuals the chance of joining in the direct marketing of an attractive line of goods, eg liquid detergents. An entrant is persuaded to pay a substantial sum for the privilege of being an agent or distributor. In fact, his main inducement for joining is not the profit he hopes to make from the sale of the product but the handsome commission fees promised for the introduction of new participants. Unless he can recruit other people to become distributors, his chances of making a profit on his joining fee are remote since in practice the marketing of the detergents in question may prove difficult and is unlikely to produce much profit by itself.

The basis of the scheme is in fact a fraud on those gullible members of the public who are persuaded to join as distributors.

Commission for recruitment of agents prohibited

Controls on this type of trading scheme are set out in the Fair Trading Act 1973, Sections 118–123. It is an offence for a promoter or participant in such a scheme to receive any payment or benefit in the following circumstances:

"Where that payment or benefit is made by some other participant who has been induced to make it by reason of the prospect held out to him of receiving similar payments or benefits for introducing other persons into the scheme."

The Secretary of State for Prices and Consumer Protection is given power to make regulations governing the content of brochures issued to attract new participants. He can also make regulations aimed at preventing participants being unfairly treated. (Section 119). These are set out in the Pyramid Selling Schemes Regulations 1973 (S.I. 1973 No. 1740).

Rights of participants

The regulations relate to the contents of advertisements and the rights of participants who must be given **written contracts** incorporating these rights.

In particular, participants have the **right to withdraw** at any time without penalty, on giving seven days written notice to the promoter.

No promoter or participant in the scheme may accept a deposit on merchandise unless it is stated in writing that such deposit is **refundable** upon the participant returning the goods in an undamaged condition.

No payment can be demanded for training facilities or services supplied. A participant who wishes to leave the scheme can insist on the promoter buying back the goods supplied to him at 90 per cent of the price he paid.

Where a participant is asked to make a payment which involves a contravention of the regulations he may recover it from the promoter or from another participant if made to him direct. No undertaking given by a participant to make any payment is enforceable in any civil proceedings.

Where goods are supplied in circumstances which involve a contravention of the regulations the participant is under no liability to pay for them. If he makes payment for any training facilities he is entitled to it back.

Anyone who circulates or distributes or arranges for the circulation of documents which contravene any of the regulations is liable to a fine of £400 or three months' imprisonment, or both. On conviction at the Crown Court the fine is unlimited and he may be imprisoned for up to two years. (Fair Trading Act 1973, Section 122).

Characteristics of those trading schemes which are regulated

Not all trading schemes come under the regulations.

A scheme is classified as pyramid selling only if it includes the following elements:

1 Goods or services or both are to be provided by the person promoting the scheme.

2 The goods or services so provided are to be supplied to other persons under transactions effected by participants in the scheme.

3 Those transactions are to be effected elsewhere than at premises at which the promoter or the participant carries on his business.

4 The prospect is held out to participants of receiving payments or other benefits for any of the following:

(a) the introduction of other persons who become participants;

(b) the promotion of participants within the trading scheme;

(c) the supply of goods to other participants;

(d) the supply of training facilities or other services for other participants;

(e) transactions effected by other participants.

N.B. The regulations do not apply to a trading scheme where there is only one participant in the United Kingdom.

CHAPTER IV

DEFECTS — LIABILITY OF THE MANUFACTURER

Primarily the consumer's claim is against the retailer. His first line of redress is to sue the retailer. However, there are three situations where the consumer may also have a claim against the manufacturer of a defective article.

The significant advantage of claiming compensation directly from the manufacturer is that he will be more likely to have the financial resources to meet a heavy claim where the purchaser has been injured. This area of the law is often referred to as "Product-Liability".

The consumer may be able to sue the manufacturer of a faulty product for compensation on the ground of **negligence.**

In respect of certain articles such as children's toys, the consumer can sue the manufacturer direct for any loss he has suffered where the manufacturer has broken statutory regulations as to safety etc imposed under the Consumer Safety Act of 1978.

Where the manufacturer gives a **guarantee** and a term of that guarantee is broken, the consumer will be entitled to compensation from the manufacturer.

Why sue the manufacturer?

Before discussing the liability of manufacturers we can consider the case of Mrs Daniels which illustrates the situation where a consumer may have no claim in law at all against the actual retailer. It was a hot summer day. Her husband, who was a street trader, went into Mrs Tabbard's pub for a jug of beer and a bottle of lemonade to make a shandy for himself and his wife. When he got home they both began by drinking some of the lemonade. Unfortunately it contained carbolic acid and both became ill.

Mr Daniels won his case against Mrs Tabbard although she was not at fault in any way, because as seller she was strictly liable under the Sale of Goods Act in the event of the lemonade not being of merchantable quality.

But Mrs Daniels had no claim against the seller because she had sold the lemonade to Mr Daniels, ie there was no contract between Mrs Daniels and the seller.

So Mrs Daniels sued the manufacturers of the lemonade. In the result her claim failed because she could not prove that the manufacturer was careless or "negligent". (*Daniels v. White* (1938)).

This situation is likely to be remedied eventually following the Law Commission's proposal that the producer of a defective article should be strictly liable in law to all consumers who suffer injury, irrespective of any fault or "negligence" on the part of the manufacturer.

In fact the Consumer Safety Act 1978 is already a step in this direction since it imposes strict liability in respect of any breach of the safety regulations towards **any person** who suffers loss.

Position of the non-purchasing consumer who is injured

There are many other instances where the strict legal guarantees contained in the Sale of Goods Act 1979 do not protect the user. Only the person who **bought** the article is entitled to sue under the Act.

Take the case of the defective rubber hot water bottle: *Priest v. Last* (1903). The husband bought it for his wife to relieve her cramp. She used it only four or five days when it burst, scalding her. The wife could not recover compensation from the shop for her injuries. **The husand only** had a legal claim and this was limited to the expense he had incurred in having her injuries treated.

Admittedly the wife could have sued the manufacturers for "negligence" but this was ruled out in practice since their operations were carried on in the USA. (This is one argument against buying a cheaper model and in favour of paying extra for a well-known brand and, incidentally, a reason for buying British. Price and patriotism apart, it is easier to complain to a firm in Birmingham than one based in the Far East).

Similarly a member of the buyer's family or a guest who is injured by a defective spin-dryer will have no claim against the shop, only against the makers for negligent manufacture. In *Godley v. Perry* (1960) a six-year-old boy was blinded in one eye by a stone from a defective catapult which broke while he was using it. The boy's claim against the local retailer succeeded because the boy had bought the catapult **himself.**

If his parents or a friend had bought it and given it to him as a present, the boy would not have had the benefit of the guarantees given by the Sale of Goods Act. Nor could the boy have sued the retailer for negligence. In practice the retailer generally will have no reason to suspect such an article might be defective. The boy's only claim for negligence would be against the manufacturer who operated abroad, so he may have had no practical way at all of getting compensation.

In the "Thalidomide" cases, had the women themselves who bought the drug suffered injuries, even nervous injury, all the retailing chemists would have been liable under Section 14 of the Sale of Goods Act, even though they could not have known the dangerous properties of the drug they were selling and accordingly were not negligent.

Where a child suffers injury before birth the Congenital Disabilities (Civil Liability) Act 1976 gives the child a specific legal right to have compensation from the **manufacturer** on the basis of **negligence.** However, the pharmacists were not negligent for they had obtained their drugs from a recognised source. In law the retailer is entitled to rely upon his supplier in the absence of circumstances suggesting an article might be defective.

The doctors who prescribed thalidomide were not negligent. They were presumably justified in relying on the testing of a reputable manufacturer. In law, the inference is that the **manufacturer is responsible** for defects in the drug he produces.

Liability of manufacturers for negligence
The liability of manufacturers to the public is of recent development. It is based on the fact that their product is intended to reach the consumer in the form it left the factory. They owe a duty to the consumer to take reasonable care in the preparation of their product to ensure that it cannot harm a consumer. The classic case is *Donoghue v. Stevenson* (1932) where the House of Lords decided that the consumer who suffers injury may sue by direct claim against manufacturers who have been negligent. The importance of this decision is that there need be no contract between the consumer and the manufacturers. Moreover he need not have bought the article himself.

It permits the consumer, where the manufacturers have been negligent, to leap-frog over all intermediate wholesalers and distributors and to sue the manufacturers direct.

Miss Donoghue's friend bought her a bottle of ginger beer in a café at Paisley and she drank some. Her friend then poured out the rest when a snail in a state of decomposition floated out of the bottle. She suffered shock and gastroenteritis.

She alleged that in the process of manufacture the snail had got into the bottle which was opaque and she suffered illness from drinking part of the contents. The House of Lords upheld her claim.

Thus all consumers whether as buyers or users will have a

legal claim against the manufacturers of a product if they can establish:

1 There is a defect in the product.
2 The defect existed when it left the factory.
3 The defect is attributable to a lack of reasonable care in the process of manufacture.
4 The defect is not of the sort the consumer could reasonably have noticed before use.
5 The consumer has suffered injury or loss.
6 Such injury or loss was caused by the defect.

There must be evidence that the defect existed when it left the manufacturer's hands and that it was not caused later. Thus the breaking of an article spontaneously one year or so after purchase is not **necessarily** evidence of careless manufacture, eg a car windscreen which shatters for no apparent reason.

A Mr Evans bought a car fitted with a windscreen made by Triplex and called "Triplex Toughened Safety Glass". After one year while he was driving, the windscreen suddenly shattered from no apparent cause and injured the occupants.

The makers of the windscreen were held not liable because of the lapse of time between purchase and breakage. Also it may have been caused by something other than a defect in manufacture.

Again using the article for a purpose materially different from that for which it was designed can also defeat a consumer's claim. If the cause of the accident is partly due to defective manufacture and partly to misuse by the consumer, compensation will be reduced. Thus where 25 per cent blame lies with the manufacturer and 75 per cent blame is owing to misuse, the consumer would forfeit 75 per cent of his compensation.

Where negligence is self-evident

It is not always easy for a consumer who has suffered injury to prove that the manufacturers have been negligent. If an article is found to contain some foreign body which would not be present if due care had been taken in manufacture, that fact is itself evidence of negligence. Where a stone is found in a bun or a bone in a chicken sandwich, or woollen underwear is found to contain a chemical irritant, none of these could have got there except through lack of care during manufacture.

Obviously the consumer cannot have access to a motor assembly plant to prove how the defect came about. Generally he will have to rely on the important legal presumption *'Res ipsa loquitur'*, ie the matter is self-evident, as in the case of a person eating a bath bun who breaks his teeth on a stone contained in it.

He is entitled to say to the court that the facts speak for themselves – the manufacturer's employees or system must have been at fault. In *Chapronière v. Mason* (1905) the manufacturer tried to argue that his production system was aimed at preventing foreign bodies getting into the buns, but this evidence was rejected. It was obvious someone in the bakery must have been careless.

However, sometimes a manufacturer is able to prove that he has taken all reasonable precautions to prevent the defect. Where carbolic acid has got into a bottle of lemonade there is a presumption of negligence. The manufacturer may avoid liability only if he satisfies the court his system of production is safe and he has proper supervision to prevent this type of defect occurring, as was proved in the case of *Daniels v. White* (1938).

Summary

1 A consumer who suffers loss or injury because an article has been manufactured negligently can claim compensation from the manufacturer direct apart from any claim he may have against the retailer.

2 The advantage of a claim in negligence is that the

consumer can claim compensation from the manufacturer although he did not himself buy the defective
article, eg if it was given to him as a gift. But he must
prove negligence whereas the original buyer need not.

3 The producer who **sells directly** to the consumer becomes
in law a retailer and so is strictly responsible under
the Sale of Goods Act. It is not necessary for the buyer
to prove there was negligence in the process of manufacture. The producer cannot escape this strict liability
to the buyer by proving he took all possible care.

4 The responsibility a manufacturer owes to the consumer
in negligence is quite separate from the contractual
liability he owes to the wholesaler or retailer under
the Sale of Goods Act.

The following list gives further examples of manufacturers' negligence where consumers have received
compensation. (The term "consumer" here covers the
ultimate user of the article or anyone who is within physical
proximity of it.)

Sweets sent out for consumption containing a piece of
wire.

Hairdyes, chemicals and drugs

Mrs Parker had been in the habit of having her hair dyed
with henna at Mrs Senior's shop. One day Mrs Senior
suggested using "Oloxo" dye and assured Mrs Parker it was
quite safe. Mrs Parker got dermatitis and claimed compensation from Mrs Senior and from Oloxo Limited, the
manufacturers of the dye. A booklet issued about the dye
stated it was dangerous if used without a prior skin test
but when the dye was supplied to Mrs Senior's shop this
warning was omitted. Mrs Parker was awarded compensation against Mrs Senior from whom she had bought the dye,
under the **contract of sale.** She also got compensation
from Oloxo Limited as manufacturers for **negligence** in
supplying it without a warning as to its danger, but Mrs

Senior was entitled to have the compensation awarded against her paid by the manufacturers. *Parker v. Oloxo & Senior* (1937) (see further p 100 regarding chemicals).

Garments or underclothing containing irritant chemicals.

Bottles, containers, packages, pipes – inadequate plastic pipes installed in a heating system which caused a fire (see p 154). Lead pipes causing water to become poisonous. Wrong labels, directions or instructions for use which accompany any product.

Warning notices
Where sufficient warning is given, the manufacturer will be absolved from liability. In *Holmes v. Ashford* (1950) hair dye was supplied to a hairdresser in labelled bottles together with a small brochure of instructions. Both labels and brochure contained a warning that the dye might be dangerous to certain skins and recommended a test should be made before it was used. The hairdresser read the label but failed to make a test. Mrs Holmes got dermatitis. She was awarded compensation against the hairdresser but **not** against the manufacturers. The Court of Appeal decided that the manufacturers had given sufficient warning of the potential danger of the dye.

Damage to the defective product itself
Note that liability for negligence on the part of the manufacturer does not amount to a guarantee of the article, eg it does not oblige them to replace, or pay for repairs to, a defective product.

However in the United States a manufacturer may be held liable where the defect in the product, say a car, causes it to sustain damage through impact or bursting into flames. This might occur where the front wheel collapses or there is a steering failure resulting in collision.

Liability of manufacturers in the United States
The Uniform Commercial Code allows an action for breach of warranty not only to the buyer but also to "members of his family or household".

In the case of *Hirst v. Elgin Metal Casket Company,* 1978, six relatives of a deceased were entitled to have compensation on the ground that they had suffered emotional distress following the opening of a defective coffin.

When the grave was opened the coffin was brought to the surface in the presence of the six relatives of the deceased. The manufacturer had claimed that the coffin was leakproof but unfortunately it turned out to the horror of the relatives that this was not so. Water had entered the coffin and the relatives had sustained considerable emotional shock.

They sued the manufacturer for breach of warranty and their claim was allowed. They had not sustained any physical injury but were entitled to damages for emotional distress.

The US District Court took the line that injury to the person was not necessarily restricted to physical injury but extended to grief, anxiety or depression. It is unlikely that any UK court would take a similar view and award compensation on these facts.

Law Commission's proposals for reform
In their report on "Liability for Defective Products" the Law Commission considers:
(a) Existing rights and remedies in English law are inadequate in respect of injury caused by defective products.
(b) Producers should as a general rule be **strictly** liable for injuries caused by defects in their products, irrespective of fault.
(c) A product should be regarded as defective if it does not comply with the standard of reasonable safety that a person is entitled to expect of it.

(d) Strict liability should rest on the producer of a component whether or not the component is later incorporated into another product by another producer.

(e) Strict liability should also be imposed on certain persons who play a part in the chain of distribution without necessarily being producers. For example a person who puts his name or trade mark on a defective product so as to present it as his own, should be strictly liable for it.

(f) In order to establish the liability of a producer, the injured person should have to prove:
  (i) that he was injured
  (ii) that the injury was attributable to a defect in or defectiveness of a product.
  (iii) that the defendant had produced the product or dealt with it under his own trade name or mark.

The Consumer Safety Act 1978

This Act enables the Secretary of State to make safety regulations to ensure that goods sold are safe and that the consumer is given proper information about them. These regulations can prescribe safety requirements as to:

(a) Composition and contents of goods
(b) Design and construction
(c) Finish and packing
(d) Safety warnings and instructions

Any supplier who in the course of business breaks these regulations or who fails to comply with a prohibition order which prohibits the supply of goods which are designated unsafe, can be fined up to £1,000 and sentenced to three months' imprisonment.

The Act enables the Secretary of State to take urgent action if unsafe goods are found to be on sale. 1. He can serve on any trader a prohibition notice prohibiting him from continuing to supply specified goods which are

80

considered to be unsafe. 2. He is able to make prohibition orders prohibiting traders supplying any goods which he considers to be unsafe. 3. He can also serve on any trader a "notice to warn" requiring him to publish a warning about goods which he has been marketing and which are considered to be dangerous. 4. He can impose labelling requirements for example, that goods must bear such information as warning symbols, names of ingredients, first-aid instructions and name and address of manufacturer or supplier.

Civil Liability is strict

The Act is important because it also imposes on the supplier a statutory duty, breach of which gives rise to strict civil liability. It expressly entitles a consumer who has suffered loss to sue a manufacturer or supplier who has failed to comply with the relevant safety regulation or prohibition order or notice. The supplier's liability to pay compensation is strict. He cannot avoid meeting any loss suffered by a consumer due to his non-compliance with any of the regulations. All exclusion clauses are void in so far as they seek to exclude or restrict financial liability. The consumer does not have to prove the manufacturer was "negligent". He need only show that a safety regulation has been broken and caused him loss.

However, in the case of a criminal charge being brought against a supplier under the Act, the supplier can avoid conviction, ie being fined or imprisoned, provided he can prove he took all reasonable steps and exercised all due diligence to avoid committing an offence.

Should the supplier be convicted the court can also make a compensation order in favour of the consumer. On the other hand, if the supplier should be acquitted on the ground that he took all reasonable steps and exercised all due diligence, a consumer who has been injured or suffered loss could still obtain compensation from the supplier since civil liability under the Act is strict and does not admit of any such defence.

The safety regulations

The Consumer Safety Act 1978 replaces the Consumer Protection Acts under which safety regulations are already in force in relation to:

Oil heaters, stands for carry-cots, nightdresses, electrical appliances, electric blankets, cooking utensils, heating appliances, pencils and graphic instruments, toys, glazed ceramic ware, electrical equipment and children's clothing (hood-cords in anoraks), aerosols, dummies, cosmetics, vitreous enamelled ware, perambulators and pushchairs and so on.

The task of enforcing the regulations lies with each Local Authority. Their trading standards officers can investigate complaints and test goods to check compliance with the regulations. They have power to prosecute either retailers, importers, wholesalers or manufacturers.

Foreign imported toys have come under scrutiny as a particular source of danger for children. Inflammability, sharp points and paint with lead in it are common hazards. Teddy bears' eyes are tested, for example, to ensure that they cannot be pulled out by the child and cause injury if swallowed.

Summary

These regulations benefit the consumer in two ways:

1 If the regulations are not complied with any consumer who suffers loss is given a right to sue the retailer or distributor for compensation for breach of statutory duty. This could be important if the manufacturer is abroad.

2 The consumer does not have the often difficult task of establishing that the process of manufacture was faulty and that the manufacturer ought to have safeguarded against the defect occurring. He need only cite the

safety regulation in question, eg lead content in paint and show his child suffered injury. In fact breach of the regulation will normally be proved at the preceding criminal trial by the Trading Standards Officer.

Manufacturers' guarantees

A statement by manufacturers "All our products are guaranteed" means no more than "They are of merchantable quality".

The manufacturers' guarantee is quite distinct from the primary liability of the retailer under the Sale of Goods Act for what he sells. (See Chapter II). Their guarantee gives the purchaser an additional right in contract to claim compensation against them direct for any defect but only if it is covered by the **terms** of their guarantee.

A manufacturers' guarantee is also known as a warranty. They may for example warrant or undertake that if their products are defective they will repair or replace them free of charge. The offer of a guarantee to the consumer involves a **separate contract** between themselves and the consumer. Usually the consumer is given a postcard to sign and return to them to confirm that he accepts the terms of their guarantee. But he is not obliged to accept it and may decline it.

Form of guarantee

Normally a manufacturers' guarantee is given in writing and contained in a document or card but a guarantee can also be spoken. (See *Shanklin Pier Ltd. v Detel Products Ltd.,* p 87). It may be announced on radio or in a television advertisement.

In the classic case of Mrs Carlill, this lady saw an advertisement by the Carbolic Smoke Ball Co, promising £100 to anyone who caught influenza after using their product as prescribed. She went to a shop, bought the smoke ball and followed the instructions as to its use but nevertheless went down with 'flu. Although she had not bought it from the manufacturing company direct, the terms of their advertisement amounted to the offer of a guarantee to all purchasers and entitled her to claim the £100 compensation from them.

Specific guarantees
Many manufacturers, particularly of machinery, vehicles or electrical goods, give a guarantee for a specific period. Often they undertake to replace defective parts free of charge. The consumer should enquire whether this includes:
- the cost of labour
- the cost of shipping a replacement

The manufacturer's guarantee is limited to what it actually states, eg defective parts only. It may not cover the cost of labour or sending the article back.

Consumer goods
Prior to the Unfair Contract Terms Act 1977 it was usual for guarantees to declare that the manufacturer was not to liable beyond remedying the actual defect. As a result the consumer could be deprived of his right to compensation from the manufacturer under common law (see p 74), in the event of the defective item causing injury, eg where a defective electric iron sets fire to the whole room and burns the consumer or someone in his family. Such exclusion clauses are now **void** so far as the ordinary consumer is concerned. As from February 1978 compensation for such consequential losses must always be given.

The Act defines a guarantee as any document which contains ". . . some promise or assurance (however worded or presented) that defects will be made good by complete or partial replacement or by repair, monetary compensation or otherwise."

It is now impossible for a guarantee which a manufacturer

gives with ordinary consumer goods to exclude or restrict **his obligation** to pay compensation to the consumer in the event of loss or damage resulting from negligence in manufacture. (In law "Negligence" means the breach of a duty to take care to ensure others do not suffer loss).

The manufacturer cannot avoid his common law responsibility in respect of goods which are of a type ordinarily supplied for **private use or consumption.** Such liability covers loss or damage (including death or personal injury) arising from the goods proving defective while in use or even if not actually in use, while simply in the possession of the consumer.

However if the item is used **exclusively** for the purposes of a **business** it will still be possible for the guarantee to exclude such liability.

Guarantees of items exclusively for BUSINESS use

Where an item is bought for **business** use the wording of the guarantee may validly still declare that the manufacturer is not to be liable for any consequential loss or injury beyond remedying the actual defect. For example, a defective power drill may break and cause injury.

• Before accepting a guarantee the business buyer should scrutinize its wording to see if it contains exclusion clauses which seek to avoid, in particular, consequential liability resulting from negligent manufacture.

• Employers should also be aware of their own liability in the case of injury to an employee through using a defective tool. Under the Employer's Liability (Defective Equipment) Act 1969 the employer is held legally responsible to pay compensation even though the defect is due to the negligence of the manufacturer. Normally the employer who is sued by an employee for compensation will have an equivalent claim to be indemnified by the manufacturer.

The business buyer should always satisfy himself that

none of these rights are taken away by the guarantee before he accepts it.

Manufacturers often try to entice business buyers into accepting their guarantee by the offer of a "free first service". The buyer will be deemed to accept all the terms of the guarantee if he signs an order form incorporating it, or returns a tear-off slip or card to register the guarantee. Even if he simply puts the article in for a free service or for a defect to be investigated under the guarantee, he will be bound by it.

However, the mere purchase of an article cannot of itself involve acceptance of the terms of the manufacturers' guarantee. When the guarantee is attached to the article with a notice stating that "purchase constitutes acceptance of the terms", the business buyer is not bound unless he accepts from the manufacturers some **advantage** such as a free service.

The chief reason for declining a guarantee which excludes his rights to sue the manufacturers for negligence is that such claims are usually for personal injuries or damage to property and may involve substantial sums of money. No small retailer could be expected to pay a very large sum by way of compensation but manufacturers usually have considerable financial resources. Moreover, manufacturers will generally be insured against product liability. Furthermore, the manufacturers' or distributors' legal ability for negligence is very wide and constitutes a major legal protection to users of their products.

Illustrations of manufacturers' liability by way of "guarantee"

A. For Advice

Manufacturers may give a consumer information in a brochure or in answer to an inquiry. This can amount to a guarantee or warranty if the consumer in reliance on such information, buys the article from a retailer. A consumer may consult the manufacturers about the suitability of their product for a certain purpose and, in reliance on what they tell him, he may be induced to buy it. A firm of paint manufacturers were asked by the owners of a pier whether their paint was suitable for repainting their pier. On being assured that it was, the pier owners instructed their contractors to use that particular paint. It turned out to be unsatisfactory and the pier had to be repainted. The manufacturers were ordered to make amends on the ground that they had warranted the suitability of their paint. *Shanklin Pier Ltd. v. Detel Products Ltd.* (1951).

B. *Advertisements*

In appropriate circumstances a manufacturer's representation as to a product's qualities, say in an advertisement, can amount to a separate warranty of its suitability on which the consumer is entitled to rely.

In the classic case the manufacturers of a patent medical preparation were held liable on an advertisement to pay £100 to anyone who used the medicine as prescribed but nevertheless caught influenza: *Carlill v. Carbolic Smoke Ball Co.* (1893). In an American case, the manufacturers of a motor car advertised it as equipped with a "shatterproof" windscreen. They were held liable to the consumer who bought it from a retailer in reliance on the advertisement and who was injured when it shattered.

C. *Statements on containers*

An unambiguous guarantee on a container as to the virtues of its contents may amount to a separate warranty or collateral contract with the purchaser. The manufacturers could be responsible to the consumer for it quite apart from the retailer's responsibility to him, should it prove defective.

Again a misstatement on a container by manufacturers as to the nature of the product within, could render them liable to the consumer for **negligence.** (See *Vacwell Engineering v. B D H Chemicals,* p 100). Thus wrongly stating that a plastic adhesive or insulation material is heat resistant could involve liability for negligence if it turns out to be inflammable.

CHAPTER V

COMPENSATION FOR
BREACH OF CONTRACT

Consequences of cancelling an order

Suppose a consumer sees in the window of a local hardware shop a refrigerator normaly sold at £100 but advertised at the specially reduced price of £80. He goes in and places an order. The legal consequences in the event of either party breaking the agreement are as follows:

● **Shop fails to deliver:** The shop must pay the customer the difference between the reduced price and the normal price, ie £20, if he insists.

● **Customer has a change of mind:** The customer must pay the shop its loss of profit on the transaction.

● **Cancelling an order for a new car:** A consumer who changes his mind and decides to cancel his order for a new car is not entitled to do so save on the ground of excessive delay. Otherwise he may have to pay the dealer the entire profit which he would have made. Whether he has to pay this depends on whether the supply of that particular model **exceeds demand.**

Assuming supplies are plentiful, the dealer will naturally have lost his profit on the particular sale as a result of cancellation. He can insist on being paid this amount even though the manufacturers are willing to accept the car back without any payment from him. He does not have to prove that he has one extra car in his showroom which he cannot sell.

However there is an important exception to this situation which is that the buyer need pay nothing if the model is **in short supply.** If there are a number of eager buyers waiting for that particular model, all the customer has done by cancelling is to shorten the suppliers' waiting list. Since they cannot obtain enough cars to meet the demand, they suffer no loss by one particular customer's cancellation.

Accordingly, Mr Sullivan was absolved from paying after cancelling his order for a new Hillman Minx which was in short supply. He had agreed to trade in his old Commer van in part-exchange.

Later he became dissatisfied with the part-exchange value of £530 and found another dealer who allowed more, so he took his custom there. The Court of Appeal came out on the side of Mr Sullivan. Since the first dealer admitted that he had a queue of buyers waiting for the Hillman, he had not suffered any real loss by the cancellation.

Cancelling an order for a second-hand car

If the dealer is able to sell the same car to another buyer at the same price or at a better price, he will have no claim against the original buyer.

Mr Wright agreed to buy a second-hand BMW for £1,670. The following day he told the dealers he had changed his mind. Six weeks later they sold the same BMW for £1,770. Despite their more profitable, subsequent sale the dealers claimed from Mr Wright their loss of profit, viz £345. The Court of Appeal refused to allow any such claim. The dealers could recover only the particular loss sustained in the transaction and nothing more. As they had sold the same car at a higher price they had suffered no loss and so could claim nothing from Mr Wright. (*Lazenby Garages Ltd. v. Wright* (1976)).

On the other hand, had the dealers been obliged to sell the car at a loss, ie below the price Mr Wright had agreed, he would have been obliged to pay them the difference.

Cancelling a special order

Suppose a consumer orders, say, a suit to be made to

measure. Should he later change his mind and cancel his order the extent of his financial liability will depend on whether the tailor has already started work on it.

In the first place the tailor will be entitled to charge his loss of profit. Strictly once a firm order has been placed and measurements taken, the consumer must pay the tailor a reasonable sum to cover the profit he would have received. This may be as much as one-third of the cost of the suit but a tradesman will usually accept a smaller sum in settlement for the sake of goodwill.

Where the tailor has actually cut out the cloth and has started sewing it, he can charge both for the value of the material used and for the work done so far, in addition to his loss of profit. This might come to almost the cost of the completed article.

Supplier's duty to mitigate loss

Against this the consumer may be entitled to certain credits since the tailor will be obliged to take reasonable steps to **mitigate his loss.** For example, he may be able to use the pieces of cloth for another order. Alternatively he may be able to sell the completed suit as a reject, though not perhaps for a very great amount. In either case he must give credit for the value of what he manages to salvage.

The same would apply where a householder cancels an order for a fitted kitchen. Assuming the supplier can return most of the fitted units to stock he would not be entitled to charge for units which were usable elsewhere. However, he would be entitled to claim a reasonable sum for labour (if any) and his loss of profit.

Suppose you agree to hire a machine for a period of three months. You then change your mind and refuse to accept the machine. It is the duty of the suppliers to take reasonable steps to re-let it to someone else. You will only have to pay for the period that they are unable to re-let it.

Cancelling and order for delay

Once a buyer has placed an order, he can ask the suppliers to notify him when delivery will be made. If this is not prompt enough for his requirements, he can cancel his order. However, by pressing for delivery after a delay has occurred, the consumer will be taken to have accepted the delay. (See also p 78).

A businessman who wanted a new Rolls Royce agreed with a firm called Jones Bros that they should build the bodywork within six months and have it ready by the following March. His hopes were disappointed and he continued to press for delivery. "Could it be ready by August, as he was planning to go to the Continent?" "Yes, it will be ready in two weeks' time", they assured him.

Finally he wrote Jones Bros. "I shall be unable to accept delivery of the Rolls you are making for me after July 25." August came – still no car, so he bought a standard model and wrote asking them for his deposit back. When it came to court Jones Bros maintained that difficulties with labour and materials were outside their control. They said it was therefore unreasonable for the buyer to have insisted on delivery by the end of July. They also said that by releasing them from the original delivery date he had waived all objection to the delay. The judges thought otherwise and ordered that he should have his deposit back. Although he had extended the time limit, when this further dead-line was again not met he was justified in cancelling the order. *Rickards v. Oppenheim* (1950).

In the same way, a woman may order a new dress for her daughter's wedding and stipulate that it be delivered "by Friday morning at the latest". A tailor who accepts this dead-line would not be entitled to deliver the dress on Saturday. Of course, in the case of a garment ordered to measure the judge must be satisfied that there was a definite dead-line.

92

Time Limits

Deadlines can cut both ways. A householder who obtains an estimate to install a new kitchen cannot accept it after an unreasonable delay. Unless he accepts fairly promptly he may not insist on having the work carried out for the sum offered. Once the offer lapses the householder will have to negotiate a new price.

Again, a man may advertise his old caravan for sale and wish to hold out as long as possible for the highest offer. A prospective buyer is entitled to state that his offer of £500 will remain open for seven days. But this does not prevent him withdrawing his offer before the dead-line arrives and before the seller accepts.

In law, notification that an offer has been withdrawn can come in a roundabout way. For example, a friend may mention to the seller that the prospective buyer has since bought a caravan from a local garage. The seller cannot insist on holding the buyer to his original offer, even though the dead-line has not passed. The offer is regarded as having been withdrawn just as if the buyer had told the seller.

Where a time is stipulated, performance must be made accordingly. The simplest instance is a catering contract for a garden fête. The buns must be delivered at the appointed time on the correct day. Any delay in performance will generally be regarded as a breach for which the customer can claim compensation.

Where no date for delivery is fixed the customer is entitled to delivery within a "reasonable" time. What is a reasonable time depends upon the circumstances. In the case of a refrigerator, delivery within 21 days or so might be considered reasonable.

If the shop writes saying it cannot deliver for three months the customer would be entitled to notify it that he proposes to buy elsewhere. Where a date for delivery is promised but not complied with, the customer can prevent further delay by making time **of the essence** of the transaction. This is done by fixing a dead-line and stating that delivery after that date will not be accepted.

Where time is of the essence
Where a **businessman** buys goods the law says that they must be delivered on the date promised. This is often an important consideration in business transactions. But where a **consumer** orders goods the date promised for delivery is not assumed to be vital unless the consumer stipulates **that it is**, eg buns for a garden fête or a caravan or boat for the family holiday, where the seller **knows** that it is vital for the consumer to have delivery on time.

Delivery here means having the article ordered available for collection not physically transporting it to the buyer's address. The Sale of Goods Act 1979, Section 51(2) determines how much a buyer may claim for non-delivery where the seller fails to supply goods on time:

"The measure of damages is the estimated loss directly and naturally resulting, in the ordinary course of events, from the seller's breach of contract."

In most situations the compensation payable is the difference between the price originally agreed and any **higher** price which is current at the date agreed for delivery.

If a date was not agreed for delivery then the relevant date will be when the seller tells the buyer he does not propose to supply the goods.

It follows that if **on that date** the buyer can obtain a similar article from a different supplier at the same price (or at a lower price) he suffers no loss and can claim no compensation. But if the current price is **higher** than the original price the buyer will have to pay more to get the same goods elsewhere. Consequently he is entitled to the difference between the agreed price and the market price as at the date promised for delivery.

The buyer is entitled to this assessment of compensation

in any event. Supposing a month later he finds the price of the article has gone down, this will be his gain but should the price rise even further, this will not increase his compensation. His duty was to buy an equivalent article **on the precise date** when the original seller failed to deliver.

Compensation for losses due to delay

So where a supplier fails to honour his contract on the date promised the buyer can notify him that he will not accept the article at a later date but will buy a similar article elsewhere. If he has to pay more than the price originally agreed he can claim the difference as compensation.

However, if he wishes, he can **accept** the item although delivered late. His compensation will then be the difference between the market value of the article on the date it should have been delivered and its value (assuming this is lower) when actually delivered.

Normally prices rise rather than fall. If so, the buyer will be entitled to nothing under Section 51(2). Nevertheless he may be able to claim compensation for consequential losses:

(1) Any loss arising **naturally** from the delay in delivery.

(2) In addition any **special** loss which at the time the order was placed both parties could have predicted as likely to result from delay in delivery.

Illustration

A laundry ordered a large boiler to replace the smaller one they already had but it was delivered five months late. During this time they had to turn away increased business which the new boiler could have coped with. The laundry was awarded compensation for this **Loss of ordinary business.**

The laundry also lost some very lucrative government

dyeing work which their old boiler could not cope with but the Court of Appeal refused them the additional profits they might have got from this exceptional business opportunity because it did not arise naturally, ie in the usual course of their business. The court would allow such loss of profits only if the firm selling the boiler was aware that the laundry was likely to obtain the lucrative dyeing work. *Victoria Laundry v. Newman* (1949).

Similarly a consumer who is prejudiced by unreasonable delay may be entitled to compensation. A contractor who promises to repair a machine or motor car within seven days but in fact takes three weeks can involve the consumer in expense, particularly if he uses it for his business. He would be justified in deducting from the repair bill the cost of having to hire a substitute machine or vehicle for two extra weeks.

In certain circumstances the contractor may be under an obligation to compensate the customer for his loss of profit due to delay. A firm of engineers may undertake to repair or to install a central heating system in a guest house in time for the winter season. If they finish the contract three or four weeks late, guests may have to be turned away. The proprietor's loss of profit for the period due to their delay would be their responsibility.

Normally the engineers would be liable only for an average loss of profits, not for an exceptionally lucrative booking, unless they had been told, say, that a special party was coming and that it was essential that the central heating was in working order on that date.

Where no business element is involved the ordinary householder could not expect to receive a great deal of compensation, unless the judge thought the inconvenience suffered was severe.

Calculating Compensation for defects

Articles which are defective can be dealt with in one

of two ways whether the defect is one of quality, fitness for purpose or failure to comply with description. Either the buyer can reject the article immediately. Alternatively, he may keep the article and claim an appropriate diminution in price.

The buyer is not obliged to return the defective article. He is obliged only to tell the retailer that he refuses to accept it.

If he decides to accept it he can insist on compensation This will cover all direct and predictable expenses he incurs which could include the cost of transport. In some instances the buyer may, if he wishes, get the defects remedied by someone else and claim the cost from the seller.

Assume an article is delivered scratched or otherwise damaged. He may prefer to retain it and claim the cost of **repair.** Compensation will be calculated as follows:

(i) Assess value of goods as of good quality (as promised).

(ii) Deduct value of goods in defective state (as delivered).

(iii) The difference is the amount the consumer is entitled to claim. (Sale of Goods Act 1979, s. 53(3).)

Loss of profit

The buyer can get higher compensation where the seller knows the buyer intends to make some profit from the article.

In one case inferior seeds were supplied. The buyer planted them and got an inferior crop worth £X. Had he got average quality seeds the value of the crop would have been far greater. The Court awarded him the difference in value between an average good crop and the worth of the crop the seeds actually produced. *Wagstaff v. Shorthorn Dairy Co,* (1884).

To claim such compensation it is essential that the use to which the buyer proposes to put the article is known or obvious to the seller. Thus where defective sugar was sold to a firm of brewers the market price of all the beer in their cellars rendered poisonous by the sugar was allowed to them.

Capital loss or profit loss?
Where a manufacturing machine is stated to produce goods at a specified rate the buyer can claim damages for loss of profit if it operates less efficiently than promised. As an alternative to assessing his loss at the difference in value between the machine as described and the one delivered, the dissatisfied buyer can claim his loss of anticipated profit. But he cannot claim both a capital loss **and** a loss of **profit.**

Take the case of the clay machine which the makers claimed could process clay at a certain rate but in fact was much slower.

The buyers sought to claim both:
(a) the difference in value between the two machines, ie the high production type specified, as compared with the more limited capacity machine they actually received.
(b) their anticipated loss of profits, calculated over a three year period, being the difference between its actual output and the output they had been promised.

The Court of Appeal said they were allowed to choose between (a) and (b) but not both. They chose (b) which was for the larger sum.

In fact, the court would have allowed the entire anticipated loss of profits for the full life expectancy of the machine, which was ten years, although in fact only three years were claimed. *Cullinane v. British Rema Mfg. Co.* (1953).

Consequential Expenses
The buyer's rights are not limited to repair or replacement. Should he suffer other incidental losses as a result of a

defect in the article, can he claim these too. Whether he keeps it or rejects it he can claim whatever loss he has sustained which has resulted, directly and naturally in the ordinary course of events, from such defect.

Thus a consumer could claim the cost of using a laundry during the weeks his own washing machine was being put right or for hiring a car whilst a defect in his was being repaired. He should notify the dealers by letter that such expenses are being incurred to allow them to expedite repairs. (Sale of Goods Act 1979, s. 53(2).)

Such expenses must be kept to a minimum. The buyer of a defective car cannot run up an unlimited bill for expenses while it is out of action. He must "mitigate" his loss. Thus he cannot hire a Rover while his new Mini is undergoing repair. Again in the case of the defective washing machine, the buyer ought to take his washing to a launderette since using a launderette is cheaper than a laundry which includes ironing. Hence a deduction might be made from the laundry bill. On the other hand, he may live too far from a launderette and have no alternative but to use the services of a laundry.

The consumer can claim too for any consequential loss he has suffered. Should his defective washing machine tear or discolour clothes, he will be entitled to their value. Similarly, if the thermostat on new electric iron malfunctions causing an expensive silk dress to be burnt. If a freezer is defective the cost of food lost through thawing is recoverable.

One man returned a tie to a well-known shop because the dye had run in the rain. He also showed them the silk shirt he had been wearing which was stained with dye from the tie. Without demur the shop repaid the cost of the tie and also paid him for the value of the shirt.

Liability for unexpectedly extensive losses
A do-it-yourself supplier who sells unsuitable, defective

or low quality materials could incur liability far beyond the mere cost of replacement of the items sold. *Smith v. Johnson* (1899) provides an illustration. Inferior lime was sold for mortar to build a wall. The mortar did not come up to building regulations standard and the wall was condemned. The buyer recovered from the seller the cost of pulling down and rebuilding the wall.

The purchaser of a carriage complained that his horses were injured when a defective pole broke. Compensation of £140 was given although the value of the pole was only £3. The injury to his horses was a natural consequence of the pole being defective. *Randall v. Newson* (1877).

In *Smith v. Green* (1876) a diseased cow was sold to a farmer and he placed her with his other cows, several of which died, as well as the cow sold. The seller was held liable for the entire loss.

The extent of the seller's liability is clearly brought out in the case of *Vacwell Engineering Co. Ltd. v B.D.H. Chemicals Ltd.* (1969). Vacwell Engineering were manufacturers of transistors. B.D.H. Ltd. who had supplied Vacwell with chemicals over a period of years advertised boron tribromide. This substance was known to react on contact with water to emit a toxic vapour but neither firm knew it could also explode (though this fact was stated in the scientific literature). In 1966 Vacwell ordered 400 glass ampoules. Each bore the warning "harmful vapour". After they were delivered and while Vacwell's technician was washing off the labels in the sink an ampoule exploded, killing him and damaging their premises. B.D.H. were held liable under an implied condition of fitness, in that Vacwell relied on B.D.H.'s skill to warn them of hazards. B.D.H. were also held negligent. (See also the Sale of Goods Act 1979, Sections 14 & 53).

CHAPTER VI

TRADE DESCRIPTIONS AND MISREPRESENTATIONS

In practice almost every sale involves a description of some sort. If a housewife selects a packet marked 'sugar' in the supermarket, she does not expect it to contain salt. If it is marked 'Demerara' but turns out to be icing sugar, she may have no use for it at all. Where goods fail to correspond with their description in all respects, the seller has broken an implied term of his contract. The Sale of Goods Act 1979, puts the position with perfect clarity in Section 13(i):

"Where there is a contract for the sale of goods by description there is an implied condition that the goods will correspond with the description."

The term "description" covers a wide area. It can refer to quality, quantity, contents, measurements, even methods of packing.

The way an article is described is likely to be particularly important in mail-order purchasing where the buyer relies on what is said and the glossy pictures in a catalogue. The sellers must (with reasonable promptness) dispatch an article corresponding to the type ordered. Even details like colour can be important. They cannot send yellow to a customer who ordered beige.

Where the item delivered is not as described it is 'defective' in the sense it is not what the buyer wants, eg it may not serve the purpose he bought it for. In any case, although perfectly sound, it is not what he ordered. Nor is it what the seller promised to deliver.

- In most cases the buyer will be entitled to reject the article and get his money back.

101

- The buyer may be entitled to be paid compensation as well for any inconvenience or loss he has suffered.
- Alternatively the buyer may choose to keep it and insist on a reduction in price by way of compensation.

Accuracy of description

The description may be on the container or on a tag or in a notice in the shop or in an advertisement. What the sales assistant tells the customer may equally be regarded as a description.

The description must be accurate:

(i) Even where the buyer has examined the item or tried it.
(ii) Even where the buyer has selected it himself, eg in a self-service store.

Accuracy means that shoes described as leather should not turn out to be plastic.

Again, a newspaper advertisement describing a car as a "Herald, convertible, white, 1961" was incorrect as to the age of the car, since the front half was of an earlier model. Although the buyer had inspected the car, he was entitled to rely on the accuracy of the description and was granted damages since the **whole** car was not 1961. *Beale v. Taylor* (1967).

A buyer who orders "staves, half an inch thick" can reject them if they vary between 9/16th and half an inch. *Arcos v. Ronaasen* (1933).

Even the packaging of goods may be part of their description. A buyer placed an order for 3,000 tins of fruit packed in cases of 30 tins. Most of the cases delivered contained 24 tins but the total was correct. The buyer was entitled to reject the consignment. Only if the difference between what is ordered and what is delivered is **minute** will the buyer be bound to accept it. *Re Moore & Landauer* (1921). Accuracy can also refer to quality. One judge remarked that an order for superior old port wine is not fulfilled by supplying wine which, in the opinion of witnesses was "almost undrinkable."

Private sellers

Mr Whipp met Mr Varley in Huddersfield and offered to sell him a 'second-hand, self-binder reaping machine' he had on his farm. He described it as 'new the previous year'. When Mr Varley received it he complained about its extreme antiquity and that it had been repaired. He sent it back. The Appeal Court held that he need not pay Mr Whipp anything, as the machine was not as Mr Whipp described it. *Varley v. Whipp* (1900). (See further p 53).

Antiques

A set of linen napkins was described as 'authentic property of Charles I' dating from the seventeenth century. An experienced antique dealer inspected the set and bought it. It turned out to be an eighteenth century set. He was entitled to reject it. *Nicholson v. Venn & Smith Marriott* (1947).

The buyer of a piece of antique silver is protected by the same basic rule of law as applies to other goods, that is, anything sold by description must corrspond exactly to that description. A man who buys a Georgian silver coffee pot cannot be fobbed off with a Victorian reproduction of a Georgian coffee pot.

In fact silver and gold articles enjoy a special protective status by virtue of the hallmark which all such articles must bear. Both the quality and date of manufacture are therefore easily ascertained.

The position regarding fake antique silver is clear. In theory it is valueless and it is unlawful knowingly to possess silver (or gold) bearing a false hallmark. The Crown Office is entitled to insist on its destruction.

New or second-hand

A motor cycle sold as 'new' was in fact four or five years old. It had been driven only five miles and had **not** been subject to a prior retail sale. The court held that a vehicle need not be

103

the **latest model** to justify being described as 'new'. *Phillips v. Cycle and General Finance Corporation Ltd.* (1976).

But an order for a **new** Singer car is not satisfied by delivery of a second-hand model (*Andrews v. Singer* (1934)). Nor is a motor car advertised as 'new' correctly described where it has been subject to a prior retail sale, eg registered with the local authority, carries number plates and has been driven away from the showrooms by the purchaser even though it has only 130 miles on the clock. *Morris Motors v. Lilley* (1959). (See further p 114).

The Misrepresentation Act 1967

This Act is much wider in its scope than Section 13(i) of the Sale of Goods Act which we have just discussed. Liability for misrepresentation is not restricted to the purchase of goods, but can apply to any pre-contract negotiations for buying or renting a house for instance, or for having your curtains dry-cleaned. It enables you to bring a civil claim for compensation for any loss you suffer as a result of a false statement of fact which leads you to enter into a contract for goods, property or services. Like Section 13(i) private sellers as well as traders are liable for misleading statements. But unlike Section 13(i), where liability is strict, a claim against a seller for misrepresentation will not succeed if he can prove he had reasonable grounds for believing his statement was true.

Misleading Sales Talk

The statement need not be part of the description of the article to give rise to a claim. A seller who tells you "This car is in excellent condition" or "a good runner" is leading you to believe it is in good mechanical order. To found a claim, the misrepresentation must be one of fact. not of opinion, on the part of the seller. Remarks like "It's the latest fashion" or "an ideal bachelor's model" are mere puffs, not statements of fact. Secondly, the statement must have induced you to buy the article or enter into the contract. If you disregard what you were told and get your own mechanic to check its working condition before you agree to buy, you will have no claim under the Act.

Rescission and Damages

A consumer who has been misled by inaccurate information can cancel or 'rescind' his purchase. He can demand his money back, just as he can return an article which is inferor to or different from what he ordered. In addition, by reason of Section 2(i) of the Misrepresentation Act 1967 he may be entitled to damages.

Take the case of a consumer who agrees to buy a 1970 Rolls Royce with 50,000 miles on the clock for £10,000. After a time he discovers the engine has done more than 100,000 and is worn out. What are his rights?

Although nothing was said about mileage the odometer has in fact 'lied' about the true mileage.

1 The seller may have been deceitful or recklessly indifferent whether the mileage was true or false.

2 On the other hand he himself may have put the clock back and so be guilty of fraud.

3 It may be the dealer was simply **negligent.** He did not examine the car carefully and check whether the mileage was correct.

In each situation the buyer has two choices: He can send the car back and buy another Rolls with 50,000 mileage at the current market price. If it costs him £12,000 he can claim the difference of £2,000 as damages from the seller. Alternatively he can keep the car and claim the cost of fitting a reconditioned engine.

Innocent Misrepresentation

Suppose the seller can convince the judge that he had reasonable grounds for believing that the mileage was correct? This in practice will be very hard for a dealer unless he was, say, relying on an independent engineer's report. But if the seller is a private person the judge may well accept that he was acting in all innocence and had reasonable grounds for believing the clock was correct. He is not an expert on cars and could not ascertain the state of the engine. In this case the judge may regard the misrepresentation as 'innocent' and not negligent. Where the seller has made an innocent misrepresentation, believing in good faith and on reasonable grounds what he said was true, the buyer can still rescind and send the car back. But if he sends it back he cannot **also** claim compensation, whereas he can if the misrepresentation is negligent or fraudulent.

However, the judge has a discretion in the case of innocent misrepresentation to refuse to allow the buyer to rescind and send the car back. Under Section 2(2) of the Misrepresentation Act 1967 he may say that the buyer has to **keep** the car and that the seller should repay part of the price. In so deciding the judge has to weigh up three considerations:

(i) The nature of the misrepresentation, eg it may be only slight.

(ii) The loss to the consumer that would be caused if he has to keep the article.

(iii) The loss to the seller if he has to take it back.

When the right to rescind is lost by acceptance

Once the buyer continues to use the article after discovering the discrepancy or defect, he will lose his right to send it back and can claim compensation only. This was what a Mr Lloyd found after he bought a second-hand lorry. Mr Long, the seller, told him it was in excellent condition but after a couple of days the buyer complained of certain defects and the seller agreed to "go halves" on the cost of a reconstructed dynamo. The buyer then sent his brother off in it to the north of England on a business trip. The Court of Appeal held that he had accepted, and lost his right to reject, the lorry. *Long v. Lloyd*(1958).

Delay bars right of rescission

A buyer who retains an article even for a comparatively short period after he has discovered it is defective may thereby lose his right to reject it. He must **immediately** notify the seller that he rejects it.

One buyer was assured that a certain chandelier was adequate to light a large assembly room. Although it did not give sufficient light the buyer kept it for nearly six months. The judge told him he was not entitled to send it back after so long a lapse of time.

Suppose the buyer does not discover the defect until some months or even years later? In 1944 a Mr Leaf bought a "Constable" painting from the International Galleries. Five years later he took it to Christie's for sale and was told it was not a Constable. He sued for his money back but the Court of Appeal refused to allow this. Even though he had no suspicion before this that the picture was not a genuine Constable, his right to reject it was lost after such a long period of time.

The Court of Appeal agreed that a painting of Salisbury Cathedral by an unknown artist was far less valuable than one by Constable but they all held that Mr Leaf had delayed far too long to be able to reject the painting. The proper time for him to have had it checked was **immediately after** he had bought it.

However, Lord Denning took the view that Mr Leaf might have had a claim for a part repayment if he could show that the gallery had given him some **positive assurance** that the painting was a Constable. For example, a certificate, or even a statement on his receipt would certainly help to establish this. In this case his claim would not have been barred for six years. *Leaf v. International Galleries* (1950).

Needless to say if the seller has been shown to be deliberately untruthful, the buyer can reject the article and demand his money back as well as having an additional claim for compensation. In Mr Leaf's case, had the misrepresentation been deliberate, the lapse of time would not have barred his claim, provided he took action as soon as he discovered he had been deceived.

Excluding Liability for Misrepresentation

Any attempt to exclude liability under the Act will have no legal effect unless the court considers that in the circumstances the exclusion clause was fair and reasonable. For example, what the shop-assistant tells the customer may conflict with what is stated on the shop's printed terms of business. Under the Act, what he actually says overrides those printed terms. However, sometimes the printed terms exclude liability for misrepresentations made by staff. They may also restrict the customer's legal remedies. Neither exemption is of any legal effect except in so far as it can satisfy the requirement of "reasonableness" stated in the Unfair Contract Terms Act 1977. (See p 132).

It is for the trader to show that such an exemption is fair and reasonable. To decide this the judge will have regard to the circumstances:

- which were or ought reasonably to have been known to the parties when the agreement was made or
- which were in the contemplation of both trader and customer when they made the agreement.

The Trade Descriptions Act 1968

This Act makes it a criminal offence for a trader to give a false or misleading description or statement relating to what he is selling or any service he is supplying. Sales talk which is misleading is just as much an offence as written information, provided the falsehood is "material".

The Trade Descriptions Act 1968 re-enforces the civil law protection already discussed which consumers have under the Sale of Goods Act and under the Misrepresentation Act, with one added advantage. In addition to imposing a fine or even imprisonment the Magistrates' Court has power to award compensation up to £400 to any consumer who has suffered by reason of the inaccurate statement.

Instead of starting a civil court action himself, the consumer can lodge a complaint with his local consumer protection department, whose trading standards officers can prosecute the trader concerned. They also have power to enter premises and inspect and seize goods as well as to start a prosecution.

The Trade Descriptions Act 1968 prohibits **traders,** by speaking or writing, misleading consumers regarding:

(i)   Goods   (Section 1)
(ii) Prices   (Section 11)
(iii) Services   (Section 14)

Goods subject to a false trade description

An offence is committed by any person who, in the course of a trade or business:

(a) **applies** a false trade description to any goods; or

(b) **supplies** or offers to supply any goods to which a false trade description has been applied.

The misleading statement does not have to be in writing and mere word of mouth is sufficient to secure conviction. It covers advertising on tv as well as radio. The only question is whether the trade description is likely to be taken as referring to the goods. It may be attached to the article itself or to anything in which it is supplied. Very often the article is described in a separate advertisement. Where a customer asks for an article in terms referring to a particular trade description, the goods supplied must in fact correspond to it.

"False"

Any description which is untrue or misleading is "false". The test is "Would it mislead an ordinary person?" It must be false to a material degree. Goods may be so altered as to lie about themselves, eg concealment of a structural weakness in a car by smoothing down and repainting areas of rusted bodywork with plastic filler to hide the rust can amount to a false trade description. A Scottish scene on a bottle of foreign whisky, even though the word "Scotch" is not used, would be misleading.

The Act applies only to traders

Only a trader (not a private seller) can be prosecuted under this Act. A man who runs a car-hire business and sells off a car which he no longer needs can be prosecuted if the mileage clock gives a false reading. He is subject to the Act not as a motor dealer but because he sells **in the course of his business.**

A trade description is an indication, direct or indirect, and by whatever means, as to any of the following:

(a) *Quantity, size or gauge:* customary sizes of shoes or clothing must be accurate.

(b) *Method of manufacture, production, processing or reconditioning:* it is wrong to describe an article as hand-made if it is machine made, even though of the same quality as the hand-made article.

(c) *Composition:* a picture on a container must accurately portray the article inside. A label on a cake tin showing a rich cake with thick fruit or cream filling must be matched by the contents. To describe shoes as leather implies that they are wholly made of leather except for minor fitments which are obviously different, eg a rubber or plastic heel. Again, an article described as "solid brass" may combine minor fittings, say, screws or clips of another metal.

(d) *Fitness for purpose, strength, performance, behaviour*

110

or accuracy: any description or advertisement must be accurate. Terms such as unbreakable, unshrinkable, moth-proof, stainless or rustless must be literally true. Waterproof means more than "shower proof". A watch described as water-proof must not let in water if left in a bowl for half-an-hour.

In *Sherratt v. Gerald's American Jewellers* (1970) a watch was engraved "water-proof" and described as a "diver's watch". The purchaser tested it by immersion in a bowl of water. It filled and stopped so the description was clearly misleading. Although the watch when supplied to the jewellers was so marked, they were convicted. They had not taken all reasonable precautions and exercised all due diligence to check the description which they could have done as easily as the purchaser did, by dipping the watch in water. (See p 123).

An advertisement in a newspaper offered a "beautiful car, all good tyres, good engine". The lady customer who bought it was impressed by its polished exterior and clean interior. Later she discovered that it suffered from serious corrosion internally and was unfit for use. The Court decided that to call a car "beautiful" referred not only to its outside but also to its quality of running and **fitness for purpose.** To call it "beautiful" was both false and misleading.

Excellent Condition

A dealer who sold a four-year-old Morris Mini with 60,000 miles on the odometer, described it as "in excellent condition throughout". This description was not accurate for subsequently the buyer found it had 15 minor defects plus two potentially dangerous defects. *Chidwick v. Beer* (1974).

"Excellent condition" means less than in "perfect condition". It is false if the facts show that the car needs a substantial number of repairs to be driven safely.

111

Any trade description must be construed in the context of the type, age and mileage of the particular vehicle. It is no defence that the car is in as good condition as might be expected of an unrepaired car of its age and mileage. If repairs are needed it will not be "excellent" until they are carried out.

The false statement need not be instrumental in **inducing** the sale, as is required to give rise to a claim under the Misrepresentation Act. But it must be made prior to the conclusion of the sale to constitute an offence. (See below).

Even though the buyer has **not** been deceived by the false trade description, it is an offence nevertheless if it is inaccurate. It is no defence for the trader to show that the buyer did not believe it, though this is relevant to mitigation.

(e) Any other physical characteristics: a vehicle described as fitted with disc brakes or a retractable aerial. A garment stated to be "permanent press".

(f) Testing by any person and the results thereof: "As tested by dentists", or "by leading car dealers", would be misleading unless a majority had approved the article. To give only part of the result of a test could also be regarded as misleading.

(g) Approval by any person: attaching the "Kite Mark" symbol to a label on a pillow means it conforms to the standard of quality prescribed by the British Standards Institution. If the filling is below this standard, an offence is committed. A salesman of educational books may falsely claim approval by a reputable body, eg a university.

(h) Place or date of manufacture, production, processing or reconditioning: Cheddar cheese or scotch broth refers not to origin but to type. Similarly "Wiltshire cut" refers not to the origin of the bacon but the type of cut. However American ham must not be called

"Scotch" and "Norfolk" turkeys must not be imported birds. "Woollen tops of the U.K." must not come from Uruguay. Whisky made outside Scotland, even though to a Scottish formula, must not be described as "Scotch Whisky". Cigarettes may not be described as "hand-made" when in fact machine-made and it is no defence that they are of equal quality to hand-made cigarettes. It is wrong to describe synthetic vinegar as "non-brewed" vinegar.

(i) Other history, including previous ownership or use: this is of particular significance to consumers when buying **antiques** or works of art as well as motor vehicles. It is an offence where the mileage clock gives a false reading, suggesting the car has had less use than is in fact the case.

A false representation as to royal approval or award amounts to an offence. So too an indirect indication that goods or services are of a kind supplied to or approved by Her Majesty or any member of the Royal Family.

No one may import into the United Kingdom goods bearing a false indication of the place of manufacture, production, processing or re-conditioning. Sometimes goods produced outside the United Kingdom bear a name or mark which is similar to a UK name of mark. Anyone offering such goods must indicate clearly the country in which they were manufactured or produced. Otherwise the name or mark must be eradicated.

A company was convicted of having sold watches described as "English lever watches" when in fact many of the most important parts came from abroad, although they were put together in England.

It is no defence that, despite the false trade description, the buyer got good value for money. Admittedly trade "puffs", even though untrue, will not involve legal liability, but the salesman must be careful not to indulge in indiscriminate praise. Thus where a car has defects, he will be liable to conviction if he refers to it as "in a showroom condition".

Altered mileometers and disclaimers

While the number of miles travelled shown on the mileometer is usually taken as an indication of the use a car has received, it is often unreliable. The car dealer can avoid liability by displaying a notice of disclaimer, ie stating that the mileage recorded on the clock is inaccurate. Such a notice must be at least as bold and clear as the reading on the clock. Alternatively, he may indicate its inaccuracy by covering over the mileage reading, preferably with a disclaimer (see p 60).

The seller must take positive steps to ensure that the customer understands that the reading shown on the clock is meaningless. Small print in a contractual document or a casual remark during negotiations is unlikely to be effective.

In *Regina v. Hammerton Cars Ltd.* (C.A.) July 14, 1976, a firm was fined £1,000 in respect of one car with a reading of 25,000 instead of 53,714 and £500 in respect of another with 25,300 instead of 34,000.

How new is a new car?

A car which has done a much greater mileage than the distance from factory to dealer would not be correctly described as new. Where the vehicle has suffered **minor damage** in the factory compound before delivery to the dealer but this has been put right, it is not a falsehood for the supplier to describe it as "new", provided it is still "as good as new".

In considering whether it is "as good as new" the quality of repair as well as the slightness of damage is to be taken into account. If serious damage, say to the chassis had occurred, it would not be fair to describe it as new even though perfectly repaired. (See also p 103).

Where the trader is buyer

Anyone trading-in a car in part-exchange is protected by the Act. Although the dealer is not selling but buying the car, he must not run it down untruthfully in order to get it at a lower price.

In one case in 1974 a car dealer told the customer that there was no possibility of repairing his car and that it was fit only for scrap. The customer accepted £2 for it but soon afterwards saw it repaired and being offered for £136. The dealer was convicted. Similarly the Act could punish a dealer in second-hand furniture who gave a housewife false information about a family heirloom she was selling to him: eg condemning it as worm-eaten, or being a Victorian reproduction when it is in fact a valuable antique.

At what stage was the statement made?

To constitute an offence the false trade description must be made **prior** to sale or be associated with the supply of the article. No offence is committed if the false statement is made **after** the sale.

In *Hall v. Wickens Motors (Gloucester) Ltd.* (1972), car dealers sold a Jaguar motor car to Mr Lunn who brought it back 40 days later complaining of the steering. They told him "There is nothing wrong with the car". An expert found later the chassis was distorted. Had the dealers given their false assurance about its condition **at the time** they supplied the car, they would have been guilty of an offence. As they gave it much later, no offence was committed under Section 1 of the Trade Descriptions Act.

N.B.—The law is different where a service is provided. Here, a false statement made **after** the contract has been made can render the supplier of the service liable to prosecution. (See p 118).

Misleading indications as to price

Although many misleading claims about prices are not covered, the Trade Descriptions Act 1968 prohibits:

(a) False comparisons with a "recommended" price. (In law, this means the price fixed by the manufacturer for the retail of goods in that area).

(b) False comparisons with the trader's **previous** selling price.

(c) False suggestions that the price is **reduced**.

Any statement that the price was previously higher means in law that it was sold at the higher price for a minimum, continuous period of 28 days, during the preceding six months.

However, a disclaimer which is sufficiently clearly worded would avoid an infringement of the Act. Thus an offence is not likely to be committed if the store puts up a notice to the following effect:

"The announcement that certain of our goods have been reduced in price does not signify that they have been offered for a period of 28 days during the preceding six months at a higher price."

To omit V.A.T. from the price of goods in an advertisement is an offence. Attracting customers by offering a discount, extra trading stamps or free gifts with certain purchases is a way of expressing a price reduction which is not caught by the Act, ie here the previous 28 days selling period does not have to be observed. The Price Marking (Bargain Offers) Order 1979, forbids **imprecise** worth and value claims or inexact price comparisons, eg. "Price elsewhere £10: our price £8"; or "Save £10 on normal shop prices" or "Up to 50% off".

The Act's operation has not yet been extended to cover:
- Prices for services and facilities and accommodation.
- House and property prices to cover comparisons with a price at which the property or similar property was previously offered.

116

False statements about services, accommodation and facilities

A trader can be prosecuted if he makes a statement which he knows to be false. It is also an offence if he makes a false statement recklessly, ie without regard to whether it is true or not. (Recklessly does not imply dishonesty).

A false statement may mislead the consumer regarding:
(a) the nature of services;
(b) the time at which they are provided;
(c) the manner in which they are provided;
(d) the persons by whom they are provided;
(e) their approval, evaluation or examination by any person;
(f) the location or amenities of any accommodation provided;
(g) the effect of any process or treatment.

"**Accommodation**" includes lodgings and rooms and holiday accommodation but not houses or property.

"**Facilities**" would include self-service facilities. It is doubtful whether services etc include insurance and financial services but these are in any event covered by special legislation.

Business only

An electrician who claims to have completely re-wired a house commits an offence if this is untrue but the private seller of a house who falsely says that it has been completely re-wired is not guilty because he is not acting in the course of business. (He could be sued for damages under the Misrepresentation Act 1967 if he makes this kind of false statement to a prospective purchaser.)

Although the Act does not expressly apply to the professions, "business" is regarded as including a professional practice, eg architects, surveyors and solicitors.

An architectural student who had not completed his examinations advertised himself as a qualified architect.

117

A Mr Armitage saw his name in the yellow pages of the telephone directory under "architects" and engaged him to draw up plans for large-scale alterations to his house. The student was convicted under Section 14(1) of the Trade Descriptions Act 1968. The Court of Appeal said his qualifications were relevant to the likely quality of the services to be provided.

How and when the false statement may be made

As we saw the false statement may be made in writing or simply spoken. A person may be guilty of an offence even though the service is to be provided by someone other than himself.

Where a service is given the false statement may be made **after** a contract has been signed. In *Breed v. Cluett* (1970) Mr and Mrs Karley signed a contract to buy a bungalow from Mr Cluett the builder. Subsequently, while he was finishing the bungalow (ie engaged in his trade) he told Mr Karley "It is subject to a 10 year N.H.B.R.C. guarantee." This was untrue. The Divisional Court said he should be convicted even though his false statement occurred **after** Mr and Mrs Karley had exchanged contracts with him and it had not induced them to buy the bungalow. The N.H.B.R.C. guarantee related to the provision of a service, ie repairs, and was covered by Section 14.

Building and building repairs involve the provision of a service. Any builder who knowingly or recklessly makes a false statement about work he **has done** under a contract commits an offence.

False statement as to existing fact, not promise as to future

However, a promise to carry out or complete building services in the future although not kept, does not amount to an offence.

A builder agreed to construct a garage for a customer. He undertook to complete it within 10 days "as the existing garage" but ran out of money and could not complete it within the time agreed, Nor was it like the existing garage. The builder was acquitted on the ground that his undertaking to complete the garage in 10 days was a **promise** which related to the future. It was not a statement about an existing fact and so it could not be either true or false at the time he made it. *Beckett v. Cohen* (1974).

It follows that to amount to an offence under Section 14 the false statement must relate to an existing fact.

Where the person who provides a service makes a promise as to what he will do and his assurance does not relate to an existing fact, nobody can say at the date when that statement is made that it is either true or false. It will be an offence only where the contractor makes a false statement at the end of the contract as to what has been done.

Holiday brochures

Here again a distinction must be drawn between false statements of fact which constitute an offence and promises as to the future which do not amount to an infringement of the Trade Descriptions Act.

Where the picture in the brochure shows an hotel which is not the one for which holiday-makers are in fact booking, this amounts to a false statement of fact.

The case of Mr and Mrs Hall involved a clear, albeit unintentional, inaccuracy with regard to the length of their holiday which was advertised as "14 nights" at the Calypso Hotel in Benidorm, Spain. The brochure described it as a 15 day holiday with 14 nights at the hotel. In fact, they and their young daughter did not arrive at the hotel until 6 a.m. Admittedly their room was available on arrival but this could not count as a first night. Unless the holiday-maker is brought to his hotel before midnight, he cannot reasonably be said to be enjoying a night at the hotel. The company was convicted of making a false statement, recklessly, as to the length of the holiday. It was fined and ordered to pay them £5 each compensation. It was acquitted on the more serious charge of intentionally misleading Mr and Mrs Hall.

Standard of accommodation

Where the complaint relates to the standard of the rooms, meals or other facilities, the tour company can generally throw the blame for such complaints onto the hotel. On arrival at their hotel in Majorca, a Mr and Mrs Dodd were put in a room without a view whereas the brochure had stated all rooms had terraces overlooking the harbour.

In their defence, the organisers explained that it was the hotel management which was at fault in not providing the room booked (in fact the hotel had offered the couple a small refund). The Court accepted that the organisers had not had any similar complaint during the previous four years they had dealt with that hotel. Rooms with terraces had always been reserved for their clients previously. It acquitted them of the charge since they could not have known the hotel might put Mr and Mrs Dodd in the wrong type of accommodation.

Facilities promised but not provided

Again tour operators escaped conviction under the Trade Descriptions Act where their brochure advertised the hotel as having a swimming pool, push chairs, as well as special meals for children. On arrival, a Mr Bateman found that none of these facilities were available. The pool was out of action undergoing repair owing to faulty construction. The court dismissed the charge of giving misleading information about the availability of push chairs and special meals, since the tour operators had no reason to believe the hotel would not supply these facilities.

As to the swimming pool, the Court of Appeal held that the brochure infringed the Trade Descriptions Act only if the tour operators **knew** the pool might not be ready for use.

120

Civil Claim

All too often on a criminal charge the tour operator will be able to pass the blame onto the hotel or the person who undertook to provide the facility or service. By contrast in a civil court the claimant will usually get damages, for breach of contract.

Mr Jackson and his family received £1,100 compensation for disappointment and distress over a spoilt holiday in Ceylon. The judge found that the hotel failed to provide the facilities for enjoyment and entertainment which Mr Jackson had been promised. He had been told that the hotel had mini-golf, an excellent restaurant, cocktail lounge, swimming pool, beauty salon, hairdressing salon and private baths. He had booked but was not given, a room connecting with his children's. There was mildew on the walls, the shower was dirty, there was no bath, no swimming pool or mini-golf and only occasionally did the restaurant offer a choice of dishes. *Jackson v. Horizon Holidays Ltd.* (1975).

Overbooking is an offence

An airline passenger who had paid in advance received a letter confirming his reservation for the flight booked. Unknown to him the airline operated a deliberate policy of overbooking. This meant that they habitually took bookings from more passengers than there were seats on each flight.

When the passenger arrived at the airport for the flight he had booked no seat was available for him owing to overbooking.

The airline was charged with contravention of Section 14(1) of the Trade Descriptions Act 1968. They were accused of recklessly making a statement in their letter about the provision of services, namely, the transportation by aeroplane of a person, which was **false** as to the time and manner in which it would be provided.

The House of Lords considered the airline had been

rightly convicted. The letter taken with the ticket and his "Earlybird" certificate was a statement of fact that the booking was certain. This statement, in view of their undisclosed overbooking policy, was false within Section 14(1) since the passenger was exposed to the risk that he might not get a place. *British Airways Board v. Taylor* (1976).

Defences under the Trade Descriptions Act

What is the legal position where a particular seat in a theatre or room in a hotel is reserved? On arrival, the customer finds someone else occupying the seat or room. The reason for this may be due to one of three situations:

(i) mistake on the part of the management. In this case they would probably have a defence under Section 24;

(ii) the manager later changed his mind because a more important guest wanted the seat or room. In this case he might escape liability under the Act because when he wrote to confirm the booking, he had correctly expressed his intention;

(iii) it may be that the manager never intended to keep the seat or room if that would require him to refuse all bookings that might possibly conflict with the first one. In this case his confirmation of the booking would be **false** because it implied that he had an intention he did not have.

Dishonesty

It is important to appreciate that dishonesty is not necessary to commit an offence under this Act. Whether or not the seller gets any benefit from the false statement is also irrelevant. A person innocently repeating a description of goods or selling goods without realizing that they have been wrongly described by someone else may be guilty.

In the case of goods an accidental inaccuracy on the part of the trader is sufficient to convict him simply because what he told the customer was in fact misleading.

It is more difficult to convict a trader who makes a false

statement regarding a service since the court must be
satisfied that the trader either:
(a) knew the statement to be false; or
(b) made it recklessly, ie regardless of whether it was true
    or false.

Mistake or accident as a defence
Under Section 24 of the Act the person charged may prove
that the false statement was due to:
(a) reliance on information supplied to him by another
    person;
(b) the act or default of another person;
(c) mistake, accident or some other cause beyond his
    control.

In addition he must also prove that he took all reasonable
precautions **and** exercised all due diligence to avoid the
commission of such offence by himself or any person under
his control.

In practice the retailer may be able to attribute the blame
to his supplier. Where he alleges the offence was due to the
act or default of another person or reliance on information
supplied by another person, he must inform the prosecution
of that person's identity at least seven days before the case
comes to court.

Where the charge is specifically one of offering to supply
goods to which a false trade description has been applied,
there are two special statutory lines of defence.

1 He may prove that he did not know and could not with
  reasonable diligence have ascertained that the goods did
  not conform to the description.
2 Alternatively, he may prove that he did not know
  and could not with reasonable diligence have ascertained
  that the description had been applied to the goods.

Time limit for prosecutions
A speedy complaint to the local trading standards officer

is essential, particularly if the misleading information was only spoken. In this case prosecution must be commenced in the Magistrates' Court within six months of when it was said.

If given in writing, say in an advertisement, the officer must start the prosecution within one year.

A trader gets away scott free if prosecution is not begun within one year of the offence being discovered. In any event, after three years the trader is immune from prosecution, if the offence is not discovered before.

CHAPTER VII

BUYING AT AUCTION

Sale to the highest bidder

An auction is an invitation to prospective buyers to "treat" and not an offer to sell to them. The characteristic of an auction sale is that goods are put up to be sold to the highest bidder but an intending purchaser will have no complaint in law if articles are withdrawn at the last moment. The auctioneer is agent of the seller and invites offers in the form of bids. Each bid is an offer to pay the price bid. Since a bid is a mere offer it can be retracted by the bidder at any time **before** the hammer falls.

The auctioneer's acceptance of the highest bid constitutes an agreement for the **sale of goods** and is governed by the same basic principles of the law of contract although certain special rules apply to sales by auction. (Sale of Goods Act 1979, Section 57).

An auction may be advertised for a certain date and then cancelled. Since it is merely an "invitation to treat" there is no legal obligation on the advertiser to hold the auction. In one case the plaintiff travelled many miles to attend an auction only to find that it had been called off. He was not entitled to claim his travelling expenses from the advertiser. *Harris v. Nickerson* (1873).

Sales without reserve

Only where the auction or a particular item has been notified as being offered **"without reserve"** is the auctioneer obliged to sell to the highest bidder. Consequently an item advertised without reserve may not be withdrawn before the fall of the hammer. *Warlow v. Harrison* (1859). If it is withdrawn there might be an infringement of Section 11 of the Trade Descriptions Act 1968 if it amounts to an indication that the goods are available for supply at a price less than that at which they are in fact available for supply.

Reserve price
Unfortunately, prospective buyers are not entitled to know the amount of the reserve price. Where the seller fixes a price below which the goods will not be sold, those attending the auction are notified only that a reserve price has been fixed.

If the reserve price is not reached the person who makes the highest bid cannot insist on buying the item even though it has been knocked down to him. However, where an auctioneer actually sells below the reserve price, he personally is liable to the purchaser.

Inflating the price?
One of the hazards of buying at auction is the possibility that someone may be bidding on behalf of the seller, not with a view to buying himself but to push up the price. This is permitted provided the seller has reserved the right to bid. Reservation of the right to bid may be announced when the lot is put up for sale. In a sale of land (not goods) it must be expressly notified in the catalogue whether the right to bid is reserved.

Unless such notification is made, it is illegal for the seller or anyone on his behalf to make a bid. It is also illegal for the auctioneer knowingly to take such a bid. Any sale contravening this rule may be treated as fraudulent. The buyer has the choice either to reject the goods and not pay anything, or take the goods and claim damages. (Sale of Goods Act 1979, Section 57).

Where the seller reserves the right to bid, **only one** person, either himself or his nominee, may bid at the auction on his behalf. The condition announcing his right to bid must be strictly complied with. In one case a seller reserved a right to bid once. Disregarding this undertaking he in fact bid three times. The Court set the sale aside.

Offence to "take bids off the wall"

An auctioneer could be convicted of deception if he pretends to accept bids which have not in fact been made, in order to push up the price. This practice is known as taking bids "out of the air" or "off the wall" and is a fraud on those bidding.

If two or more persons take part in sham bidding to induce members of the public to buy an item at an excessive price, they are guilty of criminal conspiracy.

In these cases the court has power on convicting the offenders to order compensation to the consumer who has suffered loss thereby.

"The Ring" — agreements not to bid

Where a member of the public sells a valuable item at auction it is not unknown for dealers in that type of article to get together and agree not to bid against each other. This will enable one of the dealers to buy the item at a low price to the detriment of the seller.

Afterwards the dealers hold a private auction amongst themselves. They then share the difference between the price they paid at the open auction and the price bid later at their private auction.

In the case of goods (but not buildings) this type of agreement is illegal under the Auctions (Bidding Agreements) Act 1927 and 1969.

It is an offence for a dealer to offer, or agree to give, an inducement or reward to any person for abstaining or having abstained from bidding at a sale by auction. Similarly, if any person accepts or agrees to accept from any dealer any such gift or consideration, he too is guilty of an offence. The penalty on summary conviction is a fine not exceeding £400 or a term of imprisonment not exceeding six months, or both.

In practice, it is extremely difficult for a seller to prove that dealers have formed a ring against him. However, a seller who discovers the operation of a ring may rescind the sale and claim the item back from the member of the ring who bought it. If the item has already been resold, he can claim damages from all the dealers who took part in the ring, apart from the criminal penalty imposed under the Act.

When agreements not to bid are permissible

Only members of the public who are **not** dealers may enter into an agreement not to bid against each other. In *Harrop v. Thompson* (1976) it was alleged that the plaintiff had entered into an agreement with another potential bidder who promised to stay away from the auction. As a result he acquired the property more cheaply. The judge was satisfied that he was bound to ignore the alleged agreement between the purchaser and a potential bidder. It did not invalidate the auction purchase. Where dealers are in partnership and wish to purchase an article at auction for their business they are at liberty to agree that one of them shall not bid. In this case a copy of their agreement to purchase on a **joint account** must be lodged with the auctioneer beforehand.

Verbal statements by the auctioneer

A verbal statement made to a purchaser by the auctioneer before the sale may amount to an assurance or guarantee.

Normally the printed conditions of sale will exclude liability for any defects. Nevertheless a prospective buyer is entitled to ask, for example, whether a piece of furniture is free from woodworm. If the auctioneer does give such an assurance this will be binding and will override the conditions in the sale catalogue.

A buyer who has been induced to bid owing to misleading information will be entitled to reject the goods and refuse to pay. If he has already taken the goods and paid he will be entitled to his money back. Alternatively, if he wishes, the buyer may keep the goods and claim compensation from the auctioneer.

How much Consumer Protection at Auction Sales?

The conditions of sale (which are usually printed in the catalogue) can and invariably will declare that all "guarantees" implied under the Sale of Goods Act are excluded. The seller's liability for misdescriptions and misrepresentations (see Chapter VI) will also be excluded. In practice the conditions of sale will simply state that the buyer is to have virtually no legal protection at all.

However, if it comes to a dispute, the judge has a discretion to protect the buyer if he thinks he is being treated unfairly. He can disallow the exclusion clause and reinstate the buyer's normal legal rights. To decide whether the buyer should have protection in any particular case the judge applies the test of "reasonableness". (See Chapter VIII).

The Auctioneer regarded as Expert

Owing to the Misrepresentation Act 1967 (see p 104) auctioneers may in practice find it difficult to excuse themselves from positive statements about the goods they sell, particularly antiques or paintings. This is because they are regarded as experts and must take care (as do all the more famous auction houses) to check the authenticity of items offered for sale. If it can be inferred that their staff have failed to do their "homework", the auction house will have to pay the buyer compensation and/or accept back the item in dispute.

Thus an auction catalogue may wrongly list as "Persian" a carpet originating from Turkey or Pakistan or factory-made in Persian style. The auctioneers would be responsible for this mistake and have to take it back and also possibly compensate the buyer.

Where an imitation violin was sold in the U.S. as a

Stradivarius the buyer was told by the judge he could reject it and have his money back.

In *Nicholson & Venn v. Smith-Marriott* (1947) table napkins were put up for auction, described as "the authentic property of Charles I". The purchaser bid over £700, whereas in fact they were Georgian worth only £100 or so.

The judge (Hallett, J.) ordered the seller to repay the difference.

Criminal liability and compensation under the Trade Descriptions Act 1968

This topic is dealt with in detail in Chapter VI. The auctioneer himself may be open to criminal prosecution if he aplies a false description to goods. Even an incorrect remark during the auction may be regarded as misleading bidders since dishonesty is not required to commit an offence. He may, however, under Section 24, have available several specific lines of defence if charged with an offence under the Act:

(i) he may be able to prove that the offence was due to a mistake;

(ii) that he relied on information supplied to him;

(iii) that it was due to the act or default of another person;

(iv) it was accidental;

(v) it was due to some cause beyond his control.

However, the auctioneer must also prove, in putting up any of the above defences, that he took all reasonable precautions and exercised all due diligence to avoid commission of such an offence by himself or any person under his control.

The danger of buying stolen goods

What is the legal position if goods the consumer buys at auction turn out to have been stolen?

1 Their true owner can claim from the consumer the goods or their full value.

2 Alternatively the true owner can claim their full value from the auctioneer or from the person who put them up for auction.

3 The consumer cannot sue the auctioneer for compensation. He can claim his loss only from the person who put the goods up for auction. *Willis v. British Car Auctions Ltd.* (1978).

Dangerous articles

The danger of buying articles, particularly motor vehicles, at auction was emphasised by the House of Lords in 1979 in the case of *Hurley v. Dyke.* A three-wheeled Reliant car was sold at auction, the catalogue stating that "All vehicles are offered as seen and with all faults".

A week after its purchase, the chassis, which was corroded, collapsed causing the car to veer across the road and collide with an oncoming vehicle. A passenger in the car who was injured sued Mr Dyke, the previous owner of the car, who knew it was in a dangerous condition.

The House of Lords declared that a seller is under a duty to give a purchaser adequate warning of potential dangers of which he himself knows or ought reasonably to know. A notice that a vehicle is sold "As seen with all faults" is adequate warning to any prospective purchaser that the car may be dangerous to drive without a thorough examination by a skilled mechanic.

Two of the Law Lords went even further and stated that even if the seller of a dangerously defective article knows precisely what defect the article possesses, he is under no obligation to give more than a general warning.

The implication of this for the consumer is that if he proposes to purchase a second-hand car at auction, skilled advice should always be sought beforehand.

Mock auctions

At mock auctions members of the public are induced by a skilful flow of patter to make bids for shoddy goods at inflated prices. Genuine articles are displayed which are not in fact to be sold. To generate enthusiasm amongst the crowd, the auctioneer gives away small items or sells them at a ridiculously low price, inducing bidders to believe they will get a bargain. They are then persuaded to bid for more expensive items, which are often carefully wrapped but when opened found to be of very poor quality.

The prohibition on mock auctions applies only to sales of the following articles:

Plate or plated articles, linen, china, glass, books, pictures, prints, furniture, jewellery, articles of household or personal use or ornament, any musical or scientific instrument or apparatus.

Selling methods outlawed by the Mock Auctions Act 1961 are:

(i) where the auctioneer sells any of the above goods for **less** than the highest bid;

(ii) where part of the price is repaid or credited to the bidder (or stated to be so);

(iii) where the auctioneer restricts the right to bid for any goods listed above to persons who have bought or agreed to buy one or more articles;

(iv) where any articles are **given away** or offered as gifts.

An auctioneer operating any of the above prohibited methods can be fined an amount not exceeding £100 or three months' imprisonment, or both. If the defendant is tried at the Crown Court on indictment, the maximum fine is £1,000 or two years' imprisonment, or both.

CHAPTER VIII

UNFAIR CONTRACT TERMS

Standard forms are used in a multitude of consumer transactions, when we buy a car, when we rent a tv, have our furniture stored or removed, leave an article for repair, servicing or cleaning, book a package holiday and so on. All too often his standard agreement contains clauses which nullify the trader's normal legal liability towards the consumer. Car ferries are a notorious example. Their agreement contracts out of all responsibility for damage to cars in transit. Again package tour operators reserve the right to send the holidaymaker to an alternative resort.

Lord Reid summed up the unfairness to consumers. "In the ordinary way the customer has no time to read the form and if he were to read it he would scarcely understand it and if he did understand it and objected to a particular clause he would generally be told to 'take it or leave it', If he went to another supplier the result would be the same."

In practice a consumer is generally in too much of a hurry even to attempt to read the form before signing it. The legal rule that once we sign a form we are bound by its terms, no matter how unfair they are, was changed radically by the Unfair Contract Terms Act 1977. This Act gives judges the power to strike out of an agreement exemption clauses which **unfairly avoid legal liability** on the part of the trader.

Trader excusing own breaches of contract prohibited unless reasonable

1. A trader cannot avoid liability for his own breaches of contract. His terms of business may not unfairly exclude

133

or restrict his liability for breach of contract when he himself has failed to carry out what he has undertaken. Hence a woman who sends her mink stole for cleaning is entitled to have it returned to her properly cleaned. They have broken their contract if it is lost or damaged while in their care. They cannot stipulate unreasonable terms such as "goods are held at customer's risk" or "the cleaner is not to be responsible for loss or damage however caused".

2. *Performing contract in a different way from promised*
The trader's conditions cannot unfairly entitle him to render a contractual performance substantially **different** from that which was reasonably expected of him. Thus anyone who books a summer package holiday to Greece cannot later be fobbed off with a winter holiday in Norway, even though the standard terms may provide for an alternative destination "in the discretion of the travel firm".

3. *Part avoidance forbidden unless reasonable*
Nor can his terms of business permit the trader avoiding part of what he has undertaken. For example, if a coat is sent to be cleaned and part of it, say the fur collar, is not properly cleaned, he is **not** permitted unfairly to disclaim liability.

Only "Reasonable" Exemption Clauses permitted
A trader can avoid the above prohibitions only where he can convince the judge that the term in question satisfies the requirement of **"reasonableness"**.

The judge has a discretionary power to strike it out unless the trader proves it is fair and reasonable having regard to the circumstances which ought reasonably to have been known to, or were in the contemplation of, the parties when the agreement was made.

An obvious example would be a person who takes curtains to be dry cleaned. The judge would probably consider it reasonable for the dry cleaner to say that articles which have been exposed to sunlight will be cleaned "at customer's risk".

Liability for Quality of goods cannot be excluded

The Act stipulates that the following four guarantees are always implied on a sale to a consumer. They can never be denied to the consumer or limited in any way by a term in the sale agreement. These guarantees, as we saw in Chapter II, relate to:

(a) the quality of the article sold.
(b) its fitness for any particular purpose.
(c) the accuracy of the trader's description of the article.
(d) the trader's duty to ensure that what he sells conforms with any sample previously given or shown to the consumer.

These guarantees apply only to goods of the type ordinarily supplied for private use or consumption. They are also implied in all hire-purchase agreements. The trader cannot rely on any term in his sale or hire-purchase agreement which seeks to exclude, restrict or deprive the consumer of the above four rights. Thus the credit consumer, whether on hire-purchase or credit sale, has the same four inalienable rights as the cash consumer.

Consumer Rental, hire and exchange

A consumer may obtain an article on rental or by way of exchange or for coupons or wrappers. Technically this is not a sale to him. Promotional samples given free when other goods are purchased are not strictly "sold". Similarly if the article is inserted by way of repairing something he already owns, such as a component in his tv, this does not amount to a sale. Nevertheless whatever the circumstances in which the item is supplied, the above guarantees are never excludable. (As to rental see p 261).

Agreements for work and materials

Similarly where a builder carries out repairs or work in the consumer's home or a garage repairs his car, the components or materials used must be of reasonable quality and fit for their purpose. The trader's terms of business may never avoid the legal guarantees set out above.

"Dealing as a consumer"

A person is protected by the Act where he "deals as a consumer" provided:

1 He does not make the agreement in the course of a business or pretend he is so doing, eg to get a trade discount;

2 He deals with a trader who makes the agreement in the course of **his** business.

However where you agree with someone in his **private** capacity, eg get a neighbour to carry out a building job, the court must enforce the terms agreed even if unfair to you.

Auctions

However the four guarantees can (see p 131) be excluded where anyone buys at an auction sale because anyone who buys at auction is not **"dealing as a consumer"**. The judge will consider any exclusion clause in the auction catalogue from the point of view of fairness. If it fails to pass the "reasonableness test" it will be struck out.

Business customers

Again if he is acquiring an article for business use the buyer or hire-purchaser is **not** a consumer and the above four guarantees may be excluded or restricted by a term in the supply agreement. Whether and how far they can be excluded will again depend on the **test of reasonableness** Thus a person who is buying, not as a consumer, but for the purposes of his business should read the small print carefully. (See "Guidelines" on p 138).

Liability for personal injury can never be excluded

Where death or personal injury is caused to any member of the public, liability for negligence can never be excluded or restricted by a clause in an agreement or by any notice displayed on premises, eg "All visitors enter at their own risk".

Should a visitor be injured his legal right to claim compensation for negligence will be unaffected by a "no-liability" notice or by a small-print clause on his ticket or other document he is presented with. So if the roof falls on him or an employee runs the visitor over, he cannot be deprived of his right to compensation. This protection against negligence benefits all members of the public, consumers and business visitors alike.

Negligence causing loss other than personal injury

Where the visitor is not actually hurt but suffers some financial loss, eg damage to his car or other possessions, the visitor will get compensation only if the judge considers the exclusion clause or notice unfair.

Thus a "no-liability" notice will prevent him obtaining compensation for loss due to their negligence only if it satisfies the test of **"reasonableness"** and provided there is no question of personal injury. The consumer does not have to prove the notice is unreasonable. It is up to the **trader** to show that the notice is justified, having regard to all the circumstances obtaining when the accident occurred. If it is not considered reasonable he must pay compensation.

Some notices seek to restrict liability to a specified sum of money. The question then arises whether the **limit** stipulated is reasonable. To decide this the judge must again have regard to all the circumstances and in particular to: (a) the resources which the trader could expect to be available to him for the purpose of meeting the liability should it arise.

(b) how far it was open to the trader to cover himself by insurance.

Guidelines for application of the reasonableness test

The judge may have regard to a number of considerations when deciding whether a particular exclusion clause is reasonable in the case of **business customers** (ie persons not dealing as consumers, see p 136).

1 The strength of the bargaining position of the parties relative to each other.

2 Taking into account (among other things) alternative means by which the customer's requirements could have been met.

3 Whether the customer received an inducement to agree to the term.

4 Whether in accepting the term he had an opportunity of entering into a similar contract with other persons but without having to accept a similar term.

(5) Whether the customer knew or ought reasonably to have known of the existence and extent of the term. Here the judge must have regard to any custom of the trade. He must also have regard to any previous course of dealing between the parties.

6 Sometimes liability to the customer for breach of a condition of the contract is excluded. If so, was it reasonable at the time he made the contract for the customer to expect that compliance with that condition would be practicable?

7 Whether the goods were manufactured, processed or adapted to the **special order** of the customer.

Businesses affected by the Act

"Business" includes the professions and the activities of government departments and local and public authorities, but not the insurance business.

The Act covers liability for things done in the course of a business or arising from the occupation of premises used for business purposes.

Conclusion

This Act will have sweeping effects throughout consumer and business law. In particular, it can also affect agreements **between** businessmen but only where a **standard form** is used. The Act protects consumers whether a standard form is used or not.

For the first time, non-liability clauses are forbidden in manufacturers' guarantees (see p 84). Also in the case of agreements for "work and materials", where for example a builder or garage does repairs, the quality of all materials must be up to par and the builder or garage cannot avoid this responsibility so far as the consumer is concerned. The Act applies to agreements for the hire or lease of goods or the installation of equipment (where no sale is involved).

The duty is on the trader to satisfy the judge that his exclusion clause is fair. If there is any doubt, that doubt will be exercised in favour of the consumer. Significantly the consumer can challenge a particular exemption clause on the ground that it is unfair but does not have to **prove** its unfairness. It is up to the trader to convince the judge that the clause passes the test of reasonableness.

Never before have judges been given such wide powers to strike down contract terms or notices simply on the grounds that they are unfair. There can be no doubt that judges will need little prompting to exercise their new powers under this Act.

CHAPTER IX

"QUANTUM MERUIT" — WHAT IS A FAIR PRICE?

There are many consumer situations where work is done without any price being fixed in advance, as when a householder gives hasty instructions to a plumber or builder to carry out some urgent repair work.

What are one's legal rights if a bill comes in for an unexpectedly large amount? Can the householder challenge it?

Where no price is agreed before the work is done, the consumer is bound to pay only a **reasonable** price. This means the contractor or repairer is entitled to be paid *quantum meruit,* ie the amount the job merits.

Unauthorised work

Where a contractor on his own initiative does additional work without being authorised, the consumer is not obliged to pay for it, even though the contractor considered the extra work necessary.

For example, a plumber called in to repair a leaking pipe would not be entitled to replace it without specific instructions from the householder.

Dealing with garages

The experience of a Mr Essex will illustrate some of the difficulties consumers can encounter. He left his car lights on all night and the next morning asked his garage to put the battery on "fast charge". When he came to collect his car he was given a bill not only for charging the battery but including an extra sum for checking the charging system, which he had not authorised. The garage maintained it was up to them to decide what needed to be done.

In law the garage was wrong in doing extra work without authorisation and was not entitled to charge for it. It is different if someone asks the garage to "put the battery right". In this case he must pay a reasonable charge for any necessary work.

Payment under protest

Naturally the garage would not release the car until Mr Essex paid their bill. ie they exercised their lien over the car. As they refused to reduce their bill Mr Essex had to pay it but wrote on his cheque that he paid "under protest". These words permit the person paying to reclaim the overcharged amount by way of a court action.

Deception

He would have been unwise to write out a cheque, obtain his car, and later to stop payment on the cheque. The garage could report this to the police alleging that he had got them to release their lien on the car by deception.

A garage which includes in their bill charges for work they have not carried out would equally be liable to prosecution for deception. In such a case the matter should be reported to the local Trading Standards Department for investigation with a view to possible prosecution under the Trade Descriptions Act.

Paying the Bill

What is a reasonable price? The bill should itemize the work done, time spent by workmen, materials used and so on. If it does not, the householder is entitled to demand this information. He can then submit a copy of the bill to other local contractors and ask them to estimate for the work itemized. Clearly extra may be charged if the work was done outside normal working hours or at very short notice.

The consumer should scrutinize each item. Can the builder justify 24 feet of copper tubing? A telephone call to builders' merchants will confirm the current price per foot. Again, were three men essential for the job when in fact two were standing idle much of the time?

The consumer should then write the builder a strong letter refusing to pay the amount charged, setting out his reasons. Any faulty workmanship should, of course, be emphasised. On receipt of the contractor's reply a second, more conciliatory letter should be written enclosing a cheque for such lesser sum as is considered fair payment, but making it clear that the cheque is tendered in **full settlement.** Heading this letter "without prejudice" will prevent it being produced in court, thereby suggesting that the consumer, in making the offer to settle, has a weak case.

Faulty workmanship

Where the contractor does work so badly that it is virtually useless, the consumer is under no obligation to pay. There is an implied condition that the contractor will do the job in a workmanlike and careful manner. If through lack of skill on the part of his workmen or owing to poor quality or unsuitable materials the job is defective, he is not entitled to be paid.

Duties of Contractor

Where repairs or other services are undertaken, the law places on the shoulders of the contractor three main obligations:

1 If a time limit is not stipulated he must complete the work within a reasonable length of time.
2 He will carry it out with reasonable skill, care and diligence.
3 All materials used will be of fair quality and reasonably fit for their purpose.

A contractor who does faulty work, uses poor materials

142

or who is in breach of his above duties will not be excused from legal liability by reason of small print exclusion clauses in his contract form. (See the Unfair Contract Terms Act 1977, p 133).

Payment for uncompleted work

A contractor who undertakes to do a specific job but fails to complete it cannot usually claim for work partially done. Of course, if the customer himself prevents the work being completed, the contractor is entitled to claim a fair price for work actually carried out.

Courts are not well disposed towards builders who take money on account but fail to carry out their commitments. Just before the turn of the century a builder undertook to construct two houses on a piece of land for a fixed sum. Despite substantial payments he was unable to complete the work through lack of capital, so that the owner of the land had to finish the houses himself. The builder brought a claim for a fair price (*quantum meruit*) for his half-finished work, allowing for money already received. The Court of Appeal maintained that he was not entitled to any further payment unless he completed both houses. *Sumpter v. Hedges* (1898).

This case concerned a "lump-sum" contract and laid down the rule that the builder or contractor must complete the entire contract before he can sue for his money. Because of this rule relating to lump-sum contracts, builders generally insist on terms which allow for **stage payments.**

One builder who agreed to install a central heating system for £560 received nothing in court even though the defects in his work cost only £170 to put right and the house owner's damages were assessed as low as £15. *Bolton v. Mahadeva* (1972).

Minor defects

Payment cannot be refused if the work is incomplete

only in some **minor** respect. Here the consumer can only deduct from the bill the cost of getting the work finished or making good the defect or omission.

In one case an interior designer agreed to decorate and furnish a flat for an all-in price of £750. The work was not entirely satisfactory and there were defects in the furnishing which cost £55 to put right. The court held that these defects could not be regarded as a failure by the designer to complete his part of the contract. He was allowed the agreed price of £750 less the £55 it cost to remedy the defective work. In this case the flat owner had come to the conclusion that the £750 he had originally agreed to pay, was too high but the Court held that as he had originally agreed to pay this sum he could not go back on his agreement and seek to pay only a fair price for the work.

Getting an estimate

In law an estimate may operate either as a fixed price or as an approximate indication of cost. It depends upon what the parties agree.

1 An estimate given by a contractor may amount to an offer to do the work at the price stated. If so, *quantum meruit* (fair remuneration) is not applicable.

2 Alternatively, the estimate may be understood as only a rough guide to the probable cost of the work. It may be approximate because the contractor cannot tell exactly at the outset how much work will be involved. Accordingly, where the cost of the work is only approximately assessed the contractor may not do work greatly beyond the cost stated without further authorization from the householder.

In practice, a reputable firm may well charge less than their estimate if it transpires that less work was necessary than first thought. If the repairs needed are uncertain it may not always be in the consumer's interest to fix a price in advance.

Fixing a price in advance

On the other hand he will know how much to expect if he agrees a price in advance. Once he informs the contractor that he accepts the estimate as a fixed price for the work, both contractor and consumer are equally bound by it.

If the price proves too high it must still be paid, even though it transpires that less work was necessary than originally thought. The householder cannot go back on his agreement to pay a fixed price and say that he now wishes to pay only a reasonable price, ie on the basis of *quantum meruit*.

On the other hand, if the price stated in the estimate is too low, it is the contractor who will bear the loss. For this reason, he may inflate the estimate to allow for all possible contingencies. Beware too the small builder who under-estimates in his eagerness to get work – a frequent cause of bankruptcy in the building industry. To recoup his loss through giving too low an estimate, he may over-charge on extras which arise as the work proceeds.

Extras

A fair price must be paid for all extras which the house-holder authorises. To avoid dispute the householder should insist on written notification of the cost of each extra as the work proceeds, **before** he authorises it. In other words, he will be getting a further estimated price for each extra, which he can then accept or reject as he thinks best.

Checking an estimate

It is always worth discussing an estimate on the telephone with the contractor to find out what methods he proposes to employ. For example, he may explain that plastic pipes are easier to install than cast iron, although the price is the same. Easier installation should mean that labour charges will be lower.

Obtain several estimates for the same job and compare them. If details seem imprecise telephone the firm for explanation. Information given on the telephone may be a representation and hence binding on the firm in law (see p 104). Choose a firm which seems reliable rather than the cheapest. A firm which belongs to a trade association and hence is subject to their code of practice (see p 57) is generally to be preferred since the association can bring pressure to bear in the event of a dispute.

From estimate to contract

Where an estimate operates as an offer by the contractor to do the work at the price stated, and the consumer accepts it either in writing or by telephone, the estimate then forms the basis of their contract.

Before accepting he should read the printed terms which accompany the estimate as these may allow for variations in price. Although in general a firm cannot charge more than is agreed under the estimate, there may be clauses on the back stating that "prices quoted are subject to fluctuation." There is nothing to prevent the consumer striking out a clause he disapproves.

Free Estimates

Although a fee has not been stipulated, a great deal of time and skill may be spent by the contractor in preparing an estimate. If it is not accepted by the consumer, the contractor will regard it as part of his normal overheads. There are many similar situations where a firm does work for which nothing can be claimed.

For example, an estate agent may go to considerable trouble and expense in advertising the sale of a house. If he cannot find a purchaser at a price acceptable to the seller he will not normally be entitled to a fee. The usual understanding is that he is to be paid his commission only when he secures a successful sale. For this reason, when instructing an estate agent, be careful not to sign any document binding you to pay expenses or commission save in the event of a completed sale (see p 171).

If a customer makes use of an estimate which is given free of charge he may find himself having to pay for the work which went into preparing it. One shrewd businessman got three building contractors to give him detailed estimates for re-building a war-damaged property.

Selecting the lowest he led them to believe that they would eventually get the contract. They produced for him detailed calculations of timber and steel needed and assessed the cost of a notional reconstruction of the property.

With all this information he was able to substantiate a claim for increase in his war damage assessment. He then told the builders that he had decided to employ a different firm but in fact he sold the premises. As he had no intention of employing the contractors in the first place, the judges did not hesitate to award them full recompense for their trouble, even though contracts were never finalised.

Accordingly, a consumer who proposes to make use of an estimate for some private purpose and not to employ the firm who gives it, should be prepared to pay the cost of its preparation.

Reckoning a fair price

Where a price has not been agreed in advance, in the last resort it will be for the judge to decide what is a reasonable price. The fact that watch repairers or motor mechanics do not specify what they will charge does not allow them to exploit this uncertainty.

When the work is done the repairer will often demand as much as he believes the job will stand, ie what the owner can afford or is likely to pay to settle the dispute and get his goods back. The consumer should **tender** what he considers a reasonable price.

If the repairer refuses to return the article without full payment, the consumer can pay **under protest** (see p 140).

Alternatively the consumer can sue him for its return. The repairer would then counter-claim for his full bill. The consumer must pay into court what he considers is a fair and reasonable charge. If the judge finds the consumer has been overcharged, he can order the repairer to pay him compensation for wrongfully detaining his goods.

To arrive at a fair price the judge will want to know, the average price charged in that particular trade for similar work. He will require details of how the cost of the various items on the bill was arrived at. He will take into account the length of time spent on the job, the cost of materials used, the qualifications of the worker employed to do it and how well it was done. The evidence of other local builders or someone from the appropriate trade association will also be relevant.

The right of traders to retain goods until paid

The right of a trader to keep possession of goods until payment applies particularly to those who carry out repairs. In law this right is referred to as a "lien". Similarly a seller has a lien on goods sold and need not hand them over until he is paid the full price.

A particular lien affects only those goods to which the unpaid bill relates. A motor repairer holding two cars belonging to the same person cannot retain say, the Mini as well as the Estate car if the consumer offers to pay the repair bill for the Mini. He must release the car in respect of which payment is offered.

Similarly, the lien of a dry-cleaner relates only to those clothes for which the cleaning charges remain unpaid.

The shop must hand over those articles for which the customer is prepared to pay its charges.

General liens

However, certain professions have what is known as a **general lien** or right of retention. For example, a bank can retain **all** valuables or securities deposited by a customer who overdraws his account. Solicitors, stockbrokers and auctioneers also have a general lien until **all** their bills have been paid.

A solicitor may withhold the documents relating to a transaction for which he has been paid if he can show that he has not been paid for some other work. Thus a solicitor whose costs have been paid on a house purchase may still retain the title deeds to the property if he has a bill outstanding, say, in respect of defending the same client on a motoring charge.

Disadvantage of liens

For the shopkeeper or motor-repairer, relying on his lien has one great disadvantage. It may be more trouble than it is worth for the repairer to store the goods in order to enforce payment. He cannot charge the customer for storage or the cost of garaging during the period of retention, even though several months may elapse between completion of the repairs and his charges being fully met.

When a Trader may dispose of uncollected goods

What to do when customers fail to collect articles is a particular problem for traders and repairers. The Disposal of Uncollected Goods Act 1952, entitled traders to sell such articles, but its requirements were so cumbersome that few traders made use of it.

That Act is now replaced by the Torts (Interference with Goods) Act 1977, which gives a more simplified right of disposal and sale. In particular it dispenses with the time limits required by the previous Act. Traders are empowered to sell uncollected goods (referred to as "chattels personal") eg cars, machinery, clothing and so on.

All the trader need do is to send the customer a notice which requests him to take delivery or to give directions for delivery. The notice must state the name and address of the trader and the amount owing (if any). It must describe the goods and state where they are being held, saying that they are ready for collection. It can be handed to the customer personally or sent by post to his last known address.

If he wishes, the trader can at the same time give notice of his intention to sell the goods if they are not collected. If so he must send a registered or recorded letter.

There is no need to wait any particular time. He can send these notices as soon as the item is repaired and ready for collection. Where the item was left for valuation or appraisal, the trader may give notice immediately following valuation.

It may be that he has been unable to trace the customer, eg the notice has come back in the post. Provided the trader has taken reasonable steps to trace him and is reasonably satisfied that the customer owned the article deposited, the trader may proceed to sell it.

He must sell at the highest price reasonably available. If he does not adopt the best method of sale he may have to pay the balance out of his own pocket.

Disputes

Where the customer has questioned his bill or refuses to pay all or any part of the sum claimed for the work done, the trader will have to apply to the court for authorisation to sell. This is the only method which can be used where there is a dispute over the goods or the trader's charges are questioned.

He can also apply for a court order if he suspects that the customer may not have been the owner of the article deposited. On hearing the trader's application for sale the judge may at his discretion authorise the sale subject to any conditions he deems desirable. The judge may direct that any money remaining after deduction of expenses must be paid into court and held for the credit of the customer.

Suppose the customer was not the owner of the goods but had deposited them without authorisation. The true owner can in theory claim the goods back from any one who buys them from the trader. In this case it is the trader who has to make amends. However, as between the trader and the customer who deposited the article, the customer's rights are ended by the sale.

The codes of practice for various trades often regulate the circumstances in which the trader may dispose of uncollected goods. Laundries and dry cleaners may include in their standard terms the right to sell an uncollected article without notice after a specific period. Such a term must be brought to the notice of the customer before he deposits the article. If it is unfair it will be invalid.

CHAPTER X

A FAIR DEAL FROM THE PROFESSIONS

Ever professional person, including anyone who carries on
a trade which involves special skill, must pay the consumer
compensation if he carries out his work negligently.
Negligence is the failure to exercise the care and skill
generally shown by persons in that trade or profession.
This does not mean that he must act always with the highest
expertise and skill. He is not negligent if he has done
his work with the normal standard of competence of
someone in his profession.

Three-year time limit on claims
Where personal injury is caused, eg, in a hospital, the
law allows the patient only three years from the date of
the injury in which to take legal action. Actually this
three-year period begins to run from the date when the
incorrect treatment was given.

In some cases there may be a substantial delay before the
injury makes itself apparent. If so the judge has power
to extend the three-year limitation period.

Negligence of repairers
A consumer who takes an article to be repaired is entitled
to compensation if the repair is carried out badly. He
is entitled to the cost of having the repair done properly
by another firm. Any **other loss** he has suffered, eg if he
has been injured as a result of the faulty repair, must also be
compensated. So too any third person can claim who is hurt
or suffers loss as a result of the faulty repair.

In *Stennett v. Hancock* (1939) a motor repairer replaced

the wheel of a lorry so badly that it came off and injured a pedestrian. The repairer was held liable for fitting the wheel without proper care and had to pay him compensation. However the owner of the lorry was freed from liability because he had entrusted the repair to a reputable garage.

In certain trades there is specific legislation to protect consumers. For example, in the motor trade the Road Traffic Act 1972, protects vehicle owners by making it an offence for repairers to fit defective or unsuitable parts.

The Unfair Contract Terms Act 1977, stipulates that all repairers must use components and materials which are of reasonable quality and fit for their purpose. Moreover their standard terms of business cannot exempt them from their general responsibility to perform repairs in a **workmanlike manner.** Nor can their terms of business excuse them from eg:

1 Breaking the terms of their contract.
2 Performing their contract in a different way.
3 Only partly performing what they have undertaken.
4 Liability for negligence.

Such exemption clauses are subject to the test of "reasonableness" (see p 133).

Consequently a dry cleaner who returns clothes stained or torn or fails to return them at all, must pay for their replacement. Nor may his terms of business unfairly limit the amount of compensation.

If a washing machine is wrongly repaired and stains or tears clothes, the consumer can claim the cost of replacing those clothes as well as the cost of having the repair properly done.

Should an electric iron or a tumble-drier be so badly repaired that it catches fire and damages other articles, the repairer would have to pay compensation for all the damage arising from his negligence. This will cover the cost of repiring the machine as well as the value of everything damaged by it burning out.

Services

Unfortunately a great many skilled trades which provide a service such as beauticians are not required by law to have any minimum training but membership of a trade association will usually ensure that they have. Should a customer contract some disease or suffer some injury through improper treatment or the use of uncleansed instruments, the beautician will be regarded as negligent. Similarly hairdressers are obliged to keep their equipment properly cleansed. If they use chemicals, such as dye, without a preliminary test they will be regarded as negligent if the treatment damages the consumer's hair or causes a skin complaint (see p 77).

Contractors

It is proposed to select electricians for discussion from the huge army of contractors upon whom the average consumer must depend. Many accidents arise from the faulty installation of electrical equipment or faulty wiring. Unfortunately there is no law to prevent an unskilled person carrying out electrical work and indeed many contractors have no qualification whatever.

Wherever possible one should select a tradesman who is a member of a recognised trade association which can usually be taken as a reliable indication of professional skill and competence. Repeated complaints about a trader to his association will result in his being banned from membership altogether.

Electrical Contractors Association

In the case of the Electrical Contractors Association, members are subjected to a close examination of technical competence and sound commercial background over a minimum of three years. Moreover this association, whose office is at 34 Palace Court, London W2 4HY (Telephone 01-229 1266) gives two important **guarantees** to consumers in respect of any work carried out by a member.

1 Their "Contract Completion Guarantee Scheme", introduced in 1976, guarantees a consumer that in the event of financial failure of a member, his contract will be fulfilled at the original price.
2 Under their "Guarantee of Work Scheme", the association guarantees the standard of all electrical installation wiring work of all members up to £10,000.

The consumer should obtain a contract in writing with the contractor if he is to have the backing of these two guarantee schemes.

The contractor himself remains liable (if he has the resources to meet such liability) for any loss, damage or injury which may be incurred or suffered as a result of the failure of his installation work.

Defective installations
The liability of contractors for consequential damage can in law by very extensive. Thus a householder may claim against builders, heating engineers, electricians and so on should his home be damaged by their defective installations. The Wayne Tank and Pump Co. undertook to supply and install electrically-heated tanks and piping at a factory. Because of defects in the piping the installation went up in flames and destroyed the factory. Wayne & Co. were obliged to meet the cost of building a new factory in place of the old one. *Harbutt v. Wayne* (1970).

Professional persons
The general duty not to be negligent applies to all trades and professions:

Doctors, surgeons and dentists
hospitals, nurses and anaesthetists
architects, surveyors, builders and building inspectors
estate agents, accountants and auditors
barristers (but only when engaged in non-litigious matters) and solicitors.

155

Doctors, surgeons and dentists owe a duty to their patients to show a fair, reasonable and competent degree of skill.

A doctor who failed to consider the possibility that his patient, an Englishman recently returned from Uganda, could be suffering from a tropical disease was found liable for negligence. The symptoms were fever, headache and alternate sweating and shivering which the doctor diagnosed and treated as influenza.

As he was getting no better it should have become apparent that the patient might have been suffering from a tropical disease of some kind, although malaria is not a disease with which the ordinary general practitioner normally comes into contact. Although he was not capable of diagnosing malaria he should have been alerted to the possibility. In fact a second doctor was called who had the patient transferred to a hospital where two Asian doctors immediately diagnosed malaria but in spite of treatment the patient died. Had the treatment been put in hand in time he would have stood a very good chance of recovery. His widow was awarded £15,000 damages. *Langley v. Campbell* (1975).

Responsibility of hospital for anaesthetists and nurses

One patient was awarded £93,000 compensation for brain damage which she suffered after a mistake in hospital treatment for *anorexia nervosa*. Her award was made against the Regional Health Authority which is responsible for all doctors and nurses employed in its hospitals.

The hospital is also responsible for a visiting or consulting surgeon or physician or even an anaesthetist who is not in full-time employment of the hospital.

Mr Bolton, a factory production manager, was taken to hospital after his car collided with a van and underwent an abdominal operation. The hospital **admitted** that the anaesthetist was neglectful and that during the operation Mr Bolton suffered oxygen starvation resulting in severe brain damage and consequent paralysis. He was unable to speak and his sight was damaged. He could neither feed himself nor attend to his toilet needs. He was awarded £112,000 compensation. *Bolton v. Essex Area Health Authority* (1977).

Record damages
Record damages of £243,309 were awarded in 1977 against the Camden and Islington Area Health Authority in favour of a patient who had become a hopeless invalid after a minor operation. Her brain was permanently damaged following a cardiac arrest due to failure by staff to take reasonable care for her safety. *Lim v. Camden & Islington Area Health Athority* (1977). Even larger amounts were given in similar cases in 1979.

Less skill expected of nurses
The degree of care and skill expected of a nurse is far less than that required of a trained doctor. However, the hospital would be liable for the negligence of a nurse who gives the patient the wrong dose of a drug, the correct dosage of which is clearly marked on the bottle or in the nurse's instructions from the doctor.

Risks inherent in certain operations
Although the standard of care required of a medical practitioner is a high one, he will not be considered negligent regarding risks **inherent** in an operation of the kind performed. Nor need he warn the patient of every risk involved in a proposed course of treatment.

A dentist broke the jaw of his patient while extracting a tooth. The patient claimed compensation on the ground that to break a patient's jaw must necessarily involve negligence. The court took the view that there is always the risk of a fracture of the jaw when a tooth is extracted. The patient lost because she was unable to produce an expert witness or any evidence to support her allegation of negligence. *Fish v. Kapur* (1948).

Patient's right to information

Is a patient entitled to know the precise risks involved before submitting to an operation? In a recent Canadian case the patient complained that he had not been told that the proposed operation could involve a 10% risk of disablement and a 4% risk of death. He maintained that he would never have consented to the operation in question had the surgeon advised him of the risk. The Canadian judge took the view that the operation had been conducted without the patient's true consent in law, and was thus a "battery" and awarded compensation accordingly.

Surprisingly, English law lays down no clear definition of the nature of the consent which the patient must give before submitting to an operation. Must he just consent to the operation and any necessary additional procedures, or must he give informed consent after an explanation of all the risks? Many patients might prefer to base their consent on the surgeon's advice without a detailed examination of the risks which may in practice be remote.

Proving negligence

The evidence of an independent medical specialist is almost always required if a claim in negligence is to succeed against a doctor. To press a claim for compensation an independent doctor of consultant status must give a report stating precisely why he considers the treatment given to the patient was wrong. Without such independent proof of negligence it would be virtually impossible to establish a claim in a court of law. But it is the patient who has to pay the cost of this examination and report, out of his own pocket.

One solution is to apply for legal aid and solicitors usually advise a claimant who has limited resources to apply to the local Law Society for a civil aid certificate. This will cover the cost not only of his legal advice but also of any expert report needed to establish his case.

Where negligence is obvious

In very few cases can the claimant rely on the legal rule "res ipsa loquitur" which means that the case is "obvious". An obvious example of negligence would be where a dentist removes a sound tooth by mistake or a surgeon removes a healthy limb owing to the failure of hospital staff to correctly mark the diseased limb which requires amputation. In such a case the legal burden of proof rests on the hospital to show that their negligence was **not** the cause of the patient's misfortune.

The Department of Health were quite unable to establish this defence in the case of Mr Cassidy (1951). Mr Cassidy's hand was rendered useless by negligent post-operational treatment. He went into hospital to have an operation on two fingers which were stiff. When he came out all four fingers of his hand were affected by stiffness. The court held it was for the hospital to explain how the other fingers became stiff without negligence on their part.

Mr Wood who was taken to hospital after a road accident. The doctor who saw him failed to diagnose any serious injury. The following day Mr Wood died. It was found that he had no less than 18 ribs broken as well as congestion of one lung. The doctor was held liable for making a faulty diagnosis. The fact that the patient was under the influence of alcohol made it all the more vital for the doctor to conduct his examination with particular care.

A similar case recently involved a man of 48 who became blind following prescribed treatment. This was strange because the treatment he was receiving related to a complaint in the groin. His compensation was agreed at £65,000.

Computing compensation

Where a claim is made against an individual doctor it will usually be handled on his behalf either by the Medical Defence Union or the Medical Protection Society, depending on which he belongs to. These organisations provide legal services to doctors and will indemnify them in respect of any claim for compensation. They are non profit-making organisations run by eminent members of the medical profession.

Should a patient die as a result of medical negligence leaving a wife and family, his dependants will have a substantial claim for loss of their wage earner. The amount of compensation awarded depends on what the deceased was earning and how much of his income he spent on his family. The judge will then decide how many years the deceased might normally have been expected to work. He will then multiply the two figures together, ie earnings by the number of working years ahead of him up to a maximum of about 20. For example, £5,000 a year for 15 years would give a compensation figure of £75,000.

On the other hand it is still true in English Law that it is cheaper to kill than to maim, provided the deceased has no dependants who rely on him as a wage-earner. If so his next of kin will usually receive only a modest amount "for loss of expectation of life", generally less than £1,000. Should the patient die after a period of suffering due to inadequate or wrong treatment this amount could however be substantially increased.

Medical confidences

In theory everything a doctor knows about his patient is confidential and may not be disclosed without the patient's consent.

A plastic surgeon or a dentist who has carried out improvements on a pop star may not divulge how much of the pop star's glamour has been due to his skill.

One doctor who notified the father of a young patient that she had been to a family planning clinic was brought before the General Medical Council. Although they accepted he had acted from sincere motives and not in the particular case "improperly", few doctors would risk such a breach of confidence because it lays them open to a claim for compensation by the patient. Thus before giving a medical report to an insurance company your doctor will ask you to sign a letter of authorisation.

However, the position of confidentiality relating to medical practitioners has steadily deteriorated in recent years. There are a number of statutes requiring doctors to inform on patients as a matter of routine. Infectious diseases like TB have to be notified to the local Medical Officer of Health and doctors who suspect that one of their patients has become addicted to a dangerous drug must notify the Home Office.

Again, where a person injured in a motor accident sues for compensation, the insurance company can compel both his own doctor and the hospital where he was treated to hand over **all** his medical records – not just those concerned with his injuries.

Suppose a patient goes to his doctor with injuries or cuts and the doctor realises from local knowledge that he is wanted by the police for interview in connection with a recent crime. Is the doctor under a legal obligation to notify them? Since 1967 it is now left to the doctor's own conscience whether he informs the police or not. Certainly he will not be criticised if he turns the patient in. On the other hand, he will be committing no offence if he keeps silent.

However, where a doctor is summoned to court as a witness, the judge can compel him to tell what he knows about his patient "if the interests of justice require it".

Examples of Negligence by an Architect or Surveyor

1 Failing properly to examine the foundations of a new building.

2 When superintending its construction, failing to ensure that the floors are properly laid according to the specification.

3 Failing to detect and report on obvious faults. A surveyor was asked to inspect a farm and asked to express a general opinion. He was not asked to make a detailed survey. Nevertheless he was considered negligent by the court because he did not discover dry rot and settlement.

4 An architect who designs a bridge or building so badly that it falls down is liable to everyone injured in the fall.

Architects

The advantages of having an architect when modifying or renovating your house are considerable. He will draw up detailed plans and specifications to get tenders for the work at the lowest price. The architect's duty is to see that the builder keeps rigidly to the contract price and does not run up costly extras.

Architect's fees

What does the architect himself charge? Fees are normally charged on a sliding scale varying between 6% and 10% of the cost of the work involved. Where the consumer commissions a design for, say, a new bungalow to cost between £20,000 and £25,000 he will be told the initial design fee in advance. However he should make it clear that he will not accept the design if it will cost more than a specified sum to construct.

Suppose when the plans are completed the estimated cost of building far exceeds the amount anticipated? In one case the lowest price for which any builder would undertake the construction was half as much again as the architect had estimated. The design was therefore too expensive for the owner to continue with. The court decided that the architect had not kept within his instructions. Having designed a project which was too expensive, he was not entitled to his design fee.

Nevertheless the architect must be allowed an opportunity of **modifying** his original design should all the tenders received be higher than anticipated. If he can bring down the cost of construction to the stipulated amount by redesigning the building, the owner will have to accept it. However a client need pay no fee for plans or drawings submitted for his **approval** until he approves them. But where he refuses to pay a fee he must not make any use of the plans produced by the architect.

Should he subsequently get his own builder to modify the plans and go ahead with the building on a reduced budget without the architect's assistance, he will have to pay the whole or a substantial part of the design fee. He would also have to pay a reasonable fee if he subsequently makes use of a surveyor's expertise or sketch plans even though no fee has been negotiated.

Architect's Supervision of Construction

The architect must ensure that the builder has been following his specifications. Consequently he should inspect the building site regularly as construction progresses. In particular he must check the work of sub-contractors before allowing it to be covered over by the next stage of construction. However he is not obliged actually to supervise the building work at all times, but merely to inspect it from time to time as necessary. For exercising **daily** supervision the architect would require a higher fee. The architect is responsible for any obviously defective work. He is under a duty during inspection to point this out to the contractor and see that he puts it right. But it is the contractor's responsibility to erect the building in a workmanlike manner.

A list of defects will be prepared by the architect and handed to the contractor after completion of the work, itemising what needs to be rectified. Strictly the builder is not liable for obvious defects unless the architect has actually instructed him to rectify them.

Supposing after completion the building itself begins to tilt or subside – this is prima facie evidence that the architect's design or specification was unsatisfactory. He would be responsible unless he can prove that the cause of the defect lay with the builder.

Liability of builder

Apart from obvious faults which he is asked to put right, the builder remains liable for any concealed faults of workmanship or materials which the architect could not reasonably be expected to discover by normal inspection. For example, the builder may depart from the specifications and use the wrong sort of cement or inferior materials. The architect would not be liable personally for failing to notice any such hidden defects in the work.

The consumer is protected by the Unfair Contract Terms Act 1977 which guarantees that all materials used will be of fair quality. No small print terms in the builder's contract will exonerate him if materials are not up to par, ie sound and reasonably fit for their purpose.

The principle laid down in *Donoghue v. Stevenson* has been applied to builders making them responsible to subsequent owners and occupiers of defective premises as well as to the original purchaser. Negligence means a failure to carry out repairs or building construction in a workmanlike manner. In one case a builder plugged a hole in a floor inefficiently. A woman walking in the house in high-heeled shoes caught her heel in the hole. The plug gave way and she was injured. The judge considered that a plug was not a workmanlike method of filling the hole and ordered the builder to pay her compensation.

In *Sharpe v. Sweeting Ltd* (1963) Mrs Sharpe was injured when a concrete canopy over her front door fell on her. The house was rented from the Middlesbrough Corporation for whom it had been built by Sweeting Ltd.

The builders were liable on the principle of *Donoghue v. Stevenson* for breach of their duty of care. Had the canopy been properly constructed it should have remained in position for some 60 years. The cause of the accident was faulty and negligent reinforcement of the concrete. It was found that the reinforcing mesh had not been properly placed to give sufficient support.

Where there is no NHBRC guarantee the Defective Premises Act 1972 covers all building work by way of erection, enlargement or conversion of any dwelling carried out by builders, developers, local authorities and so on. They have a duty to see that the work is done
(a) in a professional or workmanlike manner
(b) with proper materials
and to ensure it passes the "fit for habitation" test. Any subsequent tenant or purchaser can claim for six years from the date the work was completed.

The case of the attractive Show House
When a prospective buyer inspects a show house he is entitled to assume that the house to be built for him will be of equivalent construction, materials and finish.

One estate agent assured a Liverpool couple that their new house would be "just as good as the show house" although their contract merely said that their house was to be "fit for occupation and habitation". They complained about its deplorable paintwork and poor finish but the builder refused to repaint it. The Court of Appeal ordered the builder to bear the full cost of repainting. "The whole purpose of a show house", said one judge "is to give a prospective buyer the opportunity of knowing what he is going to get".

NHBC 10 year Guarantee for New Houses

Virtually every new house comes with Notice of Insurance Cover by the National House-Building Council which generally lasts 10 years.

During the first two years after certification the builder, not the NHBC, is liable. However, if he has gone bankrupt the NHBC will pay to rectify any faults.

After the end of two years the NHBC protects the buyer against "major damage requiring complete or partial rebuilding or extensive repair work". Their policy covers major settlement or subsidence, dry rot causing structural failure, collapse of joists or serious distortion of roof structure or failure of structural elements. It does not cover such items as loose or cracked tiles.

Liability of Local Authority for Building Inspectors' Survey

Where building inspectors employed by the local authority wrongly approve a house under construction, the local authority can be made to pay compensation where their inspectors have committed an error of judgment.

After buying a house in Bognor Regis built only a year or so before, Mrs Dutton noticed that cracks were beginning to appear in the walls. Taking professional advice she was told that the foundations were unsound because the house had been built on an old rubbish tip. She was advised to take legal action against the Bognor Regis UDC for compensation. The Council were ordered to pay Mrs Dutton £3,000 to put the foundations right plus her surveyor's fees and interest plus a bonus of £500 for diminution in value of her house. The judges said that the Council's inspectors owed a duty of care to subsequent purchasers of the house to carry out their inspection efficiently when they went to inspect it pursuant to their duties under the byelaws. Had they made a careful inspection they would have detected that the foundations were unsound. Hence they were negligent. *Dutton v. Bognor Regis UDC* (1972).

How Long can Liability Last?

The principle in Mrs Dutton's case was approved and strengthened by the House of Lords in 1977 in the case of *Anns v. London Borough of Merton* which concerned a block of maisonettes which had a latent defect in the foundations. The block was built in 1962 but it was 1970 before the occupants began to notice cracks in the walls and sloping floors. The reason was that the foundations were too shallow. They should have been 3' or more according to the plans deposited with the Council but in fact they were only 2'6". The Council were ordered to pay compensation to the occupants of the flats even though many of them were not the original buyers. The court held that their inspectors were negligent in not ensuring that the building was being constructed in accordance with the plans. They should have tested the foundations before permitting the builders to cover them over.

An important aspect of this case is that the statutory limitation period of six years had already passed since the block was built. The House of Lords pointed out that the six-year period starts, not when the foundations are constructed, but when the damage first appears. Architects, surveyors and builders are worried by this decision because it extends the potential period of their liability indefinitely.

Getting a Surveyor's Report

Before exchanging contracts to buy a house it is wise to employ a qualified surveyor. Although a full survey is fairly expensive, many surveyors will carry out a limited survey at a modest fee. The advantage of having a surveyor

167

is that if his report carelessly overlooks some defect, he will be responsible for the cost of putting it right. Getting a satisfactory survey report amounts to a form of insurance against major defects for years to come. If, for example, the report states that the drains are sound and they start to give trouble after the client has moved in, the surveyor must get them put right. Similarly if his report overlooks a potential structural defect it will be the surveyor's own insurance company which will have to meet the cost of putting it right.

Duty of the Building Society's Surveyor

Significantly Mrs Dutton (see above) did not have a survey carried out at the time she bought her house because it was virtually new. She relied on the fact that her building society surveyor had passed it. In so doing she was unwise because although the prospective borrower has to pay the surveyor's fee, in law the surveyor owes no legal responsibility to the borrower.

His survey report is for the benefit of the building society and is seldom shown to the house buyer. In fact it is generally little more than a valuation to ensure that if the house has to be sold by the society they will get back the amount of their loan.

Section 30 of the Building Societies Act 1962, states that when a member is given an advance to buy a property the society in law is deemed to give him a warranty that the price he is paying is reasonable. The society is obliged to make arrangements for an accurate valuation. In practice building societies avoid their obligation of having to give the borrower a warranty that the price is reasonable by handing him a disclaimer form stating that their making the advance implies no such warranty.

The lack of responsibility of the building society surveyor to house-buyers is one legal quirk that needs altering in favour of the consumer.

168

Such liability might arise under the principle enunciated by the House of Lords in 1964 in the case of Hedley Byrne v. Heller on the ground that there is a "special relationship" between surveyor and buyer. Thus, should their surveyor's report be made available to the housebuyer, the surveyor could be responsible. Where a buyer purchases on the strength of the surveyor's negligent report which is inaccurate and misleads the buyer, he could claim compensation.

The Estate Agents Act 1979 brings estate agents under the control of the Director General of Fair Trading. They must give clients in advance full information about their fees. They must also disclose any personal interest in a transaction. They must keep client's deposits in a separate account and take out insurance against possible misappropriation. Hitherto deposits paid by prospective purchasers were not safeguarded until contracts were exchanged.

Estate agents and deposits

Where a houseowner puts his house up for sale he impliedly authorises the estate agent to accept a deposit from a prospective purchaser. But if the estate agent turns out to be dishonest the owner is not responsible for it unless the purchaser has actually exchanged contracts with him to buy the property.

So the prospective purchaser ought not to pay a deposit before exchange of contracts, ie until his solicitors tell him to. Prior to exchange of contracts he should be cautious about paying more than a nominal deposit, at most £50, to an estate agent.

Interest on deposits

Where an estate agent or solicitor is authorised to hold a deposit as a **stakeholder** he is entitled to any interest

169

earned on it during the period he holds it in his bank account, ie between exchange of contracts and completion of the sale. Neither the vendor nor the purchaser can claim the interest earned. But the seller is entitled to have the deposit plus interest (if any) **immediately** where the agent or solicitor has accepted it "as agent of the vendor".

Estate agents and confidential information

An estate agent owes a duty of confidence to those members of the public who employ him. Normally an estate agent is employed by the seller although sometimes he receives instructions from a prospective buyer. Whether he acts for seller or buyer he must not disclose to anyone else confidential information which he has obtained as a result of his relationship with his client. He would be breaking this duty of confidence to his client if he tells a third party the price paid for a property. In practice local valuation officers rely on estate agents for information on sale prices and current rentals. Strictly an estate agent should not make such disclosures without obtaining his client's consent.

An estate agent is also under a duty to relay information to his client, even if obtained from a confidential source. If there is a conflict of interest between two clients or between his client and the estate agent himself, the estate agent must cease to act.

In one case estate agents were ordered to pay compensation to the owner of a farm for failing to tell him that his sitting tenant, who was proposing to buy the farm, was planning to resell it at a profit. Clearly if he had received this information he might have considered the adequacy of the price being offered by his tenant. He might even have decided not to sell to the tenant at all.

In these circumstances an estate agent would be regarded as negligent and cannot claim commission. Similarly he would not be entitled to his commission if through carelessness he fails to obtain for his client the best market price. The general rule is that he forfeits any fee if he is so negligent that the service he performs for his client is rendered valueless.

Breach of trust by the estate agent

Every agent owes a duty of honesty to the person employing him. If he dishonestly makes extra money on the side without his client's knowledge, he commits fraud. He commits a breach of trust if he buys property from a client through a nominee or arranges for the sale of a client's property to an associate who pays him secretly. Where an agent commits a breach of trust he not only forfeits his commission but could be liable to both civil and criminal proceedings for fraud.

Mr Andrews instructed a firm to find a purchaser for his property for £2,500. He agreed to pay the firm £50 commission. The agents introduced a buyer at £2,100 and Mr Andrews finally accepted this offer, telling the agents to deduct their £50 commission out of the deposit. Later Mr Andrews discovered that the agents had received a further £20 from the prospective buyer. The judge not only deprived them of their £50 commission, but also ordered them to pay to Mr Andrews the £20 they had received from the buyer, because they had broken faith with Mr Andrews.

Sales talk by estate agents

An estate agent who gives a bland assurance to a prospective buyer about the state of a propety or any other attribute could be liable to pay compensation if that assurance is unfounded, eg that there is an hourly bus service to the railway station.

Again an agent may assure a prospective buyer that the timbers of a house are sound. Should it later transpire that the timbers are infected with wood worm or dry-rot, the buyer would be entitled to demand compensation unless the agent can establish that he had reasonable grounds for believing that what he said was true.

(See further the Misrepresentation Act 1967, p 104).

When Estate Agents are Entitled to Claim Commission

An estate agent is obliged to inform clients of his rate of commission before they enter into a transaction. Normally an estate agent cannot claim commission unless and until the sale has gone through. The understanding is that he will be paid his commission out of the purchase price. The seller should not sign any document which entitles the agent to commission in any other circumstances, nor should he appoint him "sole agent" or give him "sole selling rights".

An unscrupulous estate agent may write a long letter to the seller purporting to confirm his instructions but in fact containing legal jargon, the object of which is to entitle him to his commission in the event of a sale not being completed. If so the seller should write back promptly stating that he will pay commission only on completion, ie when the buyer has paid over the full purchase price. If he fails to make this clear the seller could find himself having to pay commission although no sale in fact results.

Avoiding double commission

Beware of estate agents who inform the seller that they will be entitled to commission "in the event of their finding a ready, able and willing purchaser at the price stated or any other price the seller agrees to accept". If he accepts these terms the seller could become liable to pay them commission on a sale which does not go through.

Suppose his house is advertised at £20,000 and Smith & Co. introduce a purchaser at £17,000. After some hesitation the seller may have to accept this offer owing to financial pressure. Before contracts are exchanged another firm, Jones & Co., may come up with a purchaser who offers the original asking price of £20,000. If the seller accepts the higher offer he will then be liable to pay commission to both Smith & Co. on their abortive sale at £17,000 and also to Jones & Co. on the completed sale at £20,000.

The best advice one can give a seller is to make it clear to each estate agent whom he instructs that he will pay commission only to the agent who introduces the successful purchaser.

Sole Selling Rights and Sole Agency

It is most unwise to grant any one estate agent "sole selling rights". This means the agent must be paid commission even though the owner finds a buyer himself, or sells to a friend, or through his own advertisement.

Nor should he grant any agent "sole agency" which entitles the sole agent to commission even if another agent achieves the sale and could result in the seller being saddled with two lots of commission. However a seller who appoints a sole agent but manages to sell through his **own efforts,** is not liable to pay commission.

Accountants and Auditors

There is an implied duty on accountants not to divulge information gained as a result of advising or acting for a client. Even if the accountant discovers his client is engaged in a tax fiddle, he must not "shop" him to the Inland Revenue. What he must do is to advise his client to "come clean". The accountant can continue to act for him provided he does not become an "accomplice" in the client's attempt at tax evasion.

An accountant is liable to pay compensation to his client in the event of:
1 Disclosing confidential information without his client's permission.
2 Incompetence in handling his client's affairs or insufficient knowledge of the law.

3 Failing to take reasonable care of a client's documents.
4 Negligence.

Drawing up a balance sheet without checking the cash balance against the bank account statements or passbook will amount to negligence. If there turns out to be a discrepancy he will be liable. He must not rely solely on the cash book because its entries may not tally with the cash paid into the bank.

Even where an accountant is asked informally to give advice, eg on sale of a business, a client who suffers a loss through incorrect advice can claim compensation on the ground that he has failed to advise him properly.

When Accountants have a "Special Relationship"

The general rule used to be that only the person who actually engages the professional adviser will have a legal claim to compensation in the event of his being negligent. In 1964 this rule was altered by the leading case of *Hedley Byrne v. Heller.* The House of Lords stated that a person who has lost money through relying on a report or free advice given negligently is entitled to claim in certain circumstances. In order to succeed in his claim he must show that there is a "special relationship" between himself and the person giving the advice or report. Where a special relationship exists, it does not matter that he has not paid for the advice or report.

Similarly accountants are often asked to prepare accounts for a client who wishes to sell his business. A prospective buyer may be induced to acquire an interest in that business on the strength of those accounts. Here again there is a "special relationship" even though the accountants do not know the identity of the proposed buyer. They will be liable to compensate him if the accounts they have prepared are misleading and cause him to lose money.

Liability can be avoided only by giving a clear **disclaimer**, eg "We do not vouch for or accept responsibility for the accuracy of the information contained in this report".

Barristers and Solicitors

The legal profession in the UK is split into barristers and solicitors. One aspect of this dichotomy is that a member of the public who requires legal advice cannot approach a barrister direct but must first go to a solicitor.

Barristers (referred to as "counsel") are legal specialists. The solicitor is mainly a general practitioner. He will consult counsel where:

1 a client needs specialised advice.

2 a client requires to be represented at a court hearing.

Whilst solicitors may speak in the county court or a magistrates' court on behalf of a client, in practice most instruct a barrister to address the court. However, in the High Court or crown courts only a barrister may represent you although every private litigant may appear "in person", ie he has a right to address the court without a lawyer.

Since barristers are largely prevented from dealing directly with the general public this tends to preserve the independence and integrity of the bar from whose ranks most judges are appointed. For example, barristers may not hold money on behalf of a client, as can a solicitor. Nor may they advise or interview a client save in the presence of a solicitor.

Confidentiality and privilege

Every client can expect scrupulous fairness and secrecy from his solicitor. He may speak freely and without reserve. No solicitor is permitted to divulge what a client tells him in confidence.

Should a client confess to his legal adviser that he has broken the law, nonetheless the other may never reveal his confession and must not in any circumstances report him to the police. He may not even be called upon to state in court what his client has told him. The solicitor can refuse on the ground that the information is subject to **privilege.**

The privilege of secrecy is the client's. His solicitor may not disclose information save with his client's express permission. The privilege attaching to confidential disclosures is confined to legal advisers. This rule protects the client and allows him to speak freely to his lawyer. The rule is necessary to enable everyone to obtain legal advice without fear of recriminations.

Again your solicitor may not tell anyone the contents of your will. Even your wife is not entitled to obtain this information from him. Supposing a testator is struck with total paralysis or incapacity, can his family then insist on seeing the will? Until the testator has actually died, his solicitor must keep his will absolutely secret. However, on death the situation changes because the will then takes effect in law and the executors must be informed so that they may take control of the deceased's assets.

Even if the police are making inquiries about you, your solicitor may not tell them where to find you without obtaining your permission. In one case a husband told his solicitor to keep his new address secret from his wife. Her solicitors sent a medical certificate saying that her mental health was suffering through not knowing her husband's whereabouts. Neverthless his solicitor was forbidden to disclose his address although he was permitted to forward letters from her to his client.

If I tell my solicitor I am guilty, can he still defend me? The short answer is that he cannot. If I want to plead not guilty I must go to another lawyer. Also I must take care not to make any similar admission to him. Whatever he thinks privately about my guilt or innocence is irrelevant. Even if I have already signed a statement to the police admitting my guilt, my solicitor must always accept what I, as his client, tell him.

However anyone who consults a solicitor for advice in respect of some proposed **future** crime or fraud is not protected. Thus a solicitor may in all innocence arrange the tenancy of premises from which a dishonest client proposes to conduct a fraudulent business. The solicitor will have to give this information if called upon by the court.

Secret Profits and Commissions

The rule that an agent may not receive a secret profit or commission applies equally to solicitors. Large commissions are often paid to solicitors who arrange life insurance policies on behalf of their clients. Again, a solicitor may introduce an auctioneer or estate agent to a client who wishes to sell a property. A solicitor who receives a commission for the introduction is generally regarded as acting unprofessionally. In any case he must inform his client of any profit or commission he makes on the side. Strictly this extra commission belongs to the client and the solicitor can keep it only if the client consents. The rule is that the solicitor is entitled only to a reasonable fee for work actually done. He is not entitled to make additional profit without his client's knowledge.

Interest on clients' money

All solicitors are legally obliged to keep books of account which are audited annually. They must ensure that a client receives interest on any money they hold on his behalf. Where they hold a sum in excess of £500, they must put it in a deposit account at the bank so that the client may have interest on his money. If they should omit to place it on deposit, they must nevertheless pay the client the interest it would have earned.

A client whose money is held for an excessively long period can complain to the Law Society. He can also request them to certify how much interest he is entitled to.

Fees must be "fair and reasonable"

There are several factors in assessing a reasonable fee:

1 Basically the fee charged should reflect the work done: the number of hours spent in interviews and preparing documents, the number of letters written, telephone calls and so on.

   However all solicitors do not charge at the same hourly rate. A small firm in the provinces may charge £20 an hour for work done by a partner. If the work is done by an unqualified clerk, the charge should be less. In a large city firm with heavy overheads which is acting in an important matter, £30 to £40 an hour would not be considered unreasonable for work done by a senior solicitor. Where he is paid out of the legal aid fund, £10 to £15 per hour would be usual.

When higher rate of charge justifiable

2 A high rate of charge per hour is justified where a large sum of money or valuable property is involved. Thus a client should expect to pay more when buying a very expensive house. House buyers are not able easily to ascertain in advance exactly how much they will be charged because of the abolition of the price-related scales of fees. These used to be based on a percentage of the value of the property involved.

   However, there is nothing to prevent a solicitor agreeing to do legal work for a **fixed fee** agreed in advance. If the work turns out to be more complicated the client will benefit. If the transaction is fairly simple the solicitor can be called upon to justify his agreed fee as being fair and reasonable.

3 The basic rate chargeable may also be increased because of the importance of the matter to the client. Again, a solicitor may be justified in charging more where he hurries through a transaction or does work outside normal office hours for the client's benefit.

4 An additional sum is also chargeable for "skilled labour

and any specialised knowledge involved.". The complexity of the work as well as the time spent and the number of documents dealt with are all relevant in deciding what is a reasonable fee.

For the house buyer legal costs will usually be heavier where title is not registered because the solicitor must examine more documents. On the other hand buying an expensive town house may in fact involve the solicitor in less work where the title is registered at HM Land Registry as the documentation is simpler.

"Thinking time" is an additional item which can be charged for in a complicated transaction.

Solicitors' Bills

A solicitor may not sue a client on his bill unless it is signed by a partner or sent with a letter so signed.

A solicitor's bill for a transaction takes the form of an itemised summary of all work done, telling the client exactly what he is being asked to pay for. All special payments and disbursements, such as stamp duties, postages, telephone calls and search fees, will be set out.

Certificate of reasonableness

A client who feels he has been overcharged can insist that the solicitor sends the bill to the Law Society for a certificate as to the amount the Law Society considers fair and reasonable. Before a solicitor can sue a client for non-payment he must notify his client that he is entitled to have the bill verified by the Law Society. The solicitors' file of papers is then scrutinised to ascertain whether the amount charged is justified. A request for a certificate of reasonableness will not involve the client in any additional expense. If he is still dissatisfied, he can appeal to the county court or where the bill exceeds £2000, to the High Court.

Payment under protest

A client who thinks that his bill is too high should not pay it because this will cancel his right to have it checked by the Law Society. If he is compelled to make payment he should make it clear by letter and on his cheque that he pays "under protest". He will then be entitled to a rebate if it is later shown that he has been overcharged.

When a Solicitor may refuse to act for the Client

A solicitor may not refuse to accept work from a client **solely** on account of the client's race, colour, creed, national origins or sex.

Nor may a solicitor refuse to represent a client who is charged with a crime merely because he suspects the client is guilty. However, once the client tells him he is guilty the solicitor may not put forwards to the court a defence denying the charge. (See p 176).

Conflicting Interests

A solicitor must not act for a client:

1 Where the solicitor has some personal interest which conflicts with that of his client.
2 Where the solicitor acts for or has previously acted for another client whose interest conflicts with that of the client in question.
3 A solicitor need not act where the client insists upon his taking some action which will unnecessarily injure the other partly simply in order to gratify the malice or vindictiveness of the client.

Acting for both parties

Acting for both parties to a transaction is usually undesirable, save where their interests are identical. For example it is quite proper for a solicitor to act both for a house-buyer and the building society who is putting up the money. It is equally important for the building

180

society that the legal ownership of the property should be vested in the buyer so that his interest may be mortgaged to them.

However, as a general rule, a solicitor is forbidden from acting for both buyer and seller of property as their interests may conflict. Nor may he act for both landlord and tenant on the grant of a lease. He may act for both parties in the following instances, provided their interests do not clash:

1 A transfer between associated companies.
2 Where both buyer and seller are related by blood or marriage.
3 Where the same solicitor has acted for both clients in the past.
4 If there are no other solicitors in the vicinity whom the client can reasonably be expected to consult.
5 Where the price is less than £1,000.

How much law must a solicitor know?

A solicitor is not expected to know all the law. He is not responsible if he makes an error "being such as a cautious man might fall into". A solicitor who is in doubt about a point of law can guard himself against an allegation of negligence by taking "counsel's advice". Where he consults a barrister whose advice turns out to be wrong, a solicitor would not generally be regarded as having acted negligently. Consequently his client could not sue him for any loss incurred through following counsel's advice.

Barristers are immune from any complaint by a client in respect of the way they have conducted or managed a trial in court. More important, barristers cannot be sued for careless preparatory work leading up to a court hearing or for giving incompetent advice in any matter which might lead to litigation.

Although it has been suggested that a barrister as well as a solicitor could be sued for negligence if he makes

181

a glaring error in preparing a legal document, no one has yet successfully sued a barrister for negligence.

A solicitor could be sued for negligence if he fails to bring a witness to court or if he fails to take steps to trace a necessary witness. However, if after the witness has arrived the barrister forgets to call him to give evidence, the client has no redress.

Unpleasant advice

In practice a solicitor is expected to give not only general legal advice but common sense advice too. He is not justified in keeping silent when it is plain that the client is rushing into an unwise venture.

Occasionally he is obliged to give advice which he knows his client will find unpalatable. For example, a lady may be determined to lend money to a man with whom she has become infatuated. Even at the risk of losing her as a client, the solicitor must indicate the dangers.

Where a client is buying a house with the help of a building society advance he must advise him not to sign a contract to buy before confirmation of his mortgage comes through. A solicitor would be negligent if he exchanges contracts to buy before he receives confirmation that his client has the necessary finance available. Even if the client is in a hurry the solicitor is under a duty to warn him of the danger of signing a binding contract before getting assurance of a loan.

Examples of negligence

A typical example of negligence would be failure to issue a writ within the three-year limitation period where a client has suffered personal injuries. This would be an "open and shut" case for compensation which could be very substantial.

Mr and Mrs Piper were never told by their solicitor that the house they were buying was subject to a right of way in favour of a neighbour. After moving in they suffered grave loss of privacy through their neighbour crossing to and fro continually in front of their windows. Eventually they got so fed up that they decided to move house. They were granted compensation for their loss of privacy, but not the expense of moving home.

One woman went to a solicitor to get a court order against a man with whom she had once been friendly to stop him molesting her. The solicitor failed to take any constructive action despite the fact she had paid him a considerable sum of money. Since she could find no other solicitor who would take up her complaint against the first solicitor she started a legal action herself against the solicitor who had let her down. Not only was his firm ordered to pay back the money he had received from her, but it was also ordered to pay her compensation for the nervous stress she had suffered as a result of his failure to take action on her behalf.

"Special Relationship" of Solicitors to the Public

Farmer Green wanted his son Geoffrey to have his farm and decided to give him a 10-year option to buy it at a low price. Together they went to a solicitor who drew up an option agreement to buy it at £75 an acre. Farmer Green signed it but the solicitor forgot to have it registered under the Land Charges Act. Without registration his son's right to buy the farm was not fully protected in law.

Some years after Farmer Green broke with his son and transferred the farm to his wife for £500, thereby defeating his son's option right. Had Geoffrey's option been registered properly, she could not have got the farm in this way. As a result Geoffrey claimed more than £37,000 from the solicitor for omitting to register his option. The solicitor's firm had to compensate Geoffrey for his loss of the option right to buy the farm cheaply.

The solicitor had a "special relationship" with Geoffrey and owed him a duty to do all that was necessary in law to make the option legally "water-tight". This special relationship exists, said the judge, even though the client does not pay for the advice given. *Midland Bank v. Hett, Stubbs & Kemp* (1977).

Complaints to the Law Society

The Law Society can help a dissatisfied client in only a limited number of situations. The most important of these are **dishonesty** on the part of the solicitor, overcharging or taking advantage of his client. It will also investigate such complaints as persistent delay in paying over money owed to a client or failing to answer letters.

However, it is not able to take action against a solicitor for negligence or lack of care when conducting a client's affairs unless this is so gross as to amount to "unbefitting conduct" as would render the solicitor liable to disciplinary proceedings. This would arise, for example, where a solicitor has failed to carry out his client's instructions to defend an action or where he neglects to complete the purchase of a house after having the money.

All solicitors are covered against negligence claims under a compulsory insurance scheme. Every solicitor has guaranteed protection up to £50,000 for any one claim. Large firms have proportionately greater cover under a master policy maintained by the Law Society.

Where something has gone amiss with a client's case, the solicitor is under a duty to advise the client to obtain independent advice, ie to consult another solicitor. Failure so to advise a client would amount to unbefitting conduct.

Dishonesty of Solicitors

Finally, all solicitors are obliged to contribute annually to a compensation fund run by the Law Society. Where a solicitor goes bankrupt or disappears this fund can be used to repay even very large sums to a client who has been defrauded.

CHAPTER XI

PAYING YOUR WAY

The tender of money indicates readiness to pay. By offering the sum due the person owing it complies with his duty to pay even if the offer is refused. If so, tender of the appropriate sum prevents the creditor claiming interest after the date it was tendered.

If the creditor subsequently sues him, the person owing should pay into court the amount he considers correct. He will not then have to pay any court costs if the judge considers the creditor is entitled to no more than the amount tendered. Instead the creditor will have to pay all the legal costs (see p 297).

A creditor may refuse the amount tendered and then change his mind and later make a second demand. He is not bound by his first refusal and if he does make a subsequent demand the debtor should comply at once.

To constitute a valid tender the person owing must offer in cash the **precise** amount that is due. The creditor is not obliged to give change. To get round this point, the person paying can waive his right to change.

In theory, the creditor does not have to accept less than the full amount due. He is entitled to refuse an offer of **part** of the debt unless it is made up of several separate items. The person paying should then state to which item his payment is to be allocated. If he does not, the rules regarding appropriation of payment apply. (See below).

Tender by cash or cheque

The offer to pay must be made in legal currency. The money must actually be produced. The creditor is not obliged to accept a cheque but if he asks for a cheque in payment he is taken as waiving his right to insist on cash. Also, if when offered a cheque the creditor objects only that the **amount** is insufficient, he is again deemed to waive any objection to the cheque.

Legal tender by coins

The maximum amounts which may legally be tendered in coins are limited as follows:

A maximum of £10 can be offered in 50p coins

A maximum of £5 can be paid by 10p or 5p coins

Not more than 20p can be paid by 2p, 1p or $\frac{1}{2}$p coins.

Bank of England notes are legal tender up to any amount but no other bank notes are legal tender.

Tender must be unconditional

A tender is not invalid simply because the debtor makes payment "under protest" or because the payment is accompanied by a statement that it is all the debtor considers due. By "protesting" when paying, the debtor is able to sue later for the amount he has overpaid. However, he cannot insist on a receipt "in full discharge" or subject to such terms that, by taking the money, the creditor might afterwards be precluded from claiming that a larger amount was due.

Whilst the person paying has no right under common law to insist on being given a receipt, merely to ask for a receipt does not make the tender invalid, provided he does not make getting a receipt a **condition** of payment.

Payment by post

Payment by post is not good if lost, unless the creditor requested payment through the post. If payment by post is permitted, a postal delay will excuse late payment.

Which account is to be credited? — Common Law rules

Where a customer has a number of accounts with the

same firm, he should take care when sending his cheque to state which account he wishes to be credited. Unless he states explicitly that it is for a particular account, the recipient has the right to allocate it to any of his outstanding accounts.

Where neither the debtor nor the creditor allocates it to any particular account, the common law allocates it towards the **longest-standing** account.

Allocating a payment to a particular account

Under the Consumer Credit Act, these rules have been changed slightly where a regulated agreement is involved. Section 81 confirms the common law right of the person paying to say which account he wants to be credited. Alternatively, he can state how he wants his payment split between his various accounts.

This right could be important. Suppose one account relates to a hire-purchase agreement for his car and the creditor (or owner) is threatening to take it back. The hirer can prevent this by paying what is needed to bring his total up to one third (see p 256). However, where one of the agreements is regulated but the payer omits to specify which account he wants credited, the payment is allocated by Section 81 automatically to each of his accounts in the proportion which the sums due bear to one another.

Unlike the common law rule, the recipient may **not** allocate the payment as he wishes, where one of the agreements is either:
(a) a hire-purchase or conditional sale agreement;
(b) a consumer hire agreement;
(c) an agreement in relation to which any **security** is provided.

However, if none of the agreements is regulated, eg all are credit sale, but the person paying omits to indicate which account he wants credited, the common law rules apply

Thus the recipient can appropriate the money to the account which suits **him.** He could even apply it to meet a debt which is legally unenforceable, say, more than six years old.

Payments in advance

For the consumer to make a payment in advance is not without its hazards. Particularly in the sphere of mail order, suppliers generally ask for at least a substantial deposit.

One danger is that the company may be struggling to avoid insolvency. Too often the ordinary consumer is unlikely to hear of any impending liquidation until it is too late. (See also p 310 regarding Companies).

Where the sum is small, it is generally not worth while getting legal advice to fill in the complicated claim form and paying a fee to swear it before a solicitor, in order to claim. This leaves more money for the liquidator to distribute by way of dividend to trade creditors who benefit accordingly.

Protection of mail order payments

There are a number of mail order protection schemes. Members of the Periodical Publishers' Association have promised the Director-General of Fair Trading to guarantee all mail order advertisements which appear in their periodicals.

They will refund money sent by readers in the event of the mail order advertiser failing to supply the goods ordered. They also undertake to make a refund to readers who have lost money in the event of the liquidation or bankruptcy of mail order firms to whose advertisements readers have replied.

Claims are met only where proof of payment can be established, eg a returned cheque or postal order counterfoil must be produced. The consumer should not delay making a claim since the complaint must be lodged within **three months** of the date on which the advertisement appeared.

Claims received after the three months period are considered at the discretion of the publisher.

This scheme for refunds does not apply to goods advertised by direct mail solicitation. The consumer can claim from the publisher only where cash has to be sent in advance of goods being delivered, in answer to a direct response advertisement, display or postal bargain. Classified advertisements and catalogue mail order advertising are excluded.

Trust deposit account for customer's money

Some companies assure customers that they will hold their deposits in a special trust fund until their order is dispatched. Similarly with holiday bookings, the agent receiving the money often undertakes to hold the money in a trust fund for passengers and not to release it to the airline or travel company until the last minute. Even so, there is bound to be a period of uncertainty because the balance of the money must usually be paid some weeks before departure.

The use of a trust deposit account for customers' money was approved in the High Court in 1974 by Mr Justice Megarry. A mail order firm had gone into liquidation and the liquidators wanted to take all the money customers had paid for bedding and quilts which they had never received. This money was held in a trust account for the benefit of customers but the liquidators claimed that the trade creditors of the company were entitled to it and not the customers who had paid it.

His Lordship ordered that the money should be returned to all the customers concerned. He said that where customers had paid money in advance to a company for future supply of services or goods it was an entirely proper and honourable thing for the company to pay that money into a special trust account. The company thereby ensured that the money would be repaid to those customers if the company found that owing to its insolvency it was unable to provide them with the goods offered.

In practice, few firms are sufficiently concerned with customer protection to use this procedure.

Unless customers' payments have been placed in such a specially designated account, the liquidators will use their money to meet the debts of the company so that only a small percentage will get back by way of dividend to customers who lodge a claim.

Receipts—their form and legal significance

No particular form of words is necessary to constitute a receipt. "Settled" or "paid" or any other wording signifying an intention to give a discharge to the person paying together with the name of the creditor, is sufficient. No other words indicating payment are necessary, save the amount paid.

Whilst a receipt is evidence of payment, it is not absolutely conclusive. For example, where a receipt has been given in error, or where a firm has mistakenly credited sums to the wrong account, a judge could accept an explanation from someone in charge, that a mistake was made and that the account is still outstanding. Similarly, where a receipt is lost, a court could accept that payment had been made, provided the person who paid is prepared to declare this on oath, or some other witness confirms it.

Since receipts are only *prima facie* evidence of payment and can be contradicted, either party is at liberty to prove that the wording on a receipt does not accurately state the transaction which in fact took place.

Payment may sometimes be inferred from the length of time which has elapsed since the debt became due, even though not barred by the six-year rule. It is seldom profitable for creditors to pursue old debts unless they have a plausible explanation for their delay.

Although a consumer who owes money under a regulated agreement can demand a statement of account, there is nothing in the Consumer Credit Act 1974 which specifically entitles a person paying cash to a receipt.

The importance of getting a receipt has been highlighted by modern shopping systems whereby the shopper himself selects the goods and pays at his leisure at any one of a number of tills dotted around the shop.

Many of us will remember that prior to 1971 a receipt for a sum over £2 had to bear a 2d stamp. In fact it was an offence for a creditor to refuse to issue a receipt. Failure to issue a properly stamped receipt used to incur a penalty of £10.

Historically, the consumer's right to a receipt rested on the Stamp Act 1891 but with the abolition of the old 2d stamp duty on cheques and receipts in 1971, this right disappeared. Common law, it appears, never gave any right to demand a written receipt but it could be argued that today receipts are customary and therfore ought to be given.

A trader who refuses to supply a VAT invoice to anyone who is registered as VAT taxable can be fined up to £100 under the VAT general regulations. A tax invoice is not a receipt but nevertheless operates to entitle the taxable person to reclaim the tax stated when he sends in his own VAT return. He can claim it back even though he has not yet paid the amount in question.

Until the upsurge of convictions for shoplifting in recent years, many people regarded a receipt as superfluous and would tend to leave it on the counter. A Swedish woman shopping in Oxford Street would have been convicted of theft at Marlborough Street Magistrates' Court had the magistrate not accepted her defence that she had lost her receipt. Preservation of a receipt is therefore the consumer's best protection against unfounded suspicion. Consequently a consumer should never regard a receipt as an irritating piece of paper to be disposed of in the nearest litter basket. Not only can it prevent us having to pay the same debt twice but it could also mean the difference between innocence and guilt in the magistrates' court.

The failure of some automatic tills to provide receipts for customers is to be deplored. Not only is it proof of payment but it is a customer's only means of checking that the items purchased have been **correctly charged** on the machine.

A paid cheque is proof of payment

When we pay by cheque, a receipt is not essential. Since the Cheques Act 1957, a cheque met by your bank is proof that the payee received the money, even without his signature on the back.

Dead debts

How long should receipts or paid cheques be kept? Most judges take a dim view of creditors who forget about debts for two or three years and then suddenly wake up and issue a summons. In practice, few of us keep receipts for a great length of time but in theory we should keep them for six years. After that debts are dead and cannot be sued on. However, where the debtor has made part payment, the six-year period starts from his last payment. Similarly, an expired debt (over six years old) can be revived by a letter promising to pay. The six-year period will then run from the date of the letter in which the debt is acknowledged.

Right to demand a statement of account

Indirectly the Consumer Credit Act, Section 77 entitles the consumer to a receipt since he can demand a statement of account at any time of what he owes under his regulated agreement. To get it he need only write to the finance company, sending 15p fee. However, he cannot demand a statement of account more frequently than once a month.

A consumer who holds a fixed-sum credit agreement (see p 210) must be sent a statement showing:

(a) The total sum paid under the agreement;
(b) the total sum which has become payable but which remains outstanding, with details of the various amounts and the date on which each became due;
(c) the total sum yet to become payable under the agreement, with a breakdown of the various amounts and the dates due.

Running-accounts and rental accounts

Any consumer who holds a running-account credit agreement (see p 210) can, on payment of a like fee, obtain a statement showing:

(a) the state of the account;
(b) the amount currently payable;
(c) the amounts and dates of payments later to become due.

Similarly, a consumer who holds a rental agreement can ask for a statement of the total sum which has become payable under his agreement but remains unpaid and how it is made up, with dates of instalments missed.

Right to information without fee

A debtor who wants to pay off a regulated consumer agreement can write in for a statement showing the amount required to discharge it with particulars of how such amount is arrived at. Until the finance company gives this free of charge, it cannot take any steps to enforce the regulated agreement and if it delays more than a month it commits an offence under Section 97.

Right to termination statement without fee

Once the consumer has discharged all his obligations under a regulated agreement he can request, without fee, a formal document under Section 103 of the Consumer Credit Act that his regulated agreement is at an end and all money due under it has been fully paid. If the finance company disputes termination and is not prepared to issue a termination statement it must send him a counter-notice stating precisely why he is mistaken. Failure to give this information is an offence.

Statement of account is conclusive

The importance of getting a statutory statement of account is that it is virtually conclusive evidence against the finance company, whereas ordinary receipts are not conclusive evidence of payment. A finance company which sends out an incorrect statutory statement cannot correct it subsequently by sending out a second statement showing the true situation.

Where a statement of account or termination statement is sent out in response to a specific demand by the consumer, the finance company must take special care to ensure its accuracy since under Section 172 such a statement is binding on the finance company even if its computer has sub-stantially understated the amount owing.

However, a court has the power where the statement of account is shown to be incorrect to grant the creditor "such relief as appears to be just". For example, it could allow the creditor to recover part of the money.

Part payment

Part payment of a debt can never be regarded as settling the whole debt. A consumer who is behind with instalment payments may be approached by a representative of the finance company with the following offer: "If you pay us £400 by Saturday we will forget the extra £100 you owe us and close the account". The consumer, tempted by this offer, may scurry around to scrape together £400, perhaps at a higher rate of interest, in the hope of getting £100 knocked off his debt. Unfortunately the rule in *Pinnel's Case* (1602) says there is nothing to prevent the finance company going back on their word and suing for the balance at a later date.

The rule is illustrated by the experience of Mr Rees for whom D & C Builders had carried out certain work for which they claimed payment of £482. Mrs Rees on behalf of her husband, offered them £300 in full settlement. The company was in desperate straits financially and it seems that Mrs Rees knew this. She told them that if they did not accept £300, they would receive nothing. The company reluctantly took the £300 in settlement but later decided to sue Mr Rees for the outstanding balance of £182. The Court of Appeal decided they were entitled to this sum. Mrs Rees' payment of the smaller sum was not sufficient consideration to support the promise of the company to forego the balance.

One aspect of this rule is that it prevents businessmen using the tactical advantage of delay and the threat of litigation to avoid full payment of their debts. However, judges have sympathised with the predicament of the debtor who has perhaps scraped together his last farthing in the mistaken hope that part payment would put an end to his indebtedness. Consequently a number of exceptions have been evolved to the rule in *Pinnel's Case.*

1 The rule does not apply where the creditor's right is doubtful and the debtor disputes it in good faith. For example, he may maintain that he has made payments which were not credited, or that owing to computer error, they must have been credited to the wrong account. Any genuine dispute over the amount owed would prevent the operation of the rule.

2 The rule does not apply where the claim is "unliquidated". Suppose a motorist runs into the back of another car but does not wish to claim on his insurance policy. As the damage appears to be slight he may offer a cheque for

£20 then and there, to cover the damage. Later, when the other motorist gets to his garage he may discover that the damage is more than superficial and repairs will cost £90. Nevertheless he cannot sue the motorist who was at fault for the balance.

3 Another situation where the rule can be avoided occurs when a debt for £100 is settled by payment of £50 plus an item, such as a watch, in satisfaction. The Court will not inquire whether the value of the item given actually covers the balance.

4 Payment on an earlier date although of a smaller sum can also satisfy a larger debt. Suppose the consumer owes £100 which is due to be paid on January 1. If his creditor requests earlier payment say on December 1 and says that he will accept £75 in full satisfaction, the consumer can safely settle in this way.

5 Another situation where the rule is overridden is where payment is made by a third party. The father of a young man who was heavily in debt, sent his creditors a draft for a smaller sum which he offered in full and final settlement. The creditors cashed the draft and then sued his son for the balance. The court held that it would be a fraud on his father to allow the creditors to pursue their claim against the son.

6 Composition agreements are another exception. A consumer who cannot pay all his debts in full can offer his creditors a fixed percentage. Once a creditor accepts a dividend under a composition agreement, he cannot sue the debtor for the balance. Only if the debtor fails to pay the agreed dividend is the creditor free to sue for the full, original amount.

Rules for recovery of mistaken payments
Paradoxically the situation can arise where someone who wrongly receives a sum of money may legally keep it. Clearly, if an automatic till overpays, the customer cannot

keep the money simple because the machine has got its arithmetic wrong. Anyone knowingly marching off with too much change commits theft.

The position, however, can be very different when the wrong payment results from a mistaken view of the law as opposed to a mistake of "fact". In this case it cannot be recovered at all.

Where a person believes he is legally obliged to make a payment he cannot later claim it back on the ground that his view of the law was erroneous.

If he is in doubt he should take legal advice **before** paying. Alternatively, where his liability is uncertain he can pay **"under protest"**. This will preserve his legal right to claim it back. Alternatively he can refuse to pay altogether, leaving it to the claimant to bring an action. It will then be up to the court to decide whether payment is due.

Anyone who takes it upon himself to decide his legal position and parts with his money, cannot get it back. The object of the rule is to discourage litigation because his payment is regarded as made in settlement of a dispute. Neither party can later re-open the settlement by going to court.

If a dissatisfied person tries, the judge will dismiss his claim and award costs against him (unless he shows that his reason for coming to court is because the other party failed to keep his side of the bargain).

However, where, say, Smith lends Brown £100 and later accepts £75 in full settlement such an agreement will not prevent Smith subsequently suing for the other £25 if he changes his mind.

The distinction between fact and law is often far from clear. Suppose an insurance company pays a widow the sum assured on the death of her husband in the mistaken belief that his life policy is valid – is this a question of fact or law? If the insurance policy had lapsed because the deceased had not paid the last instalment, this would be a mistake of fact and the company could claim their money back.

An example of a mistake of law occurred when a soldier was paid too large a gratuity on demobilization. In fact, he was entitled to a much smaller gratuity. As it was the agent's fault in misreading the legal regulations, the court told the soldier he could keep the overpayment.

A mistake as to the particular transaction for which money is paid is clearly one of fact. So too, if a person is believed alive but is actually dead when the payment is made.

On the other hand, executors may misconstrue a will and make a payment to the wrong beneficiary. In this case the recipient can keep it because a mistake involving the construction of a document is regarded as a matter of law.

This rather arbitrary distinction between fact and law can operate unfairly, especially where the law is uncertain. In one case a betting company paid a totalisator levy duty because it appeared the Finance Act said they must. Another company later refused to pay and the Crown sued them.

Finally the House of Lords held that it need not be paid. The result was that the company which had obediently paid the duty could not get it back whereas the company which put up a fight was lucky.

Paying by cheque

A cheque may be crossed or it may be left "open". The payee of an open cheque, ie the person in whose favour you draw it, can request payment in cash from your bank. He cannot get cash if it is crossed.

The payee of a cheque is entitled to transfer it to another person. He does this by writing the transferee's name on the back and signing below, eg "Please pay John Smith" (signed) William Brown. This is called an endorsement.

John Smith can then present the cheque to your bank for payment.

Crossing a Cheque

Crossing a cheque involves drawing two parallel lines across it from top to bottom. This tells your bank not to pay the money over the counter. Your bank may only pay it into another bank account. Since a crossed cheque must go through a bank account, the recipient can be easily traced. Consequently, crossing a cheque is a useful safeguard in case it falls into the wrong hands. If lost it is more difficult for the finder to deal with dishonestly.

"Not Negotiable"

A cheque so marked can still be transferred and, if there is nothing wrong, the transferee can insist on payment. But if there has been dishonesty, the person who drew the cheque is safeguarded.

In Brief

When giving a cheque, make sure you cross it AND mark it "Not Negotiable" to guard against possible fraud.

"Account Payee"

Writing these words on a cheque is a further protection which you can employ in addition to crossing it. The recipient's bank, on seeing the words "account payee" is bound to ensure that it goes into the account of the person in whose favour you have drawn it. The recipient's bank will be responsible to you if it makes payment to a person who was not entitled to it (although your own bank will not).

Further Points on Drawing a Cheque

When he draws a cheque the customer authorises his bank to pay that amount out of his account. What if

199

someone alters the cheque after it has left his hands, say by increasing the amount?

A clerk wrote out a cheque for £20 to be signed by his employers but cunningly left blank the space where he should have written the amount in words. Being too trusting, one of the partners signed it, whereupon the clerk altered the £20 to £120, wrote this amount in words, took it round to the firm's bank and cashed it.

This was a clear case of forgery but the firm, not their bank, lost the money. The partner's failure to see the cheque was correctly filled out was **his** fault, not the bank's.

Moral

When writing a cheque always put the amount in words as well as numerals. Do not leave spaces which could be filled in so as to alter the amount payable.

Forgery

Apart from his own carelessness in drawing a cheque, in the normal case of forgery, say an alteration or a completely forged signature, the drawer is not responsible. His bank must stand the loss because in theory they should know the signature of their customer and be able to recognise if it is forged.

A customer is obliged to safeguard his bank from possible fraud and thus must inform them at once if he loses a cheque or cheque book, to stop payment. Also if he suspects a forgery he must tell them, so they can take steps to protect their position. Mr Greenwood failed to notify his bank that his wife had forged his signature on cheques. When she then cashed them he was held liable on the ground that by doing nothing he was assumed to have authorised her signing.

Bearer Cheques

Never write out an open cheque payable to "Wm Smith or

bearer". No indorsement is needed to cash it so, if it gets into the wrong hands, there could be a risk of fraud.

Where an uncrossed cheque is drawn "pay bearer" any person who holds the cheque can present it over the counter to your bank for payment.

Again any open (uncrossed) cheque which is drawn payable to you, once endorsed by you (ie signed on the back) becomes a "Bearer" cheque. It can be cashed by anyone so don't leave it lying around.

Out-of-date Cheques

Legally a cheque is binding on the drawer for six years from the date on it but in practice banks decline to honour "stale" cheques, ie those not presented for payment within six months (sometimes one year). Nevertheless the recipient may still sue the drawer if payment is declined, even after six months. The drawer is obliged to exchange the stale cheque for a fresh one if required, or to authorise his bank to pay the out-of-date cheque.

Undated and Post-Dated Cheques

All cheques must be dated. The bank will not pay a cheque until the date on it arrives. A cheque bearing a date in the future means payment is postponed. But if you issue a cheque without a date, the person receiving it is entitled to write in the date. He is never permitted to **alter** the date. Such a material alteration renders the cheque void.

Post-dating a cheque is a convenient method of delaying payment whilst at the same time showing a readiness to pay once the other party honours his side of the bargain. It is particularly useful where the reliability of the other party is uncertain. For example the seller of a car may undertake to carry out certain repairs before delivering it, in which case it might be unwise to make immediate payment. Post-dating gives the consumer a further period in which to stop payment if the seller defaults.

Stopping a Cheque

A cheque should never be stopped unless the consumer has good reason for complaint against the trader.

It would be fraudulent and hence criminal to stop a cheque given in payment for perfectly satisfactory goods or services simply with the intention of avoiding or delaying payment. This could amount to obtaining a pecuniary advantage by deception, contrary to the Theft Acts (see p 223). But if the consumer has a **genuine** complaint he is entitled to stop his cheque and withhold payment until it has been rectified.

If the dispute is not settled the trader can sue on the cheque and the consumer will then have to raise his complaint by way of counterclaim.

In the event of the trader having endorsed the cheque to allow payment in favour of a third party, the consumer who gave it will have no choice but to allow it to go through. This is because a cheque is a negotiable instrument and the drawer's dispute with the original payee is no concern of the third party. To prevent this the consumer should mark the cheque "**not negotiable**".

The Effect of Stopping a Cheque

A simple telephone call is sufficient notification to your bank that you wish to stop payment on a cheque. Confirmation in writing is desirable although not essential. If by oversight your bank allows the cheque to go through after receiving notice to stop, it is not permitted to charge the amount of that cheque to your account.

Computer Error

Mr Burnett had separate accounts at two different branches of the same bank. Not having to hand a cheque book from his first bank, he used a cheque from the other branch and altered the address in ink. He later told that branch to stop payment. But the bank's computer could only read the metallic printing on the cheque and ignored his penned alteration of the branch. It consequently allowed the cheque to go through on the branch whose address he had deleted. That branch, not knowing he had told the other branch to stop it, paid the cheque. The judge told the bank that it could not in those circumstances debit Mr Burnett's account.

When a Cheque is Dishonoured

A consumer is entitled to assume that his bank will honour his cheques so long as there is sufficient money in his account. If he has been allowed overdraft facilities, the bank must also honour his cheques up to the limit of his overdraft.

If there is too little in his account to meet the cheque, his bank is not bound to honour it, no matter how small the deficiency or how great the inconvenience to the customer. The bank is even within its rights in dishonouring his cheque although the customer has accounts at another branch of the same bank which can more than cover the cheque.

Claiming Compensation where a Cheque is wrongly Dishonoured

A consumer whose cheque is wrongly marked "refer to drawer" or "insufficient funds" or "please re-present", when he has sufficient funds in his account, can claim compensation from his bank for damage to his credit.

Compensation could be considerable if he is in business. Paradoxically, the smaller the cheque's cash value which his bank refuses to pay, the greater will be the injury to the customer's credit.

In the case of a private individual whose cheque is wrongly dishonoured, he will be entitled to little compensation in practice unless he can prove actual financial loss as a result of their dishonouring his cheque. For example, he may have given it to a travel agent to pay for a holiday at short notice, and, as a result of it not being met, had to forgo his holiday.

Rarely, an individual has received compensation for libel. The aspersion on his character is that he is not credit-worthy.

Protection of debtors

A debtor is someone who owes money so most of us are in fact debtors in law, even if all we owe is the amount of a newsagent's account. So too is the consumer who buys on hire-purchase and the house owner with a building society mortgage.

Traders whose customers have not paid their bills, can:
1 try to recover the money themselves by writing, calling, stopping further credit and so on,
2 take out a summons against the debtor in the county court,
3 instruct a debt-collection agency.

Debt-collection agencies are required to have a debt-collector's licence from the Department of Fair Trading under the Consumer Credit Act, Section 146(6). However a trader does not need a licence to collect a debt owing to himself provided the methods he employs are limited to sending reminder letters to the debtor or arranging to call regularly to collect instalments. He must not put pressure on the debtor which might be regarded as harassment.

Unlawful harassment

A trader or debt collector who puts too much pressure on or unfairly presses a debtor with the object of coercing him into making payment may be guilty of harassment contrary to the Administration of Justice Act 1970, Section 40(1). This offence is punishable by a fine of up to £100 or on a second or subsequent offence up to £400.

Alarm, distress or humiliation

Basically harassment is defined as making demands for payment which are calculated to subject the debtor or members of his family or household to alarm, distress or humiliation. The element of harassment may be due to the frequency of demands or their manner or occasion.

Publicity or any threat by which the demand is accompanied could amount to harassment. For example, a trader who displays a list of debtors in his shop window may be guilty of harassing them. Similarly, a van bearing the words "Debt-Collection Agency" left parked outside the debtor's home might constitute unwarranted publicity in making a demand. Any form of bullying amounts to a threat.

Court action permitted

Action which is "reasonable and otherwise permissible in law for the purpose of securing the discharge of an obligation", is not harassment, provided the person making the claim honestly believes the money to be due to himself or the person for whom he acts. Thus the trader may take reasonable action to protect himself or his business against a **future** loss. Taking enforcement action, eg refusing to make deliveries or by **legal** process, eg putting in the court bailiffs, even though very unpleasant, is of course not unlawful harassment.

But it is an offence if the person demanding the money falsely represents that criminal proceedings lie for failure to pay or suggests that he is acting in an official capacity to enforce payment, eg a police officer or officer of the court. Similarly it is an offence to use forms, letters or documents which falsely represent official documents or purport to have some official character which is untrue, eg "blue frighteners" which resemble court forms.

Even though the trader's own course of conduct does not by itself amount to harassment, he may be guilty of an offence if, for example, he allows an agency to inform the debtor's employers on the pretext of obtaining information about the debtor.

Protecting consumers against promissory notes

Prior to 1974 a finance company could avoid its responsibilities to the consumer by the device of getting him to sign a promissory note for the amount lent. A promissory note is a formal undertaking to pay a sum of money and is binding on the drawer rather like a cheque. It is not drawn on a bank, but it can operate as if it were actual money. This evasion has now been blocked by the Consumer Credit Act. The way the dodge worked was as follows:

When signing his credit agreement to repay the loan by instalments, the consumer would also be asked to sign a promissory note. This meant he was incurring a double liability to repay the amount advanced

(i) under the agreement

(ii) by virtue of the promissory note.

If it later turned out that the article sold was not working properly, all his complaints were ignored by the finance company. In desperation he would usually stop paying instalments. The finance company would not however sue him on the credit agreement because this would enable him to notify the court of his complaints by way of counterclaim and so prevent their getting judgment. Instead, they would assign the promissory note to an independent debt-collection company which would then sue him in respect of the note which in law was a quite separate debt and nothing to do with his hire-purchase agreement.

Duplicate liability of consumer prohibited

The Consumer Credit Act 1974, Section 123, prevents negotiable instruments, such as promissory notes, being taken as security to defeat the consumer's rights to a fair deal. Section 123 also forbids lenders and those selling on credit, from accepting payment by means of promissory notes or other negotiable instruments. Where money is due under a regulated agreement, they may accept only cash or cheques.

Where a cheque is taken as a down payment or as an instalment payment (not as security) the finance company is not permitted to "negotiate" (assign) the cheque to another company but must pay it into the bank in the normal way.

The lender or supplier is unable to enforce the agreement against the consumer:

(a) if a promissory note or other negotiable instrument has been taken unlawfully

(b) where a cheque is assigned unlawfully.

Only the court can permit any enforcement of the agreement. In the absence of a court order, both the consumer and his surety are free from further liability to make payment. If the court dismisses an application by the finance company to enforce the agreement, the security is treated as never having effect. Finally the finance company must indemnify the consumer in the event of his having to pay any third party to whom the cheque or other negotiable instrument has been assigned.

A word of caution. These restrictions apply only where the credit agreement is regulated. Consequently, where the credit given exceeds £5,000, there is no restriction against the lender insisting also on being given a negotiable instrument. In this higher financial bracket the consumer is without protection and in the same position he was before the passing of the Act. This contrasts with the position of a consumer who is made to pay an **extortionate** credit charge, where the court can reopen the agreement however large the amount of the loan. (See p 229).

CHAPTER XII

CONSUMER CREDIT

A consumer who lacks ready cash to buy an article he needs can:

(a) borrow the money by bank loan or overdraft or by credit card or trading check

(b) hire the article under a rental agreement. Here there is no actual **credit** element. The consumer simply pays for the use of the article for a fixed minimum period but never acquires ownership. Under the Consumer Credit Act it is referred to as a consumer **hire** agreement

(c) take it on hire-purchase. This type of transaction is intermediate between renting and buying. The consumer hires the article but can acquire ownership at the end of the hiring period provided he has paid all the rental instalments

(d) buy it on credit sale and pay for it by instalments.

Consumer Credit Terminology

The Consumer Credit Act 1974 seeks to standardise the legal terminology of credit law and introduces certain new terminology which requires some explanation. The basic agreements under the Act are consumer credit agreements which can be subdivided into:

- Debtor-creditor agreements
- Debtor-creditor-supplier agreements.

Debtor: The debtor is the consumer who borrows. He is the person who is "in debt".

Creditor: It is the creditor (lender) who provides the credit. As often as not he is a finance company or bank. He is the one who makes the loan.

Supplier: It is the supplier who supplies the goods or service.

Where the supplier is the person who also provides the finance, the supplier and the creditor will be one and the same person. However, the agreement will still be a debtor-creditor-supplier agreement and **not** a debtor-creditor agreement, which is normally a cash loan.

The Consumer Credit Act 1974 regulates the whole range of consumer-credit arrangements and brings them all under one umbrella. It covers money-lending, pawn-broking and hire-purchase.

A consumer credit agreement includes hire-purchase and credit-sale agreements as well as bank loans, check-trading and credit-card agreements.

Not all credit agreements are regulated by the Consumer Credit Act. To rank as a **regulated** a consumer credit agreement it must meet three conditions:

1 The credit provided to the debtor must not exceed £5,000.
2 It must be a **personal** credit agreement, ie granted to an individual, not to a limited company. Even loans to a sole trader or partners count as "personal".
3 It must not be classified as an "exempt" agreement.

Meaning of credit

The term "credit" covers every form of financial accommodation.

Where the credit or loan which is provided by the creditor is in excess of £5,000, the agreement is outside the protection of the Act, except that the **extortionate** credit rules (see p 229) apply to **all** agreements with individuals, even if far above the £5,000 limit.

Credit is the actual sum borrowed, either by straight cash loan or any other method of deferring payment.

The total charge for credit

Regulations defining the total charge for credit have been

made by the Secretary of State for Prices and Consumer Protection.

In determining whether the amount of credit is within the protected £5,000 limit, items which are part of the total **charge** for credit are not treated as part of the credit, even though time is allowed for their payment.

In deciding whether an agreement is protected by the Act, the cost of the credit basically refers to the interest to be paid on the loan, as distinct from the amount borrowed.

It includes all expenses of obtaining the loan, such as a broker's fee and other incidental costs, a premium payable on a policy of insurance whereby the loan is guaranteed and certain obligatory insurances required by the agreement.

The total charges for credit must be itemised.

The annual percentage rate of charge for credit must be stated in the agreement as well as in all advertisements and in quotations.

Various categories of credit

Credit may be either for a fixed sum or on a running-account basis.

An example of fixed-sum credit is a loan of a fixed amount, such as a bank loan.

Credit-sale and hire-purchase agreements are examples of fixed-sum credit; so too is check-trading since the amount of credit provided does not fluctuate, although the debt is reduced as the consumer pays his instalments.

Running-account credit can be an overdraft, a credit-card account or a shop-budget account. Once the account is opened the debtor is enabled to make further drawings against his credit. A bank overdraft is a typical case of running-account credit, sometimes referred to as a "revolving credit".

Running-account credit means the debtor or consumer can draw on it as and when he needs, without having to apply to the ceditor for an extension of credit. One example is a credit card, where the amount of the credit fluctuates according to how much the holder chooses to draw against it, usually up to a predetermined credit-limit.

Restricted-use credit

Where the loan is tied to a particular supplier or store from which the goods or services must be obtained, the credit is regarded as **restricted-use**. This is the case with all hire-purchase, credit-sale, check-trading and revolving-credit schemes operated by stores.

Unrestricted-use credit means that the consumer is free to spend the money lent where he pleases.

Credit cards can involve both restricted-use and unrestricted-use credit. If the holder uses his card to draw cash, it is for unrestricted-use, since the holder is in no way bound as to how he may spend the money he draws. If he uses the card to buy goods or services he can do so only at one of the shops or suppliers within the credit-card scheme.

This distinction is important because where the outlets are **restricted**, even though very numerous, the creditor, ie the organisation providing the credit, is responsible to ensure that the consumer is given his legal rights by all those suppliers and shops in the scheme.

Section 75 of the Consumer Credit Act provides that where the consumer has "any claim against the supplier in respect of a misrepresentation or breach of contract, he shall have a like claim against the **Creditor**," in the case of restricted-use credit. This means that the organisation running the scheme will generally have to compensate consumers who get a bad deal from any of its suppliers.

However in practice the creditor will only have to pay where the supplier has, for example, disappeared or gone bankrupt because the Act entitles the creditor to be indemnified by the supplier should the creditor have to meet any such claim for breach of contract or misrepresentation.

Restricted-use credit may limit the consumer's choice regarding:

(i) particular goods or services;

(ii) goods or services from a particular supplier;

(iii) goods or services from a limited number of suppliers.

For example, "Buy this car on HP from us" – here the credit is offered for the purchase of specific goods. "Let us insulate your roof: pay over two years" – here the credit is offered to procure a specific service. "Have a £50 loan to spend as you like at any of our branches" – here the credit is available as a specific sum of money at a particular supplier.

A credit card allows the consumer to determine as he goes along how much credit he requires, choosing amongst a limited number of suppliers.

Debtor-creditor-supplier agreements

This further sub-division of credit facilities by the Consumer Credit Act appears at first sight an unnecessary complication which is likely to confuse the layman. Briefly, the reasons for it are as follows:

(a) The creditor is responsible for the quality of the goods supplied as well as the supplier's default or misrepresentation.

(b) The consequences of cancellation are wider where a supplier is involved.

(c) The contents of the credit agreement are different where a supplier is involved.

A debtor-creditor-supplier agreement finances a transaction between the consumer and a supplier where:

(i) the credit is provided by the supplier himself; or

(ii) the credit is provided by a separate lender who has a business arrangement with the supplier to finance the transaction.

Just as suppliers who finance the supply of their own goods or services have full liability, so too, lenders who have an agreement with suppliers to provide the consumer with credit will also be responsible if their suppliers fail to give the consumer his legal rights.

Debtor-creditor agreements

By contrast lenders under a debtor-creditor agreement incur no liability for the quality of the goods, etc, which are supplied.

Basically, a debtor-creditor agreement covers the situation where lenders have no arrangement with the supplier to finance transactions.

Similarly, where the consumer receives unrestricted-use credit, say, in the form of a cash loan, he can spend the money **as he chooses**. If so a debtor-creditor situation arises and the lender is not responsible for anything the supplier "gets up to", since he has not in any way induced the consumer to go to that particular supplier.

Restriction on door-to-door canvassing for debtor-creditor-transactions

It is an offence to canvas consumers, except on trade premises, to persuade them to enter into regulated agreements, particularly for cash loans. Only where the consumer himself sends a signed, written request to see a canvasser, is canvassing permitted at his home. His sending back a printed card does not get round the restriction on home canvassing. However the Director-General of Fair Trading has power to allow it in respect of consumers who hold an existing current account, and it is intended to invite them to extend their borrowing by way of overdraft.

The rule against canvassing except on trade premises is intended to curb door-to-door loan-peddling. It does not prohibit the canvassing of consumers at any place where the consumer himself carries on any business. But generally canvassing is permitted to attract debtor-creditor business only at the premises of the lender himself or the supplier (or the canvasser).

Credit control through licensing

The Consumer Credit Act 1974 is basically concerned with transactions where consumers are given credit.

Those whose business it is to provide credit up to £5,000 are subject to controls under the Act, although certain provisions also apply where the credit exceeds £5,000. The Act empowers the Secretary of State to regulate virtually everything done in the course of credit business. An important means of control is through the system of licensing set up by the Act.

Virtually every business involved in the consumer-credit field must be licensed. Anyone who lends money, offers credit or gives customers time to pay is regarded as carrying on a consumer credit business. Simply allowing customers a reasonable period to pay their bills in the normal course of business, say, one month after delivery, would **not** require a licence.

Failure to obtain a licence from the Office of Fair Trading is punishable by a fine or imprisonment, or both.

Where a credit agreement is made by an unlicensed trader (or through an unlicensed credit-broker) the lender may well lose both money and goods, since the agreement cannot be enforced against the customer without special authorisation.

"A regulated agreement . . . if made when the creditor was **unlicensed** is enforceable against the debtor or hirer only where the Director . . . authorises it by order" (Section 40).

Although not directly granting credit or hire facilities, a trader will need to be licensed if engaged in some ancillary business operation such as:

1 Credit-brokerage.

2 Debt adjusting and debt counselling.
3 Debt collecting.
4 Credit reference agency.

Credit-brokerage

The function of the credit broker is to introduce individuals who need credit, to sources which are able to supply it. Even the trader who does not himself supply credit but simply arranges it for customers, will be regarded as a credit-broker and will require a licence.

Not only mortgage brokers but also insurance brokers, motor dealers, estate agents and solicitors may act as credit-brokers. Retailers too are regarded as credit-brokers if they introduce customers to finance houses or other sources of credit as, for example, in a hire-purchase transaction.

Consequently, a retailer will require a licence covering both consumer-credit and credit-brokerage if, as well as selling goods on credit himself, he introduces his customers to other sources of credit.

However, a retailer will **not** need a credit-brokerage licence if all he does is to accept credit cards or trading checks from customers who have obtained them from another source.

Danger of unlicensed trading as a credit-broker

"A regulated agreement made by a debtor or hirer who, for the purpose of making that agreement was introduced to the creditor by an unlicensed credit-broker is enforceable only where . . . the Director authorises it under Section 149". Although the Director can excuse unlicensed credit-dealing provided consumers have not been prejudiced, the importance of a trader obtaining a licence must be emphasised.

If he does not get a licence then all credit or hire agreements which are made following his introduction may be unenforceable, even though the credit source is properly licensed. The finance house might, therefore, seek indemnity from the trader (ie compel him to pay their loss) should it turn out that the agreements made on his introduction are unenforceable through his failure to get a licence. In any event, his business could suffer seriously as a result of being unlicensed.

Applications for licences should be made to: Consumer Credit Licensing Branch, Office of Fair Trading, Government Buildings, Bromyard Avenue, Acton, London W3 7BB.

Duty to refund brokerage fees

Mortgage brokers specialise in arranging mortgages or loans for the acquisition of property. In practice the mortgage arrangement is frequently tied in with the issue of an insurance policy on the life of the borrower in respect of which the broker receives a substantial commission from the insurance company. Some brokers also insist on receiving a fee or commission from the borrower.

Take the case of a couple who wish to borrow £2,000 by way of a second mortgage. They answer an advertisement in a newspaper and a credit broker comes to see them. He tells them he can definitely arrange a loan and asks for a fee of £50. They sign a form of application on which it is stated that this fee is **non-returnable**.

Often further fees are taken from them, eg a survey fee. They may also be asked to take out an insurance policy to ensure repayment of the loan if either of them dies.

Prior to the Consumer Credit Act the couple would have had no right to the return of their deposit if it was stated to be returnable only if the broker was unable to connect them with a willing lender. Section 155 entitles them to the return of **all** fees except £1 if the introduction does not result in their entering into a relevant loan agreement within six months following the introduction.

Penalties for non-compliance with requirements of the Consumer Credit Act

The consumer himself (ie the debtor or hirer) is not penalised in any way if legal formalities are neglected. Observance of these formalities is the worry of the creditor alone who may find it impossible or at least difficult to enforce an agreement which fails to comply with the Act. The consumer need not be concerned about legal requirements. He can still rely on his agreement and enforce it in law even though it was never signed or never put into writing. For example where goods taken on hire-purchase turn out to be defective, the consumer can sue the owner (supplier) for damages even though his agreement fails to comply with the formalities laid down by the Act.

In two situations the creditor is entirely unable to enforce the agreement:

(a) where the customer (debtor or hirer) did not sign it;

(b) in the case of a cancellable agreement (doorstep sales) if no copy is given or if the copy given to the customer did not notify him of his right of cancellation.

Where an agreement is "improperly executed" because its contents fail to comply with the requirements laid down by Section 60, the creditor will be able to enforce it but with difficulty. Since he can enforce it only by getting a court order, he will need to go to court before he can take back the goods, even though less than one third has been paid (see p 257).

In deciding whether to allow the creditor to recover his goods or money, the court must weigh up how far the consumer has been prejudiced and how far the creditor is at fault in not complying with the Act. Should the judge decide to allow the agreement, he has power:

1 to reduce what the debtor has to pay so as to compensate him for any prejudice suffered from the contravention in question. If the creditor's culpability is serious, the consumer may not have to pay anything;

2 to make an order amending the agreement as the Court considers just;

3 to strike out any terms not originally agreed by the consumer (eg to deliver up goods to the creditor) until the creditor fulfils certain conditions.

In the event of a creditor deliberately ignoring the requirements of the Act, the court would be likely to refuse any order at all in his favour but where the infringement is merely technical it could ignore it completely if the consumer has not been prejudiced. In any event, the court has wide powers to compensate him.

CHAPTER XIII

CREDIT RATING

The moment a consumer seeks credit, his financial standing is likely to be investigated. It is also likely to be checked prior to any transaction which involves instalment payments, although no sum is actually borrowed.

Finance houses and building societies do not rely wholly on the accuracy of the information given by the borrower on his application form but generally cross-check with a credit reference agency which can provide far more information about him than most people are aware.

One may assume that every individual and organisation in this country who has ever bought on credit has a credit rating. One credit register alone which operates nationwide, contains between 14m and 16m names. It augments its files with no fewer than 25,000 additional items of information daily.

A consumer's credit rating is "an estimate of his ability and intention to pay his debts in due course". His creditworthiness depends on the "Three C's" – character, capacity and capital. Ironically, the least important of these is his existing capital – the value of his home, furniture and other assets he already has.

More important is the borrower's capability to meet the proposed commitment. His ability to pay naturally depends on his present and prospective income. The most important consideration however is his general character, reputation and mode of living.

It is also vital to know whether a would-be borrower has any court judgments recorded against him. In fact about 500,000 county court judgments for debt are recorded annually at the Lord Chancellor's Department at 140 Gower Street, London WC1, which supplies them for a charge to credit organisations.

All judgments which remain unpaid for more than one month, go down as a permanent record against the debtor's name. If he pays subsequently, he can apply to have his name removed on payment of a small fee to the Lord Chancellor's Department. In fact, very few debtors are aware of this right or even appreciate that an official list of court judgments exists. Consequently the fact that a judgment is recorded does not always indicate that it remains unpaid.

Credit reference agencies
Judgments for less than £10 are not officially listed but at least one credit reference agency (Credit Data Ltd) records these on its files. Details of small debts are passed to it by an associated debt collection agency. Bankruptcy information comes to it from official sources. The electoral registers and rating lists are used to verify addresses and to trace changes of address.

In practice credit reference agencies receive considerable feed-back of information from their own members. Every time a trader makes an inquiry about a consumer, the agency makes a note on the consumer's index card showing the amount of the projected borrowing. Where a consumer's file shows a number of inquiries by traders spread over a lengthy period, this would indicate that the borrower is a good credit risk, the assumption being that each inquiry is usually followed by a loan for the projected amount.

Successful transactions noted on his file are termed "white" information and adverse entries "black" information. A note is also made whenever an unpaid debt is sent in for collection. Even though he is not actually taken to court, slow payment is recorded as a black mark against his general credit-worthiness. Similarly, where goods he holds on hire-purchase are re-possessed, this is recorded as "black" information.

The two major credit reference agencies in this country operate on a very wide scale. UAPT Ltd alone has more than 40 area offices. It is highly reputable and its origins go back to the mid-Victorian era when it was established as a non-profit-seeking society to protect its trade members.

There are at least 50 smaller agencies which furnish status reports for use by hire-purchase and rental traders, credit card companies and mail-order businesses.

Bank managers habitually give reports about customer credit-worthiness to other banks, for onward transmission to anyone inquiring. They claim that this is a well-established service available for and against all customers and that by maintaining a banking account, each customer impliedly consents to it. The information conveyed is the bank manager's personal and confidential opinion about the customer's financial position.

The Younger Committee, in fact, deprecated this practice of banks giving other banks information without getting a customer's permission. The committee considered that all banks should be obliged to tell customers when and to whom they normally give references. The customer should also be consulted every time an outsider approaches the bank for a reference.

Correcting a consumer's credit record

Every credit reference agency requires a licence to carry on its business. Licences are granted by the Director General of Fair Trading, who consequently exercises control over such agencies.

The Consumer Credit Act entitles a consumer who has sought credit or hire facilities to be told the name and address of any credit reference agency consulted about his credit-worthiness. (Creditors who refuse to tell him can be prosecuted and fined.)

He then writes to the credit reference agency in question with 25p for a copy of their file on him. If they fail to send it they will be guilty of an offence.

In fact, every consumer has the right at any time to apply to any credit reference agency for a copy of their file on him for 25p. If they do not have any information on him they must say so. Whatever information they have on him must be stated in plain English.

A consumer who considers that certain information they have about him is incorrect and likely to prejudice him if not corrected, can insist they either amend it or remove it from their file. They must within 28 days notify him whether they have done so.

If they decline to make the necessary alteration he can request that they add to their file on him **his own** statement (up to 200 words) by way of correction.

If they are unwilling to add his notice of correction to their file, the consumer or the agency can seek a ruling from the Director General of Fair Trading who can make whatever order he thinks fit, eg compel the agency to include it.

Truth in borrowing – the penalties for deception
When filling in an application form for a loan, etc, the consumer is generally asked to state the type of accommodation he lives in, whether he rents or owns it, his occupation, income and the address of his employers. Care should be taken to ensure that what he says on the proposal form is correct. Giving false information can amount to a criminal offence. Exaggerating one's income when applying for a mortgage advance could amount to attempting to obtain a pecuniary advantage (the loan from the building society) by deception. Again, overstating one's age to obtain credit

222

would be an offence if a young person wrote untruthfully "over 18".

The partner in a motor repair firm in Staffordshire some years ago stated on his application form for a building society mortgage that his income was £1,250 a year, though he was in fact getting far less. He also claimed that he was manager of the firm.

When the building society wrote to his firm for verification he intercepted their letter and replied himself, forging his partner's signature on the reply. He got his mortgage advance but when the facts came out he was sentenced to prison for six months.

At Marlborough Street Magistrates' Court a young man's unauthorised bank overdraft also involved him in a sentence of six months' imprisonment. It all began when he found his old cheque book and, knowing that he only had £5 to his credit, went to his bank and drew £20. Realising he was on to a good thing, a couple of days later he drew £40 and on the next day likewise. When he came to draw a further £40 the same afternoon, the cashier became suspicious and asked him to wait. Finding that his withdrawals had been completely unauthorised, the bank called the police, who charged him with obtaining a pecuniary advantage by deception.

"A person who by any deception dishonestly obtains for himself or another any pecuniary advantage shall on conviction on indictment be liable to imprisonment for a term not exceeding five years." (Theft Acts 1968 and 1978).

There are specific instances where the offence of obtaining a pecuniary advantage is deemed to be committed:

1 Where a person by any deception dishonestly secures the release of the whole or part of any liability to make a payment.

2 The second situation is where a person uses some form of

223

deception to obtain a bank overdraft or to take out any policy of insurance or annuity or obtain an improvement of the terms on which he is allowed to do so.

3 Thirdly, it is an offence to use, say, a false reference to get a job, where the deception gives him the opportunity to earn a remuneration (or greater remuneration) in an office or employment.

A customer ordering a meal in a restaurant implies he has the means and intention of paying for it before he leaves. If he later changes his mind and decides not to pay but slips out of the restaurant, this amounts to deception. In one case a customer was served with a dish he had not ordered and consequently left the restaurant without paying. He was held not to have incurred any debt nor to have obtained any pecuniary advantage by deception, because he was entitled to reject the dish. A person who has a valid complaint in a restaurant is entitled to refuse to pay and can avoid any accusation of deception by giving his name and address.(See below p 226).

Evading a debt

A "debt" is the obligation to pay money. By giving a worthless cheque knowing it will not be honoured, the drawer attempts to avoid that obligation. Since he knows that there is no money in the account and that he has no authority to overdraw, he commits a deception.

Oddly enough, to amount to an offence it is not necessary that the person deceived should himself suffer any loss from the deception. When Miss Kovacs drew a cheque to buy a railway ticket she used her cheque card, so her bank was obliged to honour her cheque, although she had no money in her account. Her lawyer argued that her deception had not involved the railway in any loss but this argument was rejected and she was convicted because her bank manager had told her not to overdraw.

When he draws a cheque the drawer is in law declaring:

(i)   That he has an account with the bank.

(ii) That he has authority to draw (or overdraw) on it for that amount.

(iii) That the cheque as drawn is a valid order for that amount. (See also p 242).

Overdrafts

Suppose that Smith meets his local bank manager one evening in the pub and is embarrassed when conversation turns to his overdue loan. On the spur of the moment Smith tells him that he has been ill or that he is on reduced overtime at work. Overcome with sympathy the manager tells him not to worry and to leave it for a further year. If Smith's excuse has been untruthful, he has committed a deception for which he can be prosecuted because it has resulted in the repayment of his loan being deferred. But the prosecution must prove that his intention was dishonest and that he intended **never** to pay the whole or part of what he owed.

Again, Smith may commit an offence where his glib talk enables him to borrow by way of overdraft. For example, he may tell his bank manager that he requires an overdraft to enable him to expand his business, when in fact he uses it to go on holiday. (See also p 242).

Insurance policies

Insurances and annuities are singled out a giving rise to a particular offence, because they are cases where the insurance company is peculiarly dependent on the insured's good faith since only he knows the special facts which affect the risk. For this reason the insurance company is given special protection against all possible fraud.

In civil law the effect of non-disclosure of a material fact is to make the policy void. However, a simple non-disclosure does not amount to the criminal offence of deception "by word or conduct" unless coupled with an actual falsehood.

Payment on the spot

Often goods or services are supplied on the understanding that you will pay immediately. Examples of this are hiring a cab or filling your tank at a self-service petrol station. It is an offence under the Theft Act 1978, Section 3, to make off with intent to avoid payment.

There are three points to note:

1 A consumer should leave his name and address to show he was not acting dishonestly. (He may have lost his wallet).

2 If payment is not legally enforceable, there is no offence. Thus if a meal served is uneatable the consumer would be justified in refusing to pay and leaving.

3 Where the goods supplied or the service done is contrary to law, it is no offence to make off without paying.

Suppose a person falsely claims he is a student, say, or an old age pensioner, and thus obtains a service such as a bus ride or entry to a theatre, free or at a reduced price. This is an offence under Section 2(1) (c) of the Theft Act 1978.

CHAPTER XIV

TRUTH IN LENDING

Truth in lending is a crucial theme of the Consumer Credit Act 1974. Every consumer who borrows must be told exactly how much extra he will pay when buying on credit.

For example, goods may be advertised at hire-purchase rates of say, 10 per cent per annum. The consumer is told that borrowing £1,000 over two years will cost £200. In fact, he starts repaying at the end of the first month, so at the end of the first year he will have repaid almost half the sum borrowed. Consequently he is really paying interest at the rate of nearly 20 per cent per annum.

The true rate of borrowing

Any advertisement for credit must indicate the true cost of borrowing. Thus, in the example given above, it must state that his true rate of interest is 19.7 per cent. In fact the true rate is often almost double the flat rate of interest. Advertisers must not show the flat rate of interest in large print and the true rate in smaller print. An advertiser who offers credit in false or misleading terms can be fined or sentenced to a maximum of two years' imprisonment.

Traders can purchase tables giving the effective annual rate of charge for most common transactions. In fact the full series of tables are contained in 15 volumes.

Knowing the precise annual percentage rate of interest is vital if consumers are to be able to compare offers accurately and thus to shop around for credit at the best price.

Credit charge

It is important to distinguish between the credit given and

the credit charge. Credit is the capital amount borrowed, whereas the **total charge for credit** refers to what the borrowing costs the consumer, including the interest payable. All fees and charges essential to getting the credit are regarded as part of the credit charge unless the consumer is free to choose his own source of borrowing. They must be itemised and the true annual rate of charge shown in the consumer credit agreement.

Regulations made under Section 20 prescribe in detail how the true cost of credit is to be determined, for example:

(a) Which items are to be treated as part of the total charge for credit.

(b) How the amounts of those items are ascertained.

(c) The rules for calculating the rate of the total charge for credit.

Excessive rates of interest

For the finance company the danger of charging too high a rate of interest is that the court may declare the credit bargain extortionate and re-open it.

This power of the court to investigate "credit bargains" is not restricted to regulated agreements. Any credit agreement where the loan is to an **individual** (not to a company) may be re-opened if extortionate, even though the amount of the credit exceeds £5,000.

History of moneylending

Before considering in detail how the Consumer Credit Act defines an extortionate credit bargain, we might take a brief look at the history of interest rates in this country. Originally "usury" meant simply "interest", ie payment for the use of money. Later the term usury was applied to the practice of charging excessive rates.

During the reign of Henry VIII the maximum rate of interest was fixed by statute at 10 per cent per annum. By the eighteenth century it had dropped to 5 per cent.

At this period money was so cheap that for more than 100 years loans could be had below the legal rate of 5 per cent, an indication of a stable economy. However the Napoleonic Wars pushed interest rates back to 10 per cent until eventually in 1854 the usury laws were abolished, thus leaving no limit on the rate of interest a lender could demand. Inevitably lenders began to abuse their freedom to charge what the market would stand.

To counteract abuse, courts of equity began to set aside contracts in which individuals had undertaken to pay an excessive rate of interest. What the court in fact did was to release the borrower from his obligation, by reducing the rate of interest. Finally this power of judges to re-open credit bargains and reduce oppressive rates of interest was given statutory authority by the first Moneylenders Act towards the end of Queen Victoria's reign.

The Moneylenders Acts obliged a judge, unless the contrary was proved, to presume that a rate above 48 per cent per annum was excessive. He could then re-open the whole transaction and reduce the rate to what he considered appropriate. However, it was open to the creditor to persuade the judge that the nature of the loan justified a rate of interest in excess of 48 per cent.

Extortionate credit bargains

The new powers of the court to re-open a credit transaction are wider than under the previous law and are not confined to agreements regulated by the Consumer Credit Act. These powers cover any agreement by an **individual** borrower.

The lender need **not** be a money-lender but can be a private person or an organisation not normally involved in money lending. All forms of credit as well as loans are subject to the new rules which will eventually replace those under the Moneylenders Acts 1900-1927.

Section 138 of the Consumer Credit Act ignores the old 48 per cent watershed and lays down general rules for

229

determining when a credit bargain is extortionate. The consumer does not have to **prove** it is extortionate. It is up to the lender to convince the judge that his credit bargain is **not** extortionate. The legal duty of proving it is reasonable rests on the lender.

Criteria for determining if a credit bargain is extortionate

A credit bargain is extortionate if it requires the consumer to make payments which are grossly exorbitant. It is also regarded as extortionate if it "otherwise grossly contravenes ordinary principles of fair trading." Section 138 sets out certain criteria which the court must take into account in determining whether a credit bargain is extortionate. The judge must consider evidence concerning:

(a) Interest rates prevailing at the time the agreement was made.

(b) What sort of person the borrower is, eg his age, experience, business capacity and state of health.

(c) How far the borrower was under financial pressure and what sort of pressure, when he made the credit agreement.

From the creditor's point of view the court will take into account:

(a) How much risk he accepted, having regard to the value of any security provided.

(b) The creditor's relationship with the borrower.

(c) Whether or not a colourable cash price was quoted for any goods or services included in the credit bargain, eg if the consumer was grossly overcharged for the goods in the first place, this could be a way of disguising the credit charge.

Since there is now no set rate above which interest is automatically presumed to be extortionate, the court must take into consideration all the circumstances of the transaction. Thus it will look at the credit bargain as a whole, including any linked transaction, and will not confine its investigation to the payments due under the credit agreement in isolation. Any payment which is relevant to the total charge for credit will be scrutinised.

Decisions under the Moneylenders Acts offer useful guidance to the principles on which the court may act:

- A loan to a businessman at 80 per cent a year was allowed on the ground that the money was to be used for a highly speculative and profitable enterprise.
- A borrower who proposed to use the loan to pay off debts with other moneylenders was held sufficient risk to justify 70 per cent. An added reason for allowing this higher rate was that the borrower did not offer any security.
- Whilst an annual rate of interest at 120 per cent would be extortionate in the case of an ordinary hire-purchase agreement, courts have in recent years approved as much as 120 per cent on **short term** advances where the borrower was not pressed by necessity but knew perfectly well what he was doing. For example it would not be unreasonable to charge £40 on a borrowing of £500 for four weeks although this in fact represents an annual rate of interest of over 100 per cent.
- A loan to a woman given on the security of post-dated cheques was reduced from 80 per cent to 25 per cent once the judge was satisfied the borrower was a woman lacking in business experience. Similarly, an elderly person in poor health who is talked into buying, say, central heating at instalments he cannot afford is likely to have the rate of interest cut to what is within his means.

Powers of the court

These powers are an exception to the rule that an agreement once made is "sacred" and cannot be varied or interfered with by the court. The court has a discretion to re-open a credit bargain which is extortionate. An application to have it re-opened may be made by the consumer himself, but if not his surety may apply to the court. They do not have to wait until the creditor takes them to court. The judge can cut the amount the borrower or his surety has to pay to what is fairly due and reasonable. In order to do so he may:

(i) Order accounts to be taken between any persons.

(ii) Set aside the whole or part of any obligation imposed on the borrower or his surety by the credit bargain or any related agreement.

(iii) Require the lender or finance company to repay the whole or part of any sum under the credit bargain or any related agreement.

(iv) Direct that the lender should return to the surety any property provided as security.

(v) Alter the terms of the credit agreement or any security document.

Since these powers may be exercised notwithstanding that their effect is to give an advantage unfairly to a third person, often the lender will tend to lose out. For example, a party to a linked transaction may be benefitted at the expense of the finance company.

Interest on instalments not paid on time

The Act says that consumers who pay off a regulated consumer credit agreement ahead of time will be entitled to a rebate under Section 95 because it is likely that the finance company will be able to lend out the money repaid to another borrower at a similar rate of interest.

The converse principle applies against a consumer who is late in paying an instalment due under a credit agreement. Had the instalment been paid on time the finance company could have lent out that money to someone else.

For this reason it is quite legitimate for a regulated credit agreement to stipulate that the consumer must pay additional interest for the period of delay. Thus if he pays an instalment two months late, the finance company is entitled to charge two months' further interest on that instalment. But it cannot charge a **higher** rate of interest. Charging interest on instalments in arrear is subject to the rule that the rate of interest charged must not exceed the basic rate payable under the agreement itself, ie it must not be penal.

Section 93 specifically states that the rate of interest is not to be increased on default. Accordingly his agreement cannot oblige the consumer to pay interest on outstanding instalments above the rate he is already paying.

Judgment in the county court prevents interest running

Once the county court orders a person to pay a sum of money he is freed from paying further interest. This is because judgments in county courts never carry interest. Accordingly, a person in financial difficulties may be better off once judgment is entered against him. After judgment all interest ceases completely on payments in arrear. Interest is payable only on a money judgment given in the High Court.

Consequently it is greatly to the advantage of the consumer that Section 141 stipulates that any court action in respect of a regulated agreement must be brought in the county court and not in the High Court. If the finance company improperly brings an action in the High Court to enforce a regulated agreement, it will be transferred to the county court.

Interest on High Court judgments

A creditor who gets a judgment in the High Court is entitled to interest at the rate of ten per cent from the date of judgment until the whole is paid. This rate supersedes any higher rate of interest payable previously say under a loan agreement. Here again, a consumer who is in financial difficulties may benefit once judgment has been entered against him. If he owes money at a high rate of interest, say

20 per cent or more, as soon as judgment is entered, he need pay only 10 per cent.

Interest prior to judgment

Where a consumer is sued on an agreement which stipulates for payment of interest he will be ordered to pay all interest due up to the date the court gives judgment against him. Sometimes a consumer may have to pay interest even though no interest was agreed.

The right to claim interest on an unpaid debt was given to claimants by the Law Reform Act of 1934. For example, a consumer who takes delivery of a car but fails to pay the balance until sued will have to pay interest on the amount he owes from the date he should have paid until judgment is entered.

It is commonsense that a claimant should have interest for the period he has lost the use of his capital. If he had received it on the day it was due, he could have put it on deposit at the bank or building society.

Historically however, the common law never allowed interest where payment of a debt was overdue, although courts of equity often did. Now, when any court gives judgment for an outstanding debt or awards compensation for injury, it has power to allow interest also for the period prior to judgment. For example, if a man was injured in an accident in 1976 but judgment is not given in his favour until 1979, the court can add to his compensation three years' interest up to the date of judgment. Moreover, it is not even necessary for the claimant to ask specifically for interest in his statement of claim.

The rate of interest varies according to the nature of the award. In modern cases it is usually one per cent above minimum lending rate.

CHAPTER XV

CREDIT CARDS, CHEQUE CARDS, TOKENS AND CHECK TRADING

Credit cards

The first all-purpose credit card was issued in the U.S. in 1950 by the Diner's Club. The first in the U.K. was Barclaycard in 1966, followed by Access in 1972.

The function of a credit card is to provide credit, whereas a cheque card operates simply as a guarantee by the card-holder's bank that his cheque will be met. A credit card is used without the need for a cheque. It enables the holder to obtain immediate credit from traders within the framework of the scheme and the card-holder repays the credit card company at a future date. In the meantime they pay the trader's account less a small service charge.

The advantages to the credit card holder are a short period of free credit, the convenience of drawing one cheque to cover any number of transactions and not needing to carry cash. Traders benefit because credit cards tend to encourage consumers to increase their spending. Furthermore, traders are assured of payment on submitting their account. The credit card company gets its remuneration by deducting discount from the trader's account. In some cases it also charges the card-holder a small annual fee as well as interest at an agreed rate.

Mode of employment

The credit card bears a specimen of the holder's signature, his name and account number. When a trasaction occurs the information from the card is impressed on the sales voucher which is then signed by the holder. The trader can compare his signature on the voucher with the specimen signature on his card. Where the purchase is above a certain amount the trader can check authenticity by telephoning the company.

To obtain payment the trader then sends a copy of the voucher to the credit card company or takes it to the local branch of the bank which credits him with the amount of the voucher, less the service charge.

The card holder is sent monthly statements which he is required to pay within a specified period if he wishes to avoid interest. Certain credit cards, such as Barclay and Access, allow credit card holders to pay their accounts by monthly instalments.

Credit token agreements

A credit card is an example of a credit token agreement. Not all such agreements are regulated under the provisions of the Consumer Credit Act which apply only where the holder may make repayment by instalments. The Act does not apply to cards like American Express and Diners Club which do not allow repayment by instalments. Such cards require repayment of the entire outstanding balance by a fixed date. They do not provide **term** credit but merely allow payment of a trade debt to be deferred for a short time for the convenience of the card-holder so that he does not have to carry large amounts of cash with him. Consequently, where few or no instalments are permitted, holders of such cards are likely to be denied the protection of the provisions set out in this Chapter.

Broadly, credit tokens are things given to consumers by lenders which can be used to obtain cash, goods or services on credit. A token is defined as a card, check, voucher, coupon, stamp, form, booklet, or other document or thing, given to an individual where the organisation issuing the credit token undertakes on production of the token to supply cash, goods or services on credit. Alternatively the organisation undertakes that where on the production of the token a **third party** supplies cash, goods or services, the organisation will pay the third party (whether or not deducting any discount or commission) in return for payment to it by the individual.

Examples of credit-tokens are:
1 Credit cards (but not cheque cards).
2 Cash dispenser cards.
3 Credit cards issued by a shop or store.
4 Trading vouchers.
5 Checks issued by a check trading company.

Cheques and cheque guarantee cards are not credit tokens.

How credit cards work

A consumer can use his card only at a shop or restaurant, garage etc, where the trader accepts his type of credit card. On entering into a transaction his card goes into a small machine which copies its details onto a sales voucher. The consumer settles his debt with the shop by signing the voucher. As he is legally bound by the details entered on the voucher it is important that he should check it carefully before signing to see that it has been correctly and completely filled in.

The consumer must keep within his credit limit, ie the maximum that he is permitted to owe the credit card company at any one time, and traders are at liberty to check this by referring to the credit card company.

The shop sends a copy of the sales voucher to the credit card company whose account department processes it and adds it to the consumer's account.

Period of credit without interest

Generally the card holder will have 25 days from the date of his statement to make payment. In practice, he will have interest-free credit for a total of the following periods:

(i)   say three or four days for the sales voucher to reach the credit card company accounts centre.

(ii) the time taken by the accounts centre to process the transaction – another day or two;

(iii) the time which elapses until the consumer's next statement day comes round; this could be up to a month if the transaction occurs just after the last statement day;

(iv) any interest-free period after the statement day, which is allowed by the credit card company.

Adding the above periods together means that the consumer can normally count on an interest-free period of one to two months between buying something and paying for it.

Usefulness of credit cards

Credit cards provide running-account credit, as distinct from fixed-sum credit, since the holder can use the card repeatedly to increase his borrowing provided he does not go above the maximum stipulated in his agreement. They are an extremely useful and flexible form of credit suitable for businessmen who travel frequently as well as those who dislike carrying large sums of cash.

Monthly statements provide the consumer with a record of his expenditure on which he can distinguish personal from business items. An important feature of some cards is the facility of obtaining cash. However the only similarity with a cheque card is the fact that the trader is assured of payment by the issuing company. Traders are also relieved from extending credit themselves and from the risk inherent in having large amounts of cash on the premises.

Check trading

Check trading is more common in the north of England than in the south and is in many respects similar to the credit card business but far less flexible. It provides fixed sum credit, whereas the credit card is a form of "revolving" or running account credit.

238

Trading checks and vouchers are similar in purpose but vouchers are usually for larger amounts than checks. A trading check voucher good for, say, £100 can be used only at those shops who have an arrangement with the check trading company. If the consumer buys goods for, say, £30, the shop will mark this amount on the back of the check, thus leaving him free to spend the rest of his credit in other stores.

When shops apply for payment, the check trading company generally deducts a discount from their accounts. A representative of the company then calls weekly to collect the face value of the check plus interest, by instalments at the consumer's home.

Liability for misuse of credit tokens

Credit tokens particularly cards are notoriously liable to be lost or stolen and subsequently misused by someone to obtain cash or goods fraudulently. The maximum liability of the holder is in fact limited by Section 84 of the Act to a total of £30 in respect of the whole period the card is out of his possession. Such liability encourages holders to take care of their cards. The consumer must at once notify the creditor (by telephone or in writing) that his card has been lost or stolen. After the date of such notification he is completely free of liability (not even up to £30) for its subsequent misuse.

Sometimes his agreement requires that a holder who telephones notice of loss must confirm it in writing. In any case, whether so required or not, written confirmation of loss is always a wise precaution. But any holder who consents to someone else using his credit card or token is fully liable for **all** loss arising from its subsequent use up to the time he gives the company oral or written notice that it is liable to misuse.

If the credit card company sues the holder for its misuse

and the holder disputes liability, the onus is on the company
to prove:
1 its subsequent use was authorised by the holder; or
2 its use occurred before the consumer gave them notice
  it was lost.

Liability of credit card company for suppliers

Many credit token agreements such as credit card schemes
involve a pre-existing business connection between the
company which furnishes the credit and those suppliers
who furnish the consumer with goods or services. We saw
that such an arrangement is referred to in the Act as giving
rise to a debtor-creditor-supplier agreement (see p 212).

The Consumer Credit Act makes the lender responsible
where a supplier has provided defective goods or failed to
deliver the goods at all and has gone into liquidation or
disappeared. Formerly this left the consumer legally
obliged to repay the loan to the finance company but with
no effective means of complaint or redress.

Provided his agreement is regulated, Section 75 protects
him. Where the consumer has "any claim against the
supplier in respect of a misrepresentation or breach of
contract, he will have a like claim against the creditor
(finance company)". Thus he can sue the finance company
as well as the supplier. Of course, the person primarily to
blame will be the supplier, so whilst Section 75 obliges the
finance company to settle the consumer's claim, it also
gives it a right of indemnity against the supplier, ie it can
(in theory) get back from the supplier any money it has to
pay the consumer by way of compensation.

The credit card company is responsible notwithstanding
that in entering into the transaction the consumer exceeded
his permitted credit or otherwise contravened any term
of his credit agreement. But it is not responsible where
the complaint relates to a single item costing above
£10,000 or for which the cash price was £30 or less. This

will exclude all minor purchases for which credit cards are used.

Suppose that the consumer uses his credit card to buy two bicycles, one costing £50 for himself and another at £25 for his son. Both bicycles turn out to be defective and cause an accident.

By virtue of Section 75 the father is entitled to compensation from the credit card company as well as the shop, for the cost of repairs to his bicycle. If he is injured he can claim for this too. But as his son's bicycle cost less than £30, he will have a claim against the shop only, not against the credit card company. (See further p 72 regarding problems of liability).

Cheque cards

Cheque cards or cheque guarantee cards were first issued in Britain in 1965. In the United States of America they are known as 'courtesy cards".

Cheque cards have a dual function. They enable the holder to draw cash up to £50 at other branches of the issuing bank. They can also be used to guarantee that his cheques will be honoured provided the stipulated limit – usually £50 is not exceeded. The bank is not paying for the goods or services supplied but is merely meeting the holder's cheque. The cheque card does not provide the consumer with credit since he must have sufficient money in his account to meet the amount of the cheque.

One disadvantage to the holder is that he forgoes the right to stop a cheque issued in conjunction with his card. On the other hand many traders would normally balk at the offer of a cheque unsupported by a card. The acceptance of cards for cashing cheques at banks in common market countries is particularly useful when travelling.

The rules governing the use of cheque cards are as follows:
(i) The cheque must be signed in the presence of the trader.

(ii) The trader must verify that the signature on the cheque corresponds with the specimen on the card.

(iii) The code number on the card must correspond with that printed on the cheque.

(iv) The number of the card must be written on the back of the cheque.

(v) The date on the card must show that it is current.

Misuse of cheque cards

When the card is used to obtain cash, the branch imprints a date stamp in one of the panels at the back of the cheque book. Should you go to another branch to withdraw more cash the same day, that branch will telephone your branch to ensure that the money is available. Interchanging false backs on a cheque book is a common method of obtaining cash by fraud.

A notice on the back of a cheque card usually states: "The issuing bank undertakes that any cheque not exceeding £50 will be honoured". But this guarantee does not entitle the holder to use the card to write cheques for more than he has in his bank account. If the holder requires to overdraw, he must arrange this with his bank manager **before** using the card.

Normally, anyone who issues a cheque in excess of the sum in his bank account will find his bank dishonours it unless he has arranged an overdraft. But by using his cheque card he compels the bank to honour his cheque. If he has no permission to overdraw this could involve him in being charged with "Dishonesty obtaining for himself a pecuniary advantage, namely increased borrowing by ways of overdraft from the bank by deliberately or recklessly representing that he was entitled and authorised to use the cheque card."

This is what happened to Mr Charles after he opened an account at the National Westminster Bank and was allowed overdraft facilities of £100 for two months. He

242

was later notified that he had exceeded his overdraft limit but used his cheque card to increase his overdraft to £248.

The manager knew that a cheque in his favour for £500 had been paid into another branch (although it was not met until two or three months later) and gave him a new cheque book, telling him not to cash more than one cheque a day.

That evening Mr Charles went to a gaming club and used 25 cheques to buy chips. As he used his cheque card in relation to each cheque the bank had to honour all of them.

The House of Lords considered that the jury had rightly convicted Mr Charles of dishonestly obtaining for himself a pecuniary advantage viz. increased borrowing by way of overdraft from the bank. His **deception** was that he had deliberately or recklessly represented that he was entitled and authorised to use the cheque card when issuing cheques. *Metropolitan Police Commissioner v. Charles,* House of Lords (1976).

CHAPTER XVI

HIRE-PURCHASE AND CREDIT SALES
AND CONDITIONAL SALES

Hiring and Rental

A great variety of goods can be rented for long or short periods from tv receivers to vans and building equipment. A householder who wishes to paint the outside of his house may need a ladder. Since there is no point in his having one permanently, he will probably rent one. Renting a car or tv does not involve any element of credit. Each week the renter pays for the enjoyment and use of the article including (usually) its maintenance in working order. He is in no sense investing in the article hired.

Hire-purchase

Renting (or simple hiring) is quite distinct from hire-purchase where the consumer can eventually become owner of the article. But until he pays the final instalment, the hire-purchase consumer is in the same situation as an ordinary hirer, ie he may only use the article and is not yet its legal owner.

An article held on hire-purchase does not belong to the consumer before he has finished paying for it. Until then the finance company has the security of continued ownership and the right to take it back (usually with a court order) if the consumer does not keep up his instalments. If he sells it he commits theft.

Hire-purchase involves credit because the debtor is in fact paying towards eventual ownership. He will usually be out of pocket if he terminates his agreement part-way through because he will have to pay as much as half the total hire-purchase price. Owing to the possibility of termination, a hire-purchase agreement is not a "sale". Nevertheless it has the same quality guarantees as a sale (see p 36).

Conditional sale and credit sale agreements
Except for the car trade, regulated conditional-sale agreements are not very common although conditional sale is often used in the case of motor vehicles where the amount of the loan exceeds £5,000.

Conditional sale is the same in effect as hire-purchase and both differ fundamentally from credit sale. Although the consumer under a conditional-sale agreement is allowed possession of the article, it continues to belong to the seller until all the instalments have been paid.

Credit sale
By contrast the consumer under credit sale actually owns the article although he has not yet paid the price. Consequently he is free to sell it. Admittedly, if he does sell it, his credit-sale agreement invariably requires him to pay off at once the whole amount owing. But the advantage from the consumer's point of view is that the finance company has no right to take back the article in the event of non-payment.

Before they can sue him the finance company will have to serve a **default notice** on him. If he is pressed financially he can request the court to make a **time order** to allow him to pay by such instalments as he can afford.

However, if he does not pay under the court order the bailiff could seize the article, along with his other possessions, by way of **execution.** But the bailiff may not take items which he holds on conditional sale or hire-purchase, which belong to **other** creditors.

Termination
A disadvantage of credit sale is that the consumer cannot

terminate his agreement. He has no right to send back the article if he gets tired of it or decides it was a bad buy after all and wants to cut his losses.

The right of termination applies only to hire-purchase and conditional-sale agreements, permitting the consumer to reduce his overall liability if he sends back the article ahead of time. (See p 252).

Conditional sale and hire-purchase equated

A conditional-sale agreement is defined as "an agreement for the sale of goods where the purchase price is payable in instalments but where ownership of the goods is to remain in the seller (notwithstanding that the buyer is to be in possession of the goods . . .) until such conditions as to the payment of instalments or otherwise as may be specified in the agreement, are fulfilled."

The postponement of the transfer of ownership until payment is completed, is merely a device in law to permit the finance company to get the goods back in the event of non-payment, ie to realise its security. For this reason all conditional sales are treated under the Consumer Credit Act as **identical** to hire-purchase. In both the consumer is protected by the rule that after he has paid one-third, the finance company cannot take back the article without a court order. (Sections 90 and 91).

If he cannot afford to keep up his payments the court has power, under Section 129, to reduce them, allowing him to retain the article, so long as he pays such instalments as the court thinks right, ie the court can reduce future instalments.

Complexity of credit arrangement

When a member of the public buys an article on hire-purchase he imagines he is buying it by instalments from the dealer and that the finance company is lending the money. However, their legal relationship is not so simple.

In reality the consumer will be hiring the article from a finance company, introduced by the dealer, which has never seen the goods. The legal arrangement between dealer, consumer and finance company is this:

- The dealer sells the article to the finance company.
- The finance company lets it on a hire-purchase agreement to the consumer.

In law, three separate agreements are involved:

1 A preliminary agreement (usually only by word of mouth) whereby the dealer agrees for the consumer to have the article on credit terms.
2 The dealer agrees with the finance company to sell **them** the article.
3 A hire-purchase agreement is then made between the consumer and the finance company.

When an agreement is regulated

The dominant role in these arrangements is played by the finance company. The consumer must take the terms they offer. The Consumer Credit Act seeks to protect the consumer from accepting too stringent terms to get the goods he wants. But ambitious or wealthy consumers who can afford to take on a credit liability of more than £5,000 are not protected by the Act. To have protection his total borrowing must not exceed £5,000, excluding all credit charges or interest to be paid in addition to the amount borrowed.

Suppose a consumer wishes to buy a car with a retail price of £9,000 cash. He has saved £4,000 towards it, which he pays as a deposit, and agrees to pay the balance by 50 instalments of £120 monthly, viz. £6,000.

The hire-purchase greement gives the consumer the right to buy the car for £1 once the final instalment is paid. Although the total amount payable is £6,001, nevertheless his total borrowing is only £5,000, so his transaction comes within the protection of the Act.

However, should the consumer be tempted to take any extras for an additional £50, this sum is added to the amount borrowed. The transaction would then be outside the limit set by the Act.

The salient features of credit sale may be contrasted with those of conditional sales and hire-purchase in the following summary:

	Hire-purchase and conditional sale	*compared with*	Credit sale
Form of agreement	The agreement is lengthy and complicated.		The agreement is usually short and simple.
	It will, eg, require the consumer to insure the article and keep it in good condition.		The consumer should arrange insurance cover himself since the article belongs to him from the moment he takes delivery.
	Basically the article is hired and does not belong to the consumer until the final instalment has been paid.		
Right of Sale	He must not dispose or part with possession of it without the written permission of the finance company.		If the buyer wishes, he may sell it. If so what he owes under the agreement must be repaid immediately.
Rights of finance company	The finance company remains owner of the article and has the right to take it back but must first terminate the agreement by serving notice of default. If he is still in arrear after 8 days the finance company can send its representative to take the goods back without waiting for a court order if more than two thirds of the total hp price are still outstanding.		The finance company cannot get it back. If the credit buyer defaults on even one instalment, the whole balance outstanding becomes due. This permits the finance company to sue for the whole balance at once.
Instalments	Where the hirer has paid more than one-third but then gets into arrears the court has power to fix lower instalments if his earnings are reduced.		If the customer is in financial difficulties the court can grant a **time order** in his favour, ie give him further time to pay.
Termination	The hirer has the right at any time to return the article to the		The credit buyer has no right to terminate his agreement.

248

Hire-purchase and conditional sale	*compared with*	Credit sale
hire-purchase company. In this case he must bring his total payments up to one-half of the total hire-purchase price (unless the court thinks a lesser sum would cover the company's loss). He will also have to pay all instaments up to the date of termination, if his agreement has already run more than half-way.		He cannot insist that the finance company takes the goods back, unless they are defective.
Rights if goods are defective	The hirer has the same rights as the cash buyer. He can also repudiate the agreement.	The consumer has the same rights, as if he had paid cash, to reject the article and/or claim compensation. (See p 96)
Right to cancel	The consumer who has signed on trade premises cannot cancel. The cooling-off period is allowed only where he signs at home (off trade premises) following "oral representations" (sales talk).	
Right to rebate for early repayment	Yes.	

Responsibility of the dealer

If a car on hp proves defective, the consumer cannot sue the dealer under the Sale of Goods Act since he has not bought the car from him. But he may have a claim against a dealer whose "sales patter" misled him or who was negligent, say, in failing to check its roadworthiness.

One car dealer induced a customer to sign a hire-purchase agreement with a finance company by telling him "It's a good little bus". Soon after taking delivery the customer had a crash owing to the car's defective steering. The dealer had to pay damages because his assurance caused the consumer to apply to the finance company to take it on hire-purchase terms, thereby enabling the

249

dealer to sell it to the finance company. *Andrews v. Hopkinson* (1957).

Responsibility of the finance company (creditor) for dealer
The dealer (or negotiator) is regarded as acting as **agent** for the finance company which consequently becomes responsible for what he says or does to bring off the transaction. (Section 56(2) Consumer Credit Act). Thus the consumer can also take court action against the company in respect of misrepresentations made by the dealer during negotiations, ie all statements or assurances to persuade the consumer to enter into the hire-purchase agreement. The consumer can pursue his complaint against either the company or the dealer or both.

Complaints regarding goods on hire-purchase
The consumer is, from a practical standpoint, in a stronger position to complain about an article he holds on hire-purchase than if he buys for cash. He can reinforce his complaint by the simple expedient of threatening to stop and eventually stopping paying instalments. It then lies with the finance company either to remedy his complaint or take him to court where the consumer can raise his complaint as a "counterclaim".

Take the case of Mr Attryde's motor-cycle. He paid £155 down, with instalments of £10.05 a month. He took delivery in July but had a lot of trouble and sent it back to the suppliers who tried to correct the faults without success. It then went back to the makers who kept it nine days and remedied some defects but not all.

In August he again took it back and this time they kept it three weeks, putting right some defects but not all. He used it for a further five weeks in October/November but found there were still serious faults which culminated in the chain breaking and knocking a hole in the crank case.

250

This was the last straw for Mr Attryde and he wrote telling them to repossess it. Eventually they sued him for £149.

The finance company argued that his riding it some 4,000 miles meant that he had affirmed the agreement and had to keep the machine, ie it was too late for him to repudiate it.

The judges took the opposite view. "A man only affirms a contract when he knows of the defects and by his conduct elects to go on with the contract despite them." Mr Attryde had complained from the very beginning. He did not elect to accept it **until** its defects were put right.

The hire-purchase company was ordered to pay him back all the payments he had made. Nothing was deducted for his use of the motor cycle because that was offset by the inconvenience he had experienced owing to the defects. *Farnworth Finance Facilities v. Attryde* (1970).

Terms implied in favour of credit consumer

The rights of a credit buyer against the finance company regarding defects or unfitness or inaccurate description are identical to the rights which a cash buyer has against the retailer. (See p 36). Whether the agreement is by hire-purchase, conditional sale or credit sale, these rights cannot be excluded by any clause in the actual agreement, no matter what its form of wording.

These rights are set out in Sections 8 to 11 of the Supply of Goods (Implied Terms) Act 1973, Section 10(3) of which even extends the consumer's rights slightly. Thus where the consumer requires an article for a specific purpose, it must be reasonably fit for that purpose, provided the consumer makes his purpose known to the dealer or negotiator in the course of negotiations. The consumer does not have to tell the finance house itself. Communication of the required purpose to the dealer is sufficient.

Samples and descriptions

Where under a hire-purchase agreement goods are let by

description, there is an implied condition that the goods will correspond with that description.

If the goods are let by reference to a sample as well as a description, it is not sufficient that they correspond with the sample only. They must also correspond with the description. Even where an item is selected by the hirer himself from a number of articles exposed for sale or hire, it must still correspond with its description. (See p 101).

Prior inspection by consumer
Where the consumer has inspected the goods before signing the hire-purchase agreement, the finance house is obliged to ensure that when delivered they are in substantially the same condition as when he saw them. It makes no difference that the lender is a finance company which has bought the goods without seeing them.

A Mr Wallis inspected a Buick car at the premises of the dealer and was satisfied it was all right before signing the hire-purchase forms. When delivered the Buick was in a deplorable condition and the creditor was held responsible. *Karsales v. Wallis* (1956).

Rebates for early payment
A consumer who chooses to pay off his regulated credit agreement ahead of time gets the benefit of a statutory rebate under Section 95.

He can at any time give notice in writing to the finance company (creditor) that he wishes to exercise his right of early repayment. Rental or simple hire agreements however do not qualify for a rebate in the event of early payment.

Returning hire-purchase goods
Section 99 entitles an hp consumer to terminate his agreement and return the article before he has completed all his instalment payments. Voluntary termination will not usually be to his financial advantage and he will

seldom take this course except where the value of his "equity" in the article is less than his outstanding debt.

However, he may have made a bad bargain in choosing the article in the first place. Take the case of a housewife who is dissatisfied with her dish-washer and prefers to have a newer machine. She can terminate her hp agreement and start afresh with a more recent model.

Price of termination by hp consumer
The minimum cost to terminate is one-half of the total hire-purchase price. Should the hirer (debtor) himself choose to end his hire-purchase agreement he must return the goods and bring the payments up to one-half of the total hire-purchase price. Should his instalments outstanding on termination exceed one-half, he must pay these plus the cost of any repairs if the goods have been mistreated.

In practice he will usually have to pay one-half of the total hire-purchase price. But the court has power to limit what he has to pay to the finance company's **actual loss.** Sometimes he need not pay the whole amount required to bring his payments up to one-half provided, of course, that the article has not been mistreated or been allowed to fall into disrepair.

Take the case of a car with a total hire-purchase price of £3,000, which on being returned is sold for £2,000. If the hirer has already paid £800 the court can restrict his further liability to £200 which will clear the finance company's account. In this event, the court can let him off the £700 needed to bring his payments up to one-half.

Getting into arrears with hire-purchase
More commonly the cause of termination is the consumer's failure to keep up instalment payments. If he gets into financial difficulties but would like to keep the goods he has two options:

1 Either he can wait until the finance house takes him to

court and then apply for a **time order**, ie extra time to pay, say with smaller instalments over a longer period, or

2 He can ask the finance house before they sue him if they will **agree** to accept lower instalments.

In practice they will seldom want the goods returned, with the problem of disposing of them. Nor will they want to lose the balance of the instalments. Usually they will be prepared to offer him the chance of spreading his remaining payments over an extended period.

Variation of the hire-purchase agreement

If a variation of payments is agreed by the finance company Section 82(2) of the Consumer Credit Act comes into operation: "Where an agreement (a 'modifying agreement') varies or supplements an earlier agreement, the modifying agreement shall . . . be treated as (a) revoking the earlier agreement and (b) containing provisions reproducing the combined effect of the two agreements."

Apart from the variation, the earlier agreement continues to be binding on the consumer and the finance company respectively.

Termination of non-regulated hire-purchase agreements

We saw that a consumer who exercises his right under Section 99 to terminate a **regulated** hire-purchase agreement is required to bring his payments up to one-half of the hire-purchase price.

However, his termination of a **non-regulated** hire-purchase agreement will render him liable generally to pay much more than half, often two-thirds of the hire-purchase price as a minimum payment.

To avoid the stipulated minimum payment, his best course, if he is in financial difficulties, is simply to notify the finance company and leave it to them to terminate. Where the creditor terminates the court will generally

254

declare the minimum payment to be a penalty and hence unenforceable.

If so their claim will be limited to the following amounts:
1 All instalments in arrear and unpaid.
2 Interest on late instalments at such rate as the agreement provides.
3 The cost of repair if he failed to take reasonable care of the goods.
4 The cost of repossessing the goods.

Repudiation by the consumer of his hire-purchase agreement
Whether or not the agreement is regulated, if the consumer commits a serious breach of his agreement, he is regarded as having repudiated it. For example, he may have abandoned his vehicle in a damaged state after an accident for which he was to blame or have sold it. In such cases the finance company is entitled to claim the balance of the hire-purchase price.

Default notice must be sent to the consumer
Should the consumer fall behind with his instalment payments the finance company can terminate his agreement and demand the goods be returned. In order to terminate a regulated hire-purchase agreement they must first serve a default notice giving him the chance (not less than seven days) to bring his payments up to date. (Section 87).

The default notice must specify:
(a) the nature of the alleged breach
(b) the amount required to be paid and by what date
(c) the consequences of his failure to comply (ie termination)

If within the seven days stipulated the consumer complies and pays up, his breach is treated as if it had not occurred. (Section 89). However, should he fail to comply with the notice the company is entitled to retake possession of the goods. No court order is necessary where more than two-thirds of the hp price are outstanding.

Consequences of invalid notice

A notice which does not comply with the above requirements is invalid and does not operate to terminate the agreement. It is the same as if no notice had been sent at all. Consequently, even though the hirer has paid less than one-third of the total hp price the finance company is not entitled to retake possession of the goods. If they do, they will be liable to pay compensation to the consumer.

One third minimum payment rule

Once a third of the hire-purchase price has been paid, goods held under a regulated agreement cannot be taken back by the finance company without a court order. (Section 90).

To determine one-third of the total hire-purchase price the deposit, plus all instalments plus the option money, are added together and divided by three. However, where installation charges are included in the total hire-purchase price, eg for connecting up a dish-washing machine to the plumbing system, the consumer must pay these in addition to the one-third minimum.

Penalty for wrongful "snatch-back"

Should the finance company recover goods without a court order from a consumer whose payments exceed the one-third watershed, the consumer is released from all liability under his hire-purchase agreement. Moreover the company must repay him all the money he has already paid. However, the finance company is entitled to accept the goods back from a consumer who consents to hand them over of his own volition. Also where he has abandoned the goods, eg left a damaged car at a garage and disappeared for several months without trace, the finance company is entitled to recover possession because the inference is that he has repudiated his agreement (see above).

Merely leaving a car for repair at a garage or lending it to a friend would not entitle the finance company to repossess it without a court order, but if the consumer sells it to a dealer, the finance company could seize it from the dealer's forecourt.

When a "snatch-back" is valid

Where instalments are in arrear and he fails to comply with a default notice a consumer who has failed to reach the one-third minimum is not protected from the "snatch-back" so the company can send someone to collect the goods without further warning.

Restriction on entering premises

However, in practice an important curb on the finance company retaking possession is placed in their path by Section 92. Except under an order of the court the creditor (ie finance company) shall not be entitled to **enter any premises** to take possession of goods subject to:

(a) a regulated hire-purchase agreement
(b) a regulated conditional-sale agreement
(c) a regulated consumer hire agreement (see p 261).

But a consumer whose borrowing exceeds £5,000 is not protected by the one-third minimum payment rule which applies only to regulated agreements. It is not even certain that he will get a prior warning notice although judges have indicated that some reminder that his instalments are in arrear ought to be given on similar lines to the statutory default notice mentioned above. Consequently it will be unsafe for him to withhold payments as a means of inducing the finance company to remedy his complaints. Agreements outside the protection of the Act usually permit the company to enter the consumer's premises and take back the goods immediately, if an instalment is not paid on time.

What order will the court make?

If the consumer gets into arrears with his payments under a regulated agreement (ie where less than £5,000 is borrowed) the finance company can simply sue for arrears. In this case they need not serve a default notice on him, but will simply notify him of his arrears by letter.

The consumer should state his financial circumstances on the form which he receives from the court and make an offer to pay what he can afford. The court will then decide whether to order him to pay the arrears within 14 days or allow him to pay by instalments under a **time order**.

Alternatively, if the consumer has failed to comply with their default notice, the company can issue a summons claiming the return of the goods plus all arrears outstanding. Here again it is open to the court to make a **time order** if requested by the consumer. If it sees fit the court can reduce the hp instalment payments to suit his changed financial circumstances and allow him to keep the goods so long as he makes such payments into court.

Court can vary previous orders

Should he default in the instalments fixed by the court, the finance company can request the court bailiff to repossess the goods. However this is not necessarily the end since the consumer may still have the chance to keep the goods if his financial situation has suffered a genuine setback. He can go back to court at a later date and ask for a further extension of time to catch up with his payments. The court has power to vary any order it has previously made.

Return order

Where it appears that there is no real likelihood of the consumer meeting his obligations, the court can order the return of the goods to the finance company, if "it appears to the court just to do so". (Section 133).

Transfer order
Under Section 133, as an alternative, the court can allocate to the consumer some of the items comprised in the hire-purchase agreement, eg pieces of furniture, and order the rest to be returned to the finance company.

Failure to take reasonable care of the goods
Although it has got the goods back, the finance company may seek compensation if he has failed to take reasonable care of them. In the case of a motor vehicle, an engineer will list the repairs needed and assess the cost of putting them right. The finance company is entitled to this sum as part of their loss.

Unlawful sale of goods held on hire-purchase or conditional sale
One of the dangers of buying second-hand goods is that they may be subject to an existing conditional-sale or hire-purchase agreement in which case the consumer had no right to dispose of them.

Supposing the finance company demands the goods from the innocent buyer, what are his legal rights? Apart from motor vehicles all goods which are still subject to a hire-purchase agreement must be handed over to the rightful owner, ie the finance company.

In practice, the finance company will be satisfied if it receives the balance of the hire-purchase debt. In fact, the court regards a subsequent innocent buyer as standing in the shoes of the original hirer.

However, a consumer who buys a second-hand car is safe-guarded. Where a motor vehicle is sold whilst still on hire-purchase the Hire-Purchase Act 1964, part III, protects an innocent buyer. The finance company cannot

259

get their vehicle back from him provided he is a private person (ie not a motor dealer or finance house) and bought the vehicle in good faith, unaware of any outstanding hire-purchase or conditional-sale agreement. This protection applies whether or not the agreement is regulated, ie even though the hire-purchase debt exceeds £5,000.

Should the company seize the vehicle from the buyer they will have to pay him very considerable compensation.

CHAPTER XVII

RENTAL AND HIRE

Terms to protect hirer

The terms implied by law in a hire (rental) agreement vary, according to the circumstances and nature of the hiring. In particular the hire or rental consumer is protected by the Unfair Contract Terms Act 1977. Anyone dealing as a consumer is guaranteed:

1 The article rented will correspond with the description given or any sample.
2 The article will be of reasonable quality and serviceability.
3 It will be fit for its particular use or purpose.

Exemption Clauses in Hiring

Consumer hire agreements cannot exclude these rights. However, a non-consumer, ie business renter, **can** be deprived of these guarantees if a term in his agreement takes them away but only if the test of "reasonableness" is satisfied. (See p 134 & 138).

Consumer hire agreements

Consumers often hire boats or cars on holiday or even building equipment for home repairs. Such temporary hiring is not covered by the Consumer Credit Act, nor does the Act apply if the hirer's total payments exceed £5,000 or the hiring is to a company.

The Act calls the parties to a consumer hire agreement the "owner" and the "hirer". The owner is the trader or company which offers goods for letting on hire. The hirer is the consumer who takes them on hire.

A consumer hire agreement is quite different from a

261

hire-purchase agreement because no matter how long the hiring lasts it is not intended that the hirer will ever become the owner of the article. Nevertheless a rental agreement is regulated under the Consumer Credit Act provided it has the following five characteristics:

1 The agreement must be capable of lasting for a period of more than three months. Where the hiring is continuous (say, on a monthly or weekly basis) the Act will apply but an agreement to hire a car or van for a **fixed** period of three months or less is not regulated.

2 The agreement does not oblige the hirer to make payments exceeding £5,000. In practice, few private consumers would undertake liability beyond that figure. If they do the Act will not help them.

3 It is not a hire-purchase agreement (ie no option for eventual purchase).

4 The hiring must be to an individual (or partnership).

5 The hiring must not relate to metering equipment of public utilities or post office equipment (except hired internal telephones).

Hirer's right of termination (up to £300 per annum)

Before the passing of the Consumer Credit Act, the consumer had no right to return hired goods in the event of his circumstances changing. Section 101 of that Act entitles a hirer whose payments do not exceed £300 a year to terminate the agreement after 18 months. This statutory right of termination cannot be taken away by small print clauses. No matter how long his agreement is stipulated to last, he has the choice to terminate it after 18 months.

Where the hirer's payments exceed £300 a year the Act gives him no right of termination so it is up to the hirer to ensure before signing that a suitable right is contained in his agreement, permitting him to terminate early.

262

How to terminate under Section 101

The agreement may permit the hirer to terminate **sooner** than the statutory 18 months but cannot **postpone** it beyond this period. Thus if the agreement permits termination after 9 months, then the hirer will be better off. To exercise his statutory power of termination he must give notice in writing, eg it can be handed over when the hirer pays his next instalment.

The period of notice required depends on the frequency of his instalment payments. The hirer who pays rental instalments monthly is required to give one month's notice. If he pays instalments on a fortnightly basis, two weeks' notice is sufficient.

In any event, even if he pays his rental yearly, he cannot be required to give more than three months' notice. Thus he should give notice prior to the end of the 15th month of his rental period, to take effect at the expiration of the 18th month.

Rights and duties on termination

On termination the hirer will be obliged to pay the owners compensation if he has failed to take reasonable care of the goods. He must also pay all rentals and other charges which have fallen due prior to the date of termination. On the other hand where he has paid charges in advance beyond the date of termination, he will be entitled to have them returned.

Default notice where hirer fails to keep up instalments

Where the hirer is late in making payments, the finance company must before taking any other steps, serve on him a Default Notice specifying:

(a) How much is due.
(b) The exact date by which he must pay.
(c) The consequences if he does not.

The hirer must be allowed at least seven days from

receiving it to make payment. But immediately it expires the finance company is free:

(a) To terminate the agreement and
(b) To demand payment of money due and
(c) To recover possession of the goods hired.

However, in practice it may often be unable to recover the goods, since Section 92 prevents it entering any premises to take possession of them, except under an order of the court. In other words, unless the hirer is prepared to hand them over or they are left in the open, the finance company will generally have to issue a court summons demanding their return.

When it sues for their return, it can in the same claim ask for payment of all arrears of hire instalments. If so the court can make a Time Order in the hirer's favour allowing him to pay off the arrears by instalments appropriate to his financial circumstances.

If the court decides to make an order for the return of the goods, it may suspend the operation of the return order, or make it conditional, as it sees fit under Section 135.

Hire and hire-purchase contrasted

An important respect in which a hirer is worse off than the holder of a hire-purchase agreement is that the judge cannot reduce future hire instalments, eg he cannot alter the future payment pattern as a whole, as he can in the case of hire-purchase. For example, a consumer who ought to pay £20 a month on hire-purchase of furniture could have his instalments reduced to £5 a month if his financial circumstances justify it.

Where the furniture is merely hired the judge can allow the hirer to make reduced payments only in respect of instalments he has already missed. Thus the judge could allow him to pay £5 a month off the arrears, but he must continue to pay £20 monthly in addition, to keep the furniture. This is because Section 135(3) specifically says that the judge cannot use the court's power of suspension "so as to extend the period for which, under the terms of his agreement, the hirer is entitled to possession of the goods."

Hire-purchase and hire sometimes confused

Prior to the Consumer Credit Act 1974 the court could not help a hirer who suffered financial detriment through termination of his agreement owing to non-payment. The case of Mr Galbraith illustrates the unfairness that could sometimes occur.

Mr Galbraith, who was a storeman, wanted to live near Cowley where he hoped to find work. In 1962 he decided to buy a caravan on hire-purchase to live in with his wife and children. In fact he was offered a **hire** agreement, a long document in small print, which he mistakenly accepted and signed without reading.

The cash retail price of the caravan was £1,050. He made an initial payment of £550 but failed to keep up the 60 rental payments of £12.50 monthly and the finance company repossessed the caravan after he had lived in it for only four months. They then sold it for £775 showing a profit of £275 but Mr Galbraith could not get back any of his £550 deposit. *Galbraith v. Mitchenhall Estates Ltd.* (1964).

Hirer's rights on repossession by company

Take, say, a car parked in the road and not on the hirer's own premises. There is nothing to prevent the finance company exercising their right to seize it (provided they first serve the appropriate default notice). In this case the hirer has two alternatives. He can ask the court for relief against forfeiture if he can find enough money elsewhere to clear the arrears he owes, reasonably promptly. Or, he can make an application for repayment of some of his money under Section 132 as mentioned below.

Repayment to hirer where owner recovers goods

Judges have no power to re-open hire agreements which are extortionate, since their power under Section 137 applies only to credit agreements. (See p 229).

However, a hirer who holds a regulated consumer hire agreement, may be granted financial relief under Section 132. This states that where the company recovers possession of the goods the court can let him off instalments he has missed or other money outstanding. It can also order the owners to repay to the hirer part or all of the money he has already paid.

The amount the hirer will get back will depend on what the judge considers fair, having regard to the extent the hirer has had enjoyment of the goods, ie whether the hirer has had a bad deal. Certainly today a hirer in the predicament of Mr Galbraith (above) would get back a good deal of his money. The court's power to order repayment will deter finance companies from acting unreasonably in enforcing their right of repossession.

Wrongful sale of goods held on hire

Another aspect in which hire differs from hire purchase is the position of the innocent purchaser of a motor vehicle. Clearly no hirer is entitled to sell goods he is renting. If he does so he may well be committing theft. The owners have the right to recover their goods even from an innocent purchaser (unless they were sold at a public market recognised in law as being a "market overt"). (See p 289).

Unlike hire-purchase, an innocent purchaser of a motor car from a hirer is not entitled to ownership under the Hire Purchase Act 1964, (discussed on p 259).

CHAPTER XVIII

RIGHTS OF WITHDRAWAL AND CANCELLATION

Time for withdrawal

A consumer credit agreement is not binding from the moment the consumer signs the form. No contract exists until the finance company also signs it. In law, the form he completes is merely an "offer" to the finance company. Inevitably some days will elapse for them to process his application and "accept" it. Until it reaches them and they approve and sign it, there is no agreement in existence. To put it in legal language they have to "accept" the consumer's "offer". Until they do, no regulated agreement has been made.

During this waiting period the consumer will have a breathing space of several days during which he may revoke his offer. If he does decide to withdraw he should immediately telephone the supplier or finance company. To make quite certain he should also write, the same day if possible, to confirm. If by the time he telephones they have already signed their part of the agreement and put it in the post to him, it is too late. Once they have posted it, there is a legally binding contract.

However, in certain cases (see below), notably doorstep selling, the Consumer Credit Act gives him a specific right of cancellation after the contract has been made, ie he is allowed a few days "cooling-off" period. This right to cancel is quite distinct from his right of withdrawal mentioned above.

In addition to giving him a right to cancel a "doorstep" credit agreement, the Act confirms the consumer's right to withdraw mentioned above and gives both withdrawal and cancellation the same legal consequences (see below).

Sending notice of withdrawal

Withdrawing from a prospective agreement does not have to be in any particular form. He can simply telephone or write to the credit broker, supplier or negotiator, provided that he indicates a clear intention to withdraw. (Section 57). Even though they were acting on behalf of the consumer each is regarded as the agent of the finance company (creditor) for the purpose of receiving notice of withdrawal. The consumer can tell the dealer or the finance house, whichever he finds more convenient.

Up to what moment is the consumer free to change his mind and pull out of the transaction? He must act quickly. Although he can revoke his offer at any time before the finance company posts its letter of acceptance his best course is to telephone and tell them that a letter confirming revocation is on its way.

The danger of relying simply on a letter without 'phoning first, is that he may find their letters cross in the post. If so, his letter of revocation will be ineffective, unless it arrives **before** the finance house post **their** letter of acceptance. The rule is that acceptance of an offer is final from the moment of posting. Revoking an offer operates only when the finance company are made aware of it. Until they are told, they can still accept, although the consumer's letter is lost in the post and never reaches them.

Consequence of withdrawal

Withdrawal, whether by the consumer or by the finance house, from a proposed agreement brings into operation Section 69 of the Consumer Credit Act. It is then treated in law in the same way as a cancellable agreement which has been cancelled by the consumer.

Withdrawal can put the consumer in a strong position.

For example, the dealer may allow the consumer to drive away a car as soon as he has paid the deposit and signed the proposal form. If, before the finance company accepts him, he gives notice of withdrawal, he can retain possession of the car until his deposit has been repaid.

Reclaiming the deposit on withdrawal

Where the consumer has paid money by way of deposit to the supplier or negotiator, he has the right to reclaim it from the finance company. Under the Act the person who negotiates a regulated agreement with the consumer is regarded as the agent of the finance company. (Section 56). Consequently it is responsible for what the negotiator says or does in the course of the transaction.

This is particularly important if he disappears or goes bankrupt. Although the finance company never actually receives the deposit, it must still repay the consumer. It cannot avoid liability for the supplier's acts or omissions. Whatever he says and whatever he arranges with the consumer is binding on it. Notices or small print clauses which say the finance company is not to be so liable are void.

Cancellable agreements and the cooling-off period

The consumer's statutory right to cancel is quite distinct from his choosing to withdraw. His power to withdraw after signing a regulated agreement lasts for no fixed period of time. It will depend on how long the finance company takes to process and post back their part of the agreement.

But in the case of doorstep credit, the consumer is allowed by law a minimum number of days after signing, called the "cooling-off period", during which he may cancel without obligation. The cooling-off period applies both to credit sale and hire-purchase or hiring, signed **at home.** Its object is to protect consumers from being talked into incurring a financial liability which they may later regret.

269

Every copy agreement given to the consumer or hirer must notify him of his right of cancellation—and must state the name and address of the person to whom notice of cancellation may be given.

Doorstep selling on credit

The "cooling-off" period and the right to cancel relate only to a regulated consumer credit or hire agreement where "door-step selling" methods have been employed. It is an important exception to the rule that once you have made a contract, you cannot get out of it unless the other side agrees.

The consumer will have a right of cancellation provided:

(a) he was not on "appropriate trade premises" when he signed the agreement AND

(b) he was subjected to sales patter (technically referred to as "oral representations") before signing.

Where was agreement signed?

A consumer may sign at his home or where he works himself, ie at his **own** business premises. In either case the agreement is cancellable. But if he signs at the dealer's premises it is not cancellable.

On the other hand, if after visiting the dealer's premises the consumer takes the agreement away to think about it and signs it later say at home or at his local public house, then the agreement will be cancellable.

The right of cancellation is restricted to situations where the consumer has been subjected to a line of "patter", ie the salesman or negotiator has made "oral representations" to the consumer. Thus a mail order transaction involving only advertising persuasion but **no personal contact** with the consumer prior to the agreement being signed, will be outside the "cooling-off" provisions.

Time limit for cancellation

The length of the "cooling-off" period during which he may cancel, is a minimum of five clear days but in practice it is likely to be a good deal longer. It depends on how long it takes to send the consumer a second copy of the agreement. The supplier is required to send this second copy to the consumer by post within seven days of the making of the agreement.

After receiving this second copy the consumer then has five full days to change his mind. In cases where a second copy of the agreement is not required to be sent to the consumer, his "cooling-off" period lasts for 14 days. (Section 68).

Written notice of cancellation is essential

In order to cancel, he must serve written notice stating his intention to withdraw within the time limits specified above. He can serve this notice on either of the following persons:

1 The creditor or owner.
2 The agent of the creditor or owner.
3 The person specified in the agreement.

Although a single telephone call is sufficient to withdraw from a prospective agreement, writing is necessary to cancel a "doorstep" agreement. It is not sufficient to call in at the shop and tell them you want to cancel, unless you also hand over a letter to this effect. It need not use any particular wording provided it indicates a clear intention to cancel.

Unlike a notice of withdrawal (see above), a notice of cancellation which is served by post is deemed to be effectively served when it is posted, whether or not it is actually received.

Effect of notice of cancellation

Written notice operates to cancel the agreement and any

"linked transaction". An example of a "linked transaction" would be an agreement to supply frozen foods for a freezer.

The consumer must return any goods supplied before cancellation but he is freed from any further payment under the agreement. Moreover he is entitled to have back any money he has paid. Where he has traded in an article in **part-exchange** he is entitled to have it returned to him within ten days of cancelling. If it is not returned within that period in substantially the same condition, he is entitled to have its part-exchange value instead. Thus the dealer will have a choice, either to return the article taken in part-exchange, or to pay him the part-exchange allowance in cash.

Returning goods after cancellation
The consumer must give back the goods obtained, when requested in writing, to the supplier or owner. Whilst they are in his possession he must take reasonable care of them, but he need not pay out of his own pocket to send them back.

He can simply wait until they are collected and if after 21 days following his notice of cancellation no-one comes to collect them, he is no longer under a legal duty to take reasonable care of them. He could put them out in the garden if he chooses.

When they come to collect the goods he is not entitled to retain them unless this is necessary to compel them to repay money due to him, eg his part-exchange allowance.

However in certain cases the customer is under no duty to return the goods at all:

(a) perishable goods;
(b) consumable goods which were consumed before cancellation;
(c) goods supplied to meet an emergency;
(d) materials like spare parts which the consumer has

incorporated before cancellation, into something else. But in the last two cases he will be liable to pay for the goods so used.

CHAPTER XIX

GUARANTEEING RELATIVES AND FRIENDS

If we sign to guarantee a friend or relative who is buying on credit we are in fact providing a form of security. Despite the many legal rules designed to protect them, in practice guarantors are frequently called upon to pay. Many people sign on behalf of acquaintances or workmates under the impression that they are giving little more than a character reference.

A guarantor who genuinely believed he was signing merely a reference or was misled into so believing might escape legal liability. However such a defence would be likely to succeed only in special circumstances, for example, if he was unable to read and had been deceived as to the true nature or legal consequences of the document he was signing.

A surety may be either a guarantor or indemnifier. By signing he undertakes to make good any loss the lender may suffer should the consumer fail to pay. This is not the kind of guarantee given by manufacturers in respect of their products. (See p 83). In law that type of guarantee is often called a "warranty".

Security must be written

"Any security provided in relation to a regulated agreement shall be expressed in writing," (Consumer Credit Act 1974, Section 105). In practice, a consumer is often required to provide someone to ensure he will pay under a credit agreement. The risks involved in allowing him credit often justify a finance company demanding this extra safeguard, so that if the consumer himself defaults, then his surety can be called upon to make good their loss. It may be because the consumer is not himself a householder or is under the age of 25 years.

There is also the risk that a hire-purchase consumer may be irresponsible and either damage the goods or abandon them or even sell them. It is quite understandable therefore that lenders should insist that a third person also signs to safeguard them against their making a loss in the transaction.

Where security is provided by a document of guarantee or indemnity three parties are involved:

(i)   the creditor who is lending the money
(ii) the debtor who is borrowing the money
(iii) the guarantor or indemnifier who undertakes payment if the debtor himself defaults.

Consequently a finance company or bank which takes a guarantee may look to two possible sources of repayment:

first to the debtor, but if he defaults,

then to the guarantor or indemnifier.

Simplicity and convenience

In practice, a guarantee is a very convenient form of security for a loan or credit agreement. The advantage to the consumer is simplicity, speed and absence of legal formalities. All he need do is to persuade a friend or relative to put his signature at the foot of the document of guarantee, although, as we have observed, the person taking on this responsibility does not always realise that he will be standing in the shoes of the debtor and may face heavy financial demands if he defaults.

Indemnity need not be written

The distinction between a guarantee and an indemnity goes back more than three hundred years when Parliament decreed that all guarantees must be in writing. Writing is not essential for an indemnity, even today, save as **security for a regulated agreement.**

The promise to keep another person free from loss is usually called an indemnity. It is binding even if the promise is given by word of mouth only. However, if it relates to an agreement regulated by the Consumer Credit Act, a spoken promise of indemnity is not binding, unless confirmed in writing.

Policies of insurance need not be written

One common example of an **indemnity** is an insurance policy to cover any accidental loss (excluding life or personal injury insurance). If the insured's house burns down or his car is damaged, the insurance company promises that, in return for a fixed premium, it will pay any loss the insured person suffers as a result of that particular kind of accident.

Insurance policies are in practice invariably in writing but because they are not a guarantee, a written document is **not** in law essential. Thus, if an employee of your insurance company tells you over the telephone that cover is effective, this will bind the insurance company although a policy has not been issued to you before the loss occurred.

Guarantee contrasted with indemnity

In theory a guarantee is a special kind of indemnity. It is a promise to meet all loss arising if a third person defaults in payment, say, of a debt.

One hundred years ago in the tiny fishing village of Brixham the chairman of the Board of Health asked a local builder to connect up certain drains. The builder agreed to do the work provided the Board or the chairman himself would authorise it. In order to get the work done the chairman told the builder "Go on, Mountstephen, and do the work and I will see you paid".

In fact, the Board never authorised the work so the

builder sought payment from the chairman himself. The court held that the chairman was liable on his spoken promise. Had he given a guarantee, he would not have been bound because it was not in writing, but the words "I will see you paid" constituted an indemnity, not a guarantee. *Mountstephen v. Lakeman* (1871).

If Mr Brown says to a trader, "Supply goods to my brother-in-law. If he does not pay, I will", this is a **guarantee** and **must** be in writing because Mr Brown accepts liability **only if** his brother-in-law fails to pay.

However, if Mr. Brown says, "Supply the goods to my brother-in-law. I will make sure you are paid", this is an indemnity since Mr Brown is undertaking full responsibility to **ensure payment.** His liability to pay has not been made conditional on his brother-in-law defaulting and hence written evidence of his promise is not necessary. In practice, this distinction between a guarantee and an indemnity is largely artificial but it can have important consequences in cases where the Consumer Credit Act does not apply.

Protection of indemnifiers

Before the Consumer Credit Act an indemnifier was particularly in need of protection since he could be bound by even a spoken promise. An indemnity often imposed on him a heavier financial burden than had the borrower himself. For example, he could be required, if the borrower defaulted in one instalment, to pay the whole outstanding balance in a lump sum, although the borrower himself was allowed to pay by instalments.

Where credit is given under a regulated agreement, the Act gives identical protection to guarantors and indemnifiers. They are not bound unless they sign a written document whose contents comply with regulations made under the Act. Secondly, anyone who signs to give security for a regulated agreement has the same rights, eg to pay by instalments, as the consumer has.

Rights of every surety

In all other respects too a guarantor or indemnifier enjoys the same measure of protection under the Act as does the original borrower or hirer. (Section 113). He is entitled to receive the same information and copy documents. In particular he must be sent a copy of any notice of default. He may demand an up-to-date statement of account at any time. Any agreement (or clause in it) which is unenforceable against the consumer (debtor) is likewise unenforceable against the guarantor or indemnifier. The basic rule under the Act is that his total liability may never be more onerous than that of the principal debtor for whom he signed as surety.

Consumer under eighteen

A necessary exception to this last rule is where the person obtaining credit is under 18 or is otherwise not of full capacity, eg a mental patient.

Section 113(7) of the Consumer Credit Act allows a written indemnity to be enforced where the consumer is a minor or is otherwise not of full capacity just as if he were of full age and capacity when he made the agreement. Nor surprisingly, traders are reluctant to deal with a person under 18 except on a cash basis. However credit may be obtainable if, say, his parent or a householder is prepared to sign as surety for him.

In this situation a form of indemnity and not a guarantee must be used owing to the legal rule that a debt for the supply of "non-essential" goods, or a loan, to an infant is void. If so, it follows that any guarantee of that debt is also void. However, if his parent signs a form of indemnity, the parent's liability to pay is quite independent of whether his son is legally liable or not.

Summary of protection given to guarantors and indemnifiers

As we saw, no surety may be subjected to any greater

liability than the consumer (debtor) himself. For example, he cannot be required to pay a larger sum than the consumer had to pay nor can he be obliged to make a payment at an earlier date or in a different manner than the consumer had to pay.

If the security document is unsigned or if any of the regulations made by the Director-General of Fair Trading as to the contents of the security agreement are not observed, the security, be it by way of guarantee or by indemnity, is "improperly executed".

This means that it is not effective save on an order of the court.

Where the court decides to enforce a security which is improperly executed, it has wide powers to help a guarantor or indemnifier who has been prejudiced. For example, it may vary the security document or order the amount payable by the surety to be reduced.

However an irregularity in the security agreement has no effect on the validity of the regulated credit agreement itself. The credit agreement is still valid even though the security agreement may be unenforceable.

CHAPTER XX

SHOPS AND SHOPLIFTING

Is a shop a public place?

A shop is private property. The management may request a person to leave without giving any reason. They may object to his unkempt appearance or behaviour or because he is drunk or is suspected of shoplifting, provided he is asked discreetly and no one overhears.

If he becomes troublesome and a breach of the peace is feared, the police may be called. The management may not object to serving a customer on account of his race, colour or ethnic background (Race Relations Act 1976).

However, since a shop is a place to which the public have access, a shopkeeper is not entitled to keep a firearm or offensive weapon under the counter to protect himself against possible attack.

Liability of shops for safety of customers

The management owes a duty of care to all visitors not to allow either the condition of the premises or anything done on the premises to cause harm to any customer or visitor. It must ensure that the shop floors, stairs and passages are properly maintained and their surfaces kept free of slippery substances. Hand-rails must be fitted where necessary for safety of customers. Fire precautions must also be observed and fire-fighting appliances provided.

Anyone entering a shop is regarded in law as an "invitee". A passer-by who does not intend to buy anything in the shop is an invitee if he merely uses it as a convenient short cut between two roads.

All lawful visitors, including persons permitted by

implication or custom to come into the premises, such as delivery men, salesmen, postmen, inspectors etc, are invitees in law and can expect such reasonable precautions to be taken for their safety. However, there is no such implied permission to enter for someone who comes in for an unlawful purpose, eg to commit theft. If a shoplifter injures himself on a defective stairway while making his escape, the shop would naturally not be responsible for his injury.

Danger of Spillages

May Ward was shopping in Tesco's supermarket when she slipped and fell on some yoghurt that had been spilt on the floor. The judge awarded her damages of £137 on the ground that she had proved a case of negligence on the part of the shop.

The supermarket denied negligence and gave evidence of their system for keeping the floor clean. This included brushing it as often as five or six times a day. On average, a spillage occurred about 10 times a week. The staff had instructions that if they saw a spillage on the floor they were to stay by it and call another member of the staff to clean it up.

Mrs Ward could not say how long the spillage had been on the floor but on another occasion she noticed that orange squash spilt on the floor remained there for about 15 minutes during which time no member of the staff dealt with it.

The Court of Appeal held that the supermarket knew or ought to have known of the likelihood of spillages on the floor and the danger to customers if spillages were not dealt with quickly. The supermarket could not satisfy the court that Mrs Ward would have slipped on the yoghurt **despite a proper system** designed to give reasonable protection to customers against spillage.

To escape liability the supermarket had to prove that the

yoghurt had been spilled only seconds before Mrs Ward stepped on it and consequently their staff had not had sufficient time to spot it and attend to it. *Ward v. Tesco Stores Ltd.* (1975).

Unsafe Shop Display

Bottles of fruit juice were stacked on shelving which consisted of loose sheets of glass held down by the weight of the bottles. The bottles were kept in place by sellotape. One shopper tried to remove a bottle and was cut and bruised when the display collapsed. The defence that the bottles were for display only was disallowed as insufficient notice was given to shoppers not to touch the display. Her claim for £165 for her injuries was upheld. Decision of London Small Claims Court (1977).

Shoplifting

Whilst a customer who has come under suspicion although not actually caught stealing, may be excluded from the shop, the liability of a shoplifter to arrest is strictly governed by law. The staff may arrest a shoplifter only if:
1 He is **seen** stealing.
2 A theft has occurred and there are reasonable grounds for believing that he is the one who stole the article.

Arrest and wrongful arrest

A customer who is arrested but subsequently acquitted of any charge could claim compensation for "wrongful arrest". For this reason staff should exercise extreme caution and should not act on **suspicion alone**. A vigilant employee may easily misinterpret a casual glance round the shop as a furtive check that no one is watching.

Whilst it is the duty of all employees to arrest anyone seen committing theft, the danger is that the detective or assistant may act too quickly. The usual practice, therefore, is to wait until the suspect has passed the cash counter and left the store before moving to intercept. This will usually exclude any possible claim that he intended to pay for the article. While still on the premises he may contend that he put it into a bag for convenience and did not intend to avoid payment.

Arrest by a private person

In one case a customer was seen behaving suspiciously and the staff were convinced that he had concealed an article but when he was searched nothing could be found. The outcome was that he received damages for wrongful arrest. The judge held that a private person (including a store detective) is justified in making an arrest only in the following circumstances:

- Any person may arrest without warrant anyone who is, or whom he with reasonable cause suspects to be **in the act** of committing an arrestable offence.

- Where an arrestable offence **has actually** been committed, any person may arrest without a warrant anyone who is, or whom he with **reasonable cause** suspects to be, guilty of the offence.

Consequently someone who is wrongly accused need only tell the detective he is mistaken and walk away, although to show integrity one could tender one's name and address.

However, if the detective tells the suspect that he **must** come with him, ie that he is arresting him, then it would be very unwise to resist arrest. Incidentally, it is a rule of English law that anyone being arrested is entitled to know at once the nature of the **charge**, unless this is apparent from the circumstances.

Where the store detective has used unwarranted force, this constitutes an assault. Damages would be increased if the innocent shopper has been detained in the manager's office for an unreasonable length of time or has suffered exceptional embarrassment or humiliation. However, if the shopper **voluntarily** agrees to go to the manager's office without being arrested, he cannot sue unless later kept there against his will.

Suspect's right to remain silent

Shoppers have been known to genuinely forget to pay and it is important to remember that nobody against whom an offence is alleged is bound to reply. However, if a charge is feared a concise, clear explanation as to the error is better given at the time than later. If possible, any explanation should be made in front of a witness.

A consumer unfortunate enough to be involved in such a situation should, as soon as possible, compile a note of events and details of what was said and who was present. He can then refer to this "contemporaneous" note, should the matter come to court months later, to prove what took place. When giving his evidence he will be permitted to "refresh his memory" from his note (as police officers invariably do).

Once the shopper is taken to the manager's office and the police have been called, the facts will be related to the police in the shopper's presence. The suspected person is usually cautioned by the police that he need say nothing unless he wishes to give an explanation. If the officer is satisfied that the allegation is founded he will inform the suspect that he is arresting him. The suspect must then be taken to a police station for routine documentation and formal charge. Further questions may be asked of him under caution but here again he has the right to **remain silent**. He will then be charged and given a further caution to the effect that he need not say anything in reply but whatever he does say will be taken down and may be used in evidence. Normally the police will allow the suspect to be released on bail.

The shopper's refusal to make any statement either spoken or written is in no way prejudicial. However, anything he says at this stage will be binding on him.

The fact that he has not signed a written statement does not make his remarks any the less binding. The suspect's best course is to state that he wishes to take legal advice and see a solicitor before he makes any statement.

To some extent the prevalence of shoplifting may be partly due to the layout of modern stores. It is often not easy to see where the till or cash desk is situated and not all stores have an obvious check-out point at which to pay. Displays that induce people to buy unfortunately at times induce some to steal, often in many cases articles not really needed. One young airline employee who could not speak any English ruined his career when trying on a splendid leather coat, far beyond his meagre pay and then thinking he could slip out unnoticed. The irony was that he had gone there only to buy a pullover.

By contrast, the young Italian who walked out wearing a brightly coloured sports jacket was acquitted. His excuse was that he wanted to see how it looked in the daylight and the Court accepted this.

Mistakes on the part of the shop
The law says a person is guilty of theft whenever he dishonestly appropriates something. Appropriation means assuming ownership. Even though a person is perfectly honest when another's property comes into his possession, he nevertheless commits theft the moment he decides to deal with it **dishonestly**. Thus every housewife knows that if she is given too much change it is her duty to return it.

Suppose she takes an item from the display rack knowing it is underpriced by mistake? Does she commit an offence by allowing the cashier to ring up the item at the price marked, when she knows that it should be marked at a higher price? A judge says not, because when she hands the article to the cashier this constitutes her offer to buy it at the price marked and when the cashier hands over the account slip for payment this constitutes the shop's acceptance.

By paying for the article she honours her offer to buy it at that price. There is no theft since she is not dishonestly appropriating it. However, their mistake would not prevent the shop later claiming in the county court the amount undercharged if they could prove that she knew the article was mistakenly priced.

On the other hand a housewife might be in danger of committing an offence when she asks for half a dozen electric light bulbs and the shop assistant puts eight in her basket but charges for six only. On her return home she counts the bulbs and finds two extra for which she has not paid.

Before the Theft Act 1968, she would not have been guilty of an offence if she kept the extra bulbs but under the present law, she is technically guilty of theft unless she takes immediate steps to return the bulbs or pay for them as soon as the mistake is discovered.

Dishonest intention necessary

The Magistrate must be sure beyond reasonable doubt, that there was an intention to cheat the shop. Where guilt is not proved beyond reasonable doubt, she must be acquitted but her acquittal does not necessarily imply proof of payment by the accused. When he acquits, the magistrate is not saying "I am certain she is not guilty". He is simply saying "I am not certain she is guilty".

The problem of proof of guilt is, in practice, sometimes very difficult. Even when a magistrate convicts, he can never be absolutely certain of guilt. If faced with the alternative of believing either the professional witness, eg a store detective or police officer – as against a private person, a magistrate will tend usually, to believe the professional.

Previous convictions

One difficulty from the Magistrate's point of view is that

he is not allowed to know (as English law stands at present) whether the accused has any previous convictions. Naturally, a person can cite his good character in his defence but where the accused has previous convictions, this will not come out in court, unless he attacks the character of one of the prosecution witnesses or pretends that he has no convictions. In practice, a magistrate can read between the lines. Failure of defence counsel to assert previous good character can generally be taken as implying at least one conviction for dishonesty.

Legal Costs

Under the Costs in Criminal Cases Act 1952, magistrates' courts have power to order a convicted person to pay the prosecutor's costs. Conversely, if he is acquitted, the court can order the prosecutor to pay the accused's defence costs, 'as it thinks just and reasonable'. The snag is that the court is not obliged to award legal costs to the winner. All too often an accused person who has been acquitted will be left to pay his own legal bill because at present magistrates have a discretion, but no duty, to give costs. In practice, lawyers generally find that magistrates will exercise this discretionary power to award costs more often against an accused person on conviction than in his favour on acquittal.

Although free legal aid is now common, not all defendants are financially eligible. Paradoxically, whereas the poorer person who gets legal aid will not suffer financially, the wealthier person may still find himself landed with a heavy legal bill despite having been acquitted.

CHAPTER XXI

CRIME AND THE CONSUMER

Buying Stolen Goods

It is quite possible for a consumer to buy an article which was originally stolen without being aware of its origin. If he buys it in all **innocence** he will not be guilty of the offence of receiving stolen property. Under the Theft Act 1968, this offence is now termed "dishonest handling".

If the police make investigations and accuse the consumer of dishonest handling, it is not for him to prove his innocence. It is for the police to prove dishonesty on his part, ie that he knew or believed the article to be stolen.

Such proof may be apparent from the circumstances in which the article has been bought. Typically buying a camera or a leather coat in a pub or from a chance acquaintance is ·obviously foolish and dangerous. In such circumstances one's suspicions ought immediately to be aroused as to the origin of the goods. Such a buyer will find it hard to convince a court of his innocence particularly if he has paid a very low price for the article.

The moral is not to risk buying from unusual sources or in suspicious circumstances. If in doubt, do not be tempted.

Guilty Knowledge

Although in some cases the court will inevitably infer guilty knowledge from the circumstances of the purchase, nevertheless the test of guilty knowledge is subjective. A court must decide what the buyer himself knew or must have suspected. If the buyer deliberately closed his eyes to the circumstances a court will be likely to infer that he must have realised the article was "bent". A buyer is not entitled to shut his eyes if the circumstances seem suspicious.

It must be proved that the buyer had guilty knowledge at the moment of purchase. Should he subsequently be told, eg by the police, that the jewellery he has bought in good faith came from a burglary, he will not be guilty of dishonestly handling stolen goods. **To retain** an article innocently acquired after being told of its true origin is not in itself a breach of the law.

Recovering stolen goods from an innocent buyer

In theory the Magistarates' or Crown Court has power to order the return of stolen goods to the true owner when it convicts the thief. But in practice a criminal court will seldom order an **innocent** buyer to relinquish them.

The tendency is to leave disputes about ownership to the civil courts. However, when convicting the thief it will often order **him** to compensate the person from whom he stole. But conviction of the thief does not mean the loser gets his goods back automatically.

Whether the true owner can claim back an article which was originally stolen from him will depend on the circumstances in which the buyer obtained it. Strictly the buyer has no right to keep it and the loser can obtain an order from the county court for its return to him. If the buyer has parted with it he can be compelled to pay its value to the loser.

Suppose your car is stolen. You discover eventually that it was bought at auction by Smith. You can sue Smith for the return of your car or its value. You can if you wish also sue the auctioneer for its value on the ground that he "converted" it in law. Both the auctioneer and Smith, although innocent parties, are liable to recompense you. It is not necessary for you to trace who stole your car.

Marker overt

However, S. 22(1), Sale of Goods Act, can sometimes protect

a consumer who has in good faith bought an article without knowledge that the seller had no legal right to sell it. This protection applies only if you buy at a public market in England. It does not apply to public markets in Scotland or Wales. Also buyers from shops in the City of London are protected provided they buy during normal shopping hours.

Buyers at shops outside the city boundary, eg in the Strand or West End, are not protected if the goods they purchase turn out to be stolen. But there is no list of markets where we may safely shop. In practice it is impossible for the consumer to know whether a market is protected as being "constituted by law".

The Law Reform Committee in 1966 recommended that anyone who innocently buys stolen goods, either at retail trade premises or at a public auction, should be entitled to keep them but unfortunately this sweeping protection has not been implemented.

The consumer's difficulty in ascertaining whether a particular market or fair counts as a market overt came before the Court of Appeal some years ago. A man who had hired a car from the Bishopsgate Motor Finance Corporation took it to Maidstone and tried to sell it by auction there without success. Later in the day he managed to sell it privately in the market at Maidstone. The man who bought the car proved that Maidstone Market had been legally established in 1747 and consequently ranked as a market overt. Being an innocent buyer he was allowed by the court to retain ownership of the vehicle so that the company's claim to the car failed.

Cars on hire-purchase

What if a car is not bought in an established market? Since 1964 a private buyer is protected by law even though the car is still on hire-purchase or subject to a credit agreement. Legally a car which is on hire-purchase belongs to the finance company, but a private buyer may be quite unaware of their interest in the car. If he buys it in good faith, without any suspicion, the finance company cannot claim the car from him.

However, this protection only applies to buyers of cars which are on hire-purchase. it would not apply to a car which was **hired** or subject to a rental agreement.

A buyer who is suspicious can check to confirm that no finance company owns the car by getting in touch with the AA or the RAC or any Citizens' Advice Bureau. They will check free of charge within 48 hours with the National Hire-Purchase Records and tell the prospective purchaser if the car is still subject to an unpaid hire-purchase agreement.

Although the log book is not proof of ownership, a seller who cannot produce it should arouse suspicion. A buyer who pays before he receives the log book may not be able to keep the car if the dealer has been guilty of fraud. The safest course for the buyer is to hand over his cheque or cash in exchange for the log book. Alternatively, he could give a post-dated cheque and inform the seller that he will stop the cheque if the log book does not arrive by a stated date.

Registration of sale of vehicle compulsory
One way in which the law tries to keep a check on stolen cars is by insisting that anyone who sells his car must promptly notify the Vehicle Registration Office. Failure to do so can involve a fine of £20.

The buyer too must register the change of ownership at once by sending in the log book. He is not entitled to wait until he needs to renew the excise licence before registering his ownership. Failure to register the purchase promptly can involve a fine of £50.

Theft by finding
A person who finds something which has been lost is usually

entitled to keep it provided it is impossible to trace the owner. He commits theft who **dishonestly** appropriates property belonging to another with the intention of permanently depriving the other of it. He will be guilty of theft also where the person to whom it belongs can be discovered by taking reasonable steps. The obvious step when something is found is to report it to the nearest police station.

It is not necessary to hand the item found to the police. It is sufficient to notify them by letter. The finder can keep it until the owner becomes known.

Finders Keepers

The normal rule is that anything found in a public place belongs to the finder only if the true owner cannot be traced. Thus anyone finding bank notes in the street or in a place to which the public have access, for example, on the floor of a shop or supermarket, can keep the notes if no one claims them. The notes do not belong to the proprietor of the shop because it is a public place. One exception to this rule is that anyone who finds an article on a London bus must declare his find to the London Transport Board. Nevertheless, if the owner cannot be traced, the Board must return the item to the finder.

Items found on Private Property

Anyone lawfully on someone else's land, for example, a farm worker or contractor or even a neighbour paying a social visit will have a better claim to any unattached, **ownerless** object which he finds on the surface than has the owner of the land himself (although a trespasser does not).

Where the finder is not entitled to access to the land the rule "finders keepers" is not applicable because he is a trespasser. Thus lost golf balls lying loose on the course belong to the club and no stranger may come onto the course to pick them up.

Some years ago the owners of a golf course received complaints that strangers were making a practice of coming on to the course to look for lost golf balls which they would then sell. The owners prosecuted one of the finders (who was not a member of their club) for theft of the golf balls he had found. The court agreed that the finder had committed theft.

However, golfers who are **lawfully** on the course can keep any lost balls they come across – unless they happen to have the owner's name printed on them – an uncommon practice and one not well-regarded in golfing circles despite the fact that it establishes ownership.

Buried Treasure

Where ownerless articles are found fixed to property or lying under the surface, the rule is that the **occupier** of the property has the right to keep them, not the finder. In 1963 two workmen found a safe full of banknotes fixed into the basement wall of a house they were demolishing. Since the legal tenants of the property were the Corporation of London the court accordingly held that the money found belonged to the Corporation. In another case some contractors who were engaged to clean out a pool found two rings **buried** in the mud at the bottom. The owner of the land was entitled to the rings found.

In the case of *Hannah v. Peel* a soldier found a brooch lying loose in a crevice on top of a window frame in the house in which he was billeted. The owner of the house had never been in occupation since he bought it. As the article was found lying loose in the house the soldier was allowed to keep it. Had it been buried he would have had to surrender it to the owner of the house.

How Long does Ownership Last?

Mr Russell hid a biscuit tin containing almost £2,000

in the roof of his house. He was a very forgetful man, according to his widow, and forgot to get it out when they moved some years later. Three years after the new owners had taken possession some workmen who were installing a cooker dislodged a few bricks and discovered the biscuit tin. The tin and contents were handed over to the police. They disregarded Mr Russell's claim and gave the money to the owners of the house. Mr Russell died before the case was heard but the judge believed his widow's story that **she** was the one entitled to the money. The judge reasoned that when Mr Russell sold the house he had no intention of parting with the money in the biscuit tin as well. He continued therefore to be the legal owner of the money.

In such circumstances the loser of the item has six years from the date on which it was **found** to make his claim. He does not have to make a legal claim within six years of the date on which he **lost** it.

Treasure Seekers

A popular and often profitable hobby is the use of electronic devices to discover buried metal. Favourite hunting grounds are the sites of ancient monuments of which there are about 9,000 in Great Britain. The majority of these sites are in fact privately owned so that anything dug up on them by a treasure seeker will belong to the owner of the land. Accordingly unlawful diggers could be prosecuted for theft if they keep their finds, even though it is a site to which the public have free access.

Treasure trove belongs to the Crown but its concealment is no longer an offence. Items termed "treasure trove" are not simply lost. They are called treasure trove only if they are of gold or silver and have been buried in time of peril, the owner intending but never in fact returning to retrieve them. Such finds are usually of considerable historical interest and the Crown invariably pays their full value to the finder. By this means the

Government encourages finders to hand them in so that they may be purchased by an appropriate museum. Nevertheless failure to report the finding of treasure trove is not a criminal offence these days.

Picking Wild Fruit

Children and grown-ups often go into fields to gather blackberries or mushrooms. In the UK farmers and land-owners are tolerant since trespass is not a crime provided no damage is done and there is no intention to be dishonest. Thus no one is entitled to steal apples or other produce. But the law makes an exception in the case of picking certain items:

mushrooms or fungus growing wild

fruit growing wild

fruit or foliage of a plant, shrub or tree growing wild. Provided you do not propose to sell them and do not gather them for reward or for commercial purposes, taking them is not theft.

CHAPTER XXII

TAKING THE TRADER TO COURT

We saw in Chapter I the distinction between a civil and a criminal action. Bringing an offender before a criminal court is almost exclusively the task of the police or governmental officials like Trading Standards Officers. Criminal proceedings are begun in the magistrates' court but if the matter is serious are transferred to the crown court.

We saw how a criminal court can, when it convicts a trader of an offence, also order him to pay compensation to the individual consumer. Generally, however, it will be up to the consumer himself to bring a civil claim.

Our civil courts are arranged in a two-tier system. The High Court deals with claims above £2,000. Claims for smaller amounts are dealt with in the county court.

The High Court

The average consumer will seldom have any need to concern himself with the High Court. It is based in the Law Courts in the Strand, London WC2, but has district registries in all the larger towns, usually in the same building as the local county court office.

The High Court is divided into three sections, each for a different area of law. A person wishing to petition for divorce will apply to the Family Division which deals with all family matters. Anyone making an application in connection with a trust or the estate of a deceased person will apply to the Chancery Division. The Queen's Bench Division deals with other general areas of the law, eg commercial claims.

Legal Costs

Bringing a claim in the High Court is far more complicated than in the county court and in practice a claimant would need to employ a solicitor to handle the legal work. But if his claim is successful his cost of employing a lawyer is usually added to the bill of the person who loses, except in the following two situations:

1 A defendant in the High Court who is ordered to pay less than £350 will not have to pay any legal costs to the successful claimant. This means that all legal fees and expenses incurred by the claimant will have to come out of his own pocket.

2 Where the High Court awards a claimant less than £1,200, it will not allow him his **full** legal costs. The party who loses will not be ordered to pay legal costs and expenses except on the county court scale, which is much lower.

For these reasons claims for less than £2,000 are seldom brought in the High Court.

Insurance against legal costs and expenses

It is well known that legal costs sometimes exceed the amount recovered. One householder who complained that his garden fence had been damaged instructed solicitors to claim £19 from a firm whose driver had knocked it down. In the outcome the solicitors' charges alone amounted to £20. In another case a consumer's complaint against contractors who had installed central heating resulted in his receiving an allowance of £30 on the ground that their work had not been completed properly. But his solicitors' fees, which fortunately were covered by his insurance policy, amounted to £99.

A consumer who has been dissuaded from taking legal action on account of the potential cost involved, could consider insuring under a family, general and consumer protection policy. The fact that the other side knows he is insured and consequently has the financial resources of the insurance company behind him can result in an early settlement, often without the need to go to court at all.

Some insurance companies offer a "legal expenses" insurance policy to individuals and families. Insurance is usful for those whose income group is too high to qualify for legal aid, yet lack the personal resources to take court action themselves.

Under a scheme offered by Lloyd's the policy-holder contributes 10 per cent of the cost of the legal expenses incurred, the remaining 90 per cent being met by the insurance company. Another scheme called DAS Legal Expenses Insurance offered by Phoenix Assurance in conjunction with a German-based company meets legal costs in full.

The County Courts

Since most consumer claims are below the £2,000 ceiling, the county court will deal with them. The county court will also deal with any claim to which the Consumer Credit Act applies. Thus a claim by a lender for arrears due under a regulated agreement (up to £5,000) will normally come before the county court.

To encourage consumers taking their complaints to the county court without legal help, important changes have been introduced in recent years. First, the county court has simplified its form of "request" so that it can be filled in without legal assistance.

Secondly there is a new rule which denies legal expenses to a person who wins a claim for less than £200. This rule discourages both claimants and defendants employing a solicitor since even if they win, all their legal expenses will have to come out of their own pocket. In the past the risk of having to pay the trader's legal costs if he lost tended to discourage a consumer from going to court.

Similarly where a trader sues for less than £200, the

consumer will not have to pay any additional legal costs if he disputes the claim even though he loses.

Arbitration in the County Court

Another modernisation aimed at encouraging consumers coming to court has been the introduction of simple arbitration hearings to deal with small claims. Arbitration cuts out intimidating formalities and legal rules and normally takes place in private.

Although heard in the county court, strict rules of procedure do not apply to an arbitration. Formalities are kept to a minimum to encourage the ordinary person to handle his own case. As the investigation by the arbitrator usually takes the form of a discussion, no one needs a lawyer.

Either the claimant or the defendant can request arbitration if the amount in dispute is not above £200. If the amount exceeds £200, neither party is obliged to accept arbitration unless the judge orders it.

Arbitration by voluntary Small Claims Court

Arbitration to settle disputes between traders and consumers can also be requested in the London Small Claims Court which is a voluntary organisation dealing with disputes up to £350. It does not come under the official county court system. There is a similar small claims court in Manchester. The advantage of a small claims court is that its fee for arbitration is less than at the official county court. The disadvantage is that it can only decide a dispute and has no power to enforce payment. If the trader does not comply with an order of the small claims court, the consumer will have to transfer the order to the county court to get payment.

Arbitration under trade codes of practice

The codes of practice laid down by the major trade

associations and approved by the Office of Fair Trading provide for conciliation and arbitration of disputes between a trader and his customer. If conciliation fails the documents can be sent for arbitration to the Institute of Arbitrators, 75 Cannon Street, London EC4N 5BH. In order to keep costs as low as possible the arbitrator will normally consider only the relevant documents, so it will not be necessary for either the trader or consumer to be present.

The customer has the right to take his dispute to the county court instead of arbitration if he prefers. He can also apply to the county court to enforce the decision of the arbitrator.

Which County Court has jurisdiction?

There are more than 350 county courts. There is a county court office in most towns to cover the surrounding area.

If the person you propose to sue, ie the defendant, is not in your local area, inquire at your nearest county court office. They will tell you in which county court to start your claim. This will be the court nearest which the person you wish to sue lives or carries on business.

When you can sue in your local county court

However even if the person you wish to sue does not live locally, often you may make your claim in your **local** court. The test is whether the events giving rise to your claim occurred locally.

Where you have bought a defective item from the **local branch** of a chain of stores, you can still sue the head office of the chain in your local court even though the local branch has closed down.

If you lent some money to a neighbour who has **moved** to another town without repaying, you can sue him in your local county court (ie where the loan was made). Alternatively you can start your claim in the court nearest which he now lives.

If you have bought something **by post** you can also sue in your local county court, should you have sent money in answer to an advertisement which promises to send the item on receipt of the correct price.

Starting a court action

To bring a claim in the county court you must fill in a form called a "Request". On this form the claimant who starts the action is called the plaintiff. The person against whom the claim is made is called the defendant. Forms of request can be obtained from any county court office. Although the officials at the court cannot give actual legal advice, the court staff will help the claimant to complete this form. In fact the form contains a number of questions which involve legal terminology. These may be left to the court staff, who will tell you if any further information is required. Basically all the information you need to insert on the form is your own full name and address and the name and address of the person against whom you are bringing the claim. You must also state the amount which you are claiming. On this depends the court fee required. You must keep the receipt for this fee because you will need it again, eg to draw money out of court at the end of the action. If you would like your case to be dealt with in private under the arbitration scheme, say so on your request form.

Particulars of claim

You will need to write on a separate sheet of paper a note saying what your claim is all about. A clear and concise letter will serve the purpose. The court will require two copies of this letter. You will also need to keep a copy for yourself. The court sends a copy to the defendant together with a form of summons.

You should set out quite briefly the facts of your complaint. You do not have to tell the whole story from start to finish because you will have a chance to state this when you come to court.

You can state that you wish to claim because:

(i) The article bought is defective
(ii) Goods ordered and paid for have not been delivered
(iii) Goods have been delivered but in a damaged condition
(iv) The article delivered was not the article ordered
(v) Repair work carried out by a garage or by a builder is faulty
(vi) A carpet sent off to be dry-cleaned was returned torn or not returned at all.

Example of particulars of claim

1 On July 5 1978 I bought an XYZ bicycle from the ABC bicycle shop.
2 Ten days after I bought it the frame cracked.
3 Consequently the bicycle is useless. I asked the shop to replace it but they said I should write to the manufacturer.
4 I claim from the ABC bicycle shop the sum of £50 which I paid for the bicycle.
5 I would like this case dealt with by arbitration.

Default Summons

In the above case the claimant or plaintiff is seeking a specific sum of money, ie the amount he paid for the bicycle. The court staff will probably tell you that a Default Summons can be issued. This means that no court hearing will have to take place unless the shop states its defence within 14 days.

Getting judgment without a court hearing

The great majority of legal claims are in fact not defended. Once a court summons is received by the defendant, very often he pays the amount claimed into court. Alternatively he may pay into court a lesser amount than is claimed.

If this is accepted by the claimant in satisfaction, the court action need proceed no further.

If no defence reaches the court office within 14 days you will be entitled to have judgment entered against the shop. This is done by a very simple form obtainable at the court office. But you must bring with you the form of receipt which you got when you paid your court fee (the plaint note).

If the shop disputes your claim, it must send to the court within 14 days its statement of defence. For example, it may reply that the bicycle is not defective. A copy of this defence will then be sent to you. The court will then fix a date for hearing.

An Ordinary Summons

The court office will issue an ordinary summons where no exact debt is owing and the appropriate amount of compensation will have to be assessed by the judge. Take the case of a bicycle being defective, eg the handlebars breaking while you are riding. You have fallen off and injured your hand and wish to claim compensation for your injury, time off work, cost of repairs to the bicycle and so on. An ordinary summons has a date fixed for hearing in about two months' time. This date will be written on your receipt. (If you cannot attend on the date given you should write to the court registrar immediately stating the reason and requesting a different date.)

If your claim is not disputed judgment will be given in your favour on that date. But if the defendant disputes your claim, the court registrar will hold a preliminary investigation. This is called a "pre-trial review".

The Pre-Trial Review

Where you have issued an ordinary summons the pre-trial review takes place in private at the court offices on the date shown on your plaint note. Where you have issued a default summons the court will write to you in the event of a defence being sent in, enclosing a copy and giving the date for pre-trial review. You should bring your documents to the pre-trial review becuse if the defendant does not attend you will most likely be given judgment after telling the registrar all about your complaint. Consequently the registrar will want to see any letters, bills, receipts and other documents relating to your claim.

If the defendant attends the hearing the registrar will try to sort the case out then and there.

Is there any chance of coming to an agreement without a trial? For example, the shop may offer to repay half the cost of the bicycle. If you are prepared to accept this, then the registrar will enter judgment for that amount.

If no agreement is possible the registrar will then give any directions he feels necessary to clarify what the dispute is all about and will fix a final hearing date. For example, if the defendant has not stated what his defence is, or the defence is not entirely clear, the registrar will order the defendant to give written details of his defence.

Proving your case
We saw in Chapter II that a dissatisfied buyer can reject a defective item and/or claim compensation from the seller for his financial loss. How must he establish to the satisfaction of the judge that the item bought was not of "merchantable" quality?

A pair of child's shoes may begin to disintegrate well before the end of their normal life expectancy. What is the standard of durability the consumer can expect? In theory, of course, this is a question for a shoe expert to assess but the consumer would be able to argue, eg

- my child's shoes normally last one year;
- these lasted two months;
- the shoes came apart before there were real signs of wear;

- they are not up to the normal standard of shoes at that price.

If the shoe broke and injured the wearer's ankle, compensation can be claimed for pain and suffering and time lost from work etc.

In the case of a mechanical item such as a car or washing machine, the retailers may have given a guarantee for a specific period during which they undertake to keep it in working order. Such a specific guarantee by the retailers reinforces their basic obligation to provide defect-free goods but does not limit the duration of their liability for the product.

Take for instance the case of a washing machine whose motor breaks down after 14 months' use. Assuming the year's guarantee has expired, has the consumer a claim against the retailers? To establish his claim he needs to call as a witness an expert on electric motors to say: "The normal life expectancy of this type of motor is five years. The motor seized up because it was poorly made so that it now needs to be replaced. Otherwise the machine is in good condition and has not been misused." On these facts the consumer would be entitled to the cost of a replacement motor. He is also entitled to the labour costs involved.

What evidence is required?
Evidence is what a person tells the judge on oath in court. The judge has to decide between the plaintiff and the defendant. Upon the evidence presented by each will depend his decision. Suppose the plaintiff is complaining that the motor of his spin-drier burnt out after only six months use. In proving his case in court he could produce, for example, the code of practice of the electrical trade association which lists how long various types of appliance can be expected to last.

In a claim for faulty goods, it may be necessary to have

the evidence of an expert witness. An "expert" is a person who through knowledge or experience is skilled in the matters on which he is asked to give an opinion. To establish his complaint that the brakes of his car were negligently repaired, the motorist could call as an expert witness the garage mechanic who subsequently discovered this and put the brakes right.

Again the plaintiff could send the defective article for examination by a product testing centre. For example, in the case of footwear, testing is carried out at Kettering by the Shoe and Allied Trades Research Association which will give a test report. This report can be produced as evidence at the trial to support his claim.

Where an expert's report has been obtained and the defendant raises no objection, the expert himself need not come to court. However, if the defendant refuses to accept it, the expert witness may have come to court to give evidence.

Any witness not prepared to attend voluntarily can be compelled to do so by the issue of a witness summons.

You can ask for this in the court office. However, you must remember that you will have to pay the witness his expenses which may include travelling and loss of earnings.

Documents can be very important in proving your case. Letters, drawings, agreements, bills, invoices, receipts, bank statements, paid cheques and any other relevant papers should be brought to court.

Keep notes of your telephone conversations with the retailer. These may be used to "refresh your memory" when telling the judge what excuses were given or proposals and suggestions put forward by the trader.

Further, any broken or damaged parts of the article complained of, if they are small enough, should be brought to court. With larger, non-portable items, the registrar or judge, at the pre-trial review, can be requested to make an on-the-spot inspection, eg of a suite of furniture, and if he decides this is necessary he will do so.

In appropriate circumstances photographs may be accepted as evidence, eg of paint flaking off a wall to show that the decorating of a room was not carried out in a workmanlike manner.

Giving evidence in court

If you lack confidence, take a friend or relative for moral support. The judge can allow him or her to speak on your behalf.

Before your case is called, the court is likely to be trying other cases. Sit in court to hear how questions are put and answered and pick up hints.

If your case is heard by the judge, address him as "your honour": a registrar or arbitrator can be called "sir". If in doubt use no form of address. Calling him "my lord" could sound slightly facetious (unless he is a High Court judge). "Your worship" is used to address magistrates. You will not go far wrong with a polite "Sir". Remember too when answering questions not to get indignant or excited.

When the usher calls your case stand up and go forward into the witness box on the judge's right, assuming you are the plaintiff (claimant). The defendant goes into the box on the judge's left. Lawyers stay on the bench in front of the court.

Once in the witness box you will be handed the testament and a card and asked to read out the oath. The judge or registrar will then invite you to tell him all the facts, when, where and from whom you bought the goods, what went wrong, when you complained and so on. Speak slowly as he will be writing it all down so keep an eye on his pen and pause between sentences until he has stopped writing. He will help your story along by asking questions. He may stop you saying certain things he consideres irrelevant or inadmissible (eg what your brother George told you), so do not be offended or feel he is against you if he cuts you short.

When you have finished your story, the defendant can ask **you** questions. You will have the same opportunity to question **him** later. Even if you fancy yourself as a lawyer do not attempt to overwhelm your opponent with questions. Leave this to the judge or registrar who, if neither you nor your opponent have a lawyer, will question each of you in turn.

Remember the rule against "hearsay" evidence. You can tell the court about conversations you had with the defendant or his staff but you may not recite conversations you had with third parties, eg What you were told by Mrs Smith down the road or the lady at the Citizens Advice Bureau.

Enforcing Judgement

At the end of the case the judge or registrar will usually sum up what the case was about and give his decision. Sometimes he will reserve judgement and give it another day but this would be unlikely for a small claim.

Where judgement is given against the trader he will be ordered to make payment within, say, 14 days. What if he ignores the court order? Judgement can be enforced by filling in a form at the court office and paying the appropriate fee for "execution". The court bailiffs then visit the trader to obtain payment with the threat of seizing his goods in default. It follows that if he has gone out of business or the shop has closed down, there will be no goods to seize and sell to satisfy your judgement.

If the trader has gone out of business and got a job elsewhere it will be possible to fill in another form to "attach his earnings". The court will order his employers (once you have found out where he is working) to deduct a weekly sum from his wages and pay it into court.

Alternatively he can be summoned to court for oral

examination by the registrar to answer questions about his means and to explain his failure to pay. This method can also be used if he was running a company. Complications are particularly likely to arise when a customer seeks to get money back from a limited company.

Consumers and Companies

One particular danger for the unsuspecting consumer arises when dealing with a limited company because a trader who conducts his business through the legal apparatus of a limited company is not himself liable for its debts in the event of it becoming insolvent. Nor need he ensure that the company honours its obligations.

As a result all too often the consumer is left with a right which he is not able to enforce. For example, he may be entitled to claim back from the company a deposit he has paid or compensation for a defective purchase. Even if the court gives judgment in his favour, the court bailiff cannot compel the company to pay unless the company has assets which can be sold. If it has none, the person running the company as director cannot be made personaly liable for the debt. Nor can the shareholders be made to pay because each shareholder's liability to meet the company's debts is limited to the value of his shares.

Trade Names

Again the consumer may be dealing with "Whizz Electronics" but who is responsible to meet the firm's liabilities and debts? It may be that this imposing title is merely the trade name of an individual called John Smith. If so the consumer can sue "John Smith trading as Whizz Electronics" and judgment can be enforced against John Smith personally.

On the other hand John Smith maybe running his business through the medium of a limited company, eg J. Smith & Co. Ltd. so that the **company** will be registered as trading as "Whizz Electronics". Accordingly the consumer can sue the company only.

Where a company carries on business under a trade name which is **different** from its registered name it must register it in the Business Names Registry at 55 City Road, London EC1Y 1BB. Members of the public can inquire at the Registry to discover the identity of the company or person who is trading under that particular trade name.

How can the consumer find out whether he is in fact dealing with a limited company? To start with, the name of the company must always be followed by the word "limited" to warn the public that its liability to meet claims is limited by law and all business and other documents and letters must show it.

To ensure that members of the public are aware that they are dealing with a company which has only limited liability, its name must also be displayed in a conspicuous position at every place its business is carried on. Since only a small fine is payable for not displaying the company name, in practice many shops and other places of business omit to show it.

A limited company must show the names of all directors on all letters, trade circulars and similar documents. Any member of the public who wishes to know what a limited company is worth can go to the Companies Registry at Companies House, 55 City Road, London EC1Y 1BB (tel. 01-253 9393) and look at its accounts. These are open to inspection by anyone on payment of a small fee. Since every limited company must file its accounts yearly, the public can find out how credit-worthy a particular company is.

Dangers of limited liability to consumer

If the company has no assets, suing it will generally be a waste of time. The consumer cannot sue John Smith himself for the return of money paid to John Smith Ltd, because

310

in law the company is a separate "person". This legal separateness can go so far that John Smith may **himself** be listed as a creditor of his own company.

The risks of doing business with a limited company are illustrated by the leading case of *Salomon v. Salomon & Co. Ltd.* (1897) which establishes that a limited company is a distinct legal entity from its directors and shareholders. Mr Salomon, who ran a leather business, formed the company to buy his business from him for £30,000. In exchange he accepted 20,000 £1 shares in the company. The remaining £10,000 was regarded as a loan from him. This loan was secured on the assets of the company by a document known as a debenture.

When the company was wound up it showed debts of £7,000 and assets of £6,000. Relying on his debenture Mr Salomon claimed repayment of his loan in preference to all the other people to whom the company owed money. The other creditors argued they should come first as Mr Salomon and Salomon & Co. Ltd. were one and the same person and that a man could not owe money to himself.

The House of Lords decided otherwise. Salomon & Co. Ltd. as a company had a separate legal identity from Mr Salomon himself. Accordingly the company had to repay the debt it owed to him under the debenture before paying anyone else.

Safeguarding against Company Insolvency

One way round the limited liability trap is for the consumer to insist on making his agreement with the trader personally, avoiding any reference to the limited company. Thus cheques should be made payable to J. Smith and all correspondence addressed to him with no mention of the company. If the consumer can satisfy the judge that he was dealing with the trader **as an individual** and not with his company, the trader will be personally responsible to meet any court order for compensation.

Another method of making a director of a company personally responsible is to ask him to give a personal guarantee. A second-hand car dealer could be asked for a letter in which he undertakes personally to put right defects free of charge, for a minimum period.

When Credit Supplier is responsible for Limited Company's Default

A third method by which the consumer can protect himself in the event of the company with which he is dealing becoming insolvent is to buy on credit and not for cash. Where he buys on hire-purchase the finance house will be responsible for any defects in the goods or other default by the dealer.

If the consumer does not want to incur interest charges he could use his **credit card** where the purchase price is £30 or more. Although the consumer pays off his debt to the credit card company immediately, he still has special indemnity rights under any credit card issued after 1st July 1977. Section 75 of the Consumer Credit Act 1974, makes the credit card company liable where goods or services are purchased with the use of a credit card but a dispute arises between the card-holder and the supplier relating for example to the quality of goods or services.

Section 75 enables the card-holder to join the credit card company as a party to any proceedings which he brings against the supplier. Alternatively the card-holder can bring a separate action against the credit card company, for example it may be that Whizz Electronics Limited has gone out of business and has delivered only part of the Hi-Fi equipment for which the card holder has signed.

This right of indemnity applies to all purchases of goods or services whose cash price is between £30 and £10,000. The moral for the consumer is that if in doubt about the reliability of a supplier he should use his credit card to make the purchase.

Unfair Contract Terms
Act 1977

1977 CHAPTER 50

ARRANGEMENT OF SECTIONS

PART I

AMENDMENT OF LAW FOR ENGLAND AND WALES AND NORTHERN IRELAND

Introductory

PART II

AMENDMENT OF LAW FOR SCOTLAND

A

ELIZABETH II

Unfair Contract Terms Act 1977

1977 CHAPTER 50

An Act to impose further limits on the extent to which under the law of England and Wales and Northern Ireland civil liability for breach of contract, or for negligence or other breach of duty, can be avoided by means of contract terms and otherwise, and under the law of Scotland civil liability can be avoided by means of contract terms.   [26th October 1977]

BE IT ENACTED by the Queen's most Excellent Majesty, by and with the advice and consent of the Lords Spiritual and Temporal, and Commons, in this present Parliament assembled, and by the authority of the same, as follows:—

PART I

AMENDMENT OF LAW FOR ENGLAND AND WALES AND NORTHERN IRELAND

Introductory

1.—(1) For the purposes of this Part of this Act, " negligence " means the breach— {.marginal} Scope of Part I.

    (*a*) of any obligation, arising from the express or implied terms of a contract, to take reasonable care or exercise reasonable skill in the performance of the contract ;

    (*b*) of any common law duty to take reasonable care or exercise reasonable skill (but not any stricter duty) ;

PART I
1957 c. 31.
1957 c. 25
(N.I.).

(c) of the common duty of care imposed by the Occupiers' Liability Act 1957 or the Occupiers' Liability Act (Northern Ireland) 1957.

(2) This Part of this Act is subject to Part III ; and in relation to contracts, the operation of sections 2 to 4 and 7 is subject to the exceptions made by Schedule 1.

(3) In the case of both contract and tort, sections 2 to 7 apply (except where the contrary is stated in section 6(4)) only to business liability, that is liability for breach of obligations or duties arising—

(a) from things done or to be done by a person in the course of a business (whether his own business or another's) ; or

(b) from the occupation of premises used for business purposes of the occupier ;

and references to liability are to be read accordingly.

(4) In relation to any breach of duty or obligation, it is immaterial for any purpose of this Part of this Act whether the breach was inadvertent or intentional, or whether liability for it arises directly or vicariously.

Avoidance of liability for negligence, breach of contract, etc.

Negligence liability.

2.—(1) A person cannot by reference to any contract term or to a notice given to persons generally or to particular persons exclude or restrict his liability for death or personal injury resulting from negligence.

(2) In the case of other loss or damage, a person cannot so exclude or restrict his liability for negligence except in so far as the term or notice satisfies the requirement of reasonableness.

(3) Where a contract term or notice purports to exclude or restrict liability for negligence a person's agreement to or awareness of it is not of itself to be taken as indicating his voluntary acceptance of any risk.

Liability arising in contract.

3.—(1) This section applies as between contracting parties where one of them deals as consumer or on the other's written standard terms of business.

(2) As against that party, the other cannot by reference to any contract term—

(a) when himself in breach of contract, exclude or restrict any liability of his in respect of the breach ; or

(b) claim to be entitled—

(i) to render a contractual performance substantially different from that which was reasonably expected of him, or

> > (ii) in respect of the whole or any part of his
> > contractual obligation, to render no performance
> > at all,

except in so far as (in any of the cases mentioned above in this subsection) the contract term satisfies the requirement of reasonableness.

4.—(1) A person dealing as consumer cannot by reference to Unreasonable any contract term be made to indemnify another person (whether indemnity a party to the contract or not) in respect of liability that may be clauses. incurred by the other for negligence or breach of contract, except in so far as the contract term satisfies the requirement of reasonableness.

(2) This section applies whether the liability in question—

> (a) is directly that of the person to be indemnified or is incurred by him vicariously ;
>
> (b) is to the person dealing as consumer or to someone else.

Liability arising from sale or supply of goods

5.—(1) In the case of goods of a type ordinarily supplied for " Guarantee " private use or consumption, where loss or damage— of consumer goods.

> (a) arises from the goods proving defective while in consumer use ; and
>
> (b) results from the negligence of a person concerned in the manufacture or distribution of the goods,

liability for the loss or damage cannot be excluded or restricted by reference to any contract term or notice contained in or operating by reference to a guarantee of the goods.

(2) For these purposes—

> (a) goods are to be regarded as " in consumer use " when a person is using them, or has them in his possession for use, otherwise than exclusively for the purposes of a business ; and
>
> (b) anything in writing is a guarantee if it contains or purports to contain some promise or assurance (however worded or presented) that defects will be made good by complete or partial replacement, or by repair, monetary compensation or otherwise.

(3) This section does not apply as between the parties to a contract under or in pursuance of which possession or ownership of the goods passed.

6.—(1) Liability for breach of the obligations arising from— Sale and

> (a) section 12 of the Sale of Goods Act 1893 (seller's hire-purchase. implied undertakings as to title, etc.) ; 56 & 57 Vict. c. 71.

B

(b) section 8 of the Supply of Goods (Implied Terms) Act 1973 (the corresponding thing in relation to hire-purchase),

cannot be excluded or restricted by reference to any contract term.

(2) As against a person dealing as consumer, liability for breach of the obligations arising from—

   (a) section 13, 14 or 15 of the 1893 Act (seller's implied undertakings as to conformity of goods with description or sample, or as to their quality or fitness for a particular purpose) ;

   (b) section 9, 10 or 11 of the 1973 Act (the corresponding things in relation to hire-purchase),

cannot be excluded or restricted by reference to any contract term.

(3) As against a person dealing otherwise than as consumer, the liability specified in subsection (2) above can be excluded or restricted by reference to a contract term, but only in so far as the term satisfies the requirement of reasonableness.

(4) The liabilities referred to in this section are not only the business liabilities defined by section 1(3), but include those arising under any contract of sale of goods or hire-purchase agreement.

Miscellaneous contracts under which goods pass.

7.—(1) Where the possession or ownership of goods passes under or in pursuance of a contract not governed by the law of sale of goods or hire-purchase, subsections (2) to (4) below apply as regards the effect (if any) to be given to contract terms excluding or restricting liability for breach of obligation arising by implication of law from the nature of the contract.

(2) As against a person dealing as consumer, liability in respect of the goods' correspondence with description or sample, or their quality or fitness for any particular purpose, cannot be excluded or restricted by reference to any such term.

(3) As against a person dealing otherwise than as consumer, that liability can be excluded or restricted by reference to such a term, but only in so far as the term satisfies the requirement of reasonableness.

(4) Liability in respect of—

   (a) the right to transfer ownership of the goods, or give possession ; or

   (b) the assurance of quiet possession to a person taking goods in pursuance of the contract,

cannot be excluded or restricted by reference to any such term   PART I
except in so far as the term satisfies the requirement of
reasonableness.

(5) This section does not apply in the case of goods passing 1964 c. 71.
on a redemption of trading stamps within the Trading Stamps 1965 c. 6.
Act 1964 or the Trading Stamps Act (Northern Ireland) 1965.   (N.I.).

Other provisions about contracts

8.—(1) In the Misrepresentation Act 1967, the following is Misrepre-
substituted for section 3—   sentation.

" Avoidance   3. If a contract contains a term which would 1967 c. 7.
of provision   exclude or restrict—
excluding
liability for
misrepre-   (a) any liability to which a party to a contract
sentation.   may be subject by reason of any misrepre-
                        sentation made by him before the contract
                        was made ; or

                   (b) any remedy available to another party to the
                        contract by reason of such a misrepresenta-
                        tion,

that term shall be of no effect except in so far as it
satisfies the requirement of reasonableness as stated
in section 11(1) of the Unfair Contract Terms Act
1977 ; and it is for those claiming that the term
satisfies that requirement to show that it does.".

(2) The same section is substituted for section 3 of the Mis- 1967 c. 14
representation Act (Northern Ireland) 1967.   (N.I.).

9.—(1) Where for reliance upon it a contract term has to Effect of
satisfy the requirement of reasonableness, it may be found to breach.
do so and be given effect accordingly notwithstanding that the
contract has been terminated either by breach or by a party
electing to treat it as repudiated.

(2) Where on a breach the contract is nevertheless affirmed
by a party entitled to treat it as repudiated, this does not of itself
exclude the requirement of reasonableness in relation to any
contract term.

10. A person is not bound by any contract term prejudicing Evasion by
or taking away rights of his which arise under, or in connection means of
with the performance of, another contract, so far as those rights secondary
extend to the enforcement of another's liability which this Part contract.
of this Act prevents that other from excluding or restricting.

Explanatory provisions

11.—(1) In relation to a contract term, the requirement of reasonableness for the purposes of this Part of this Act, section 3 of the Misrepresentation Act 1967 and section 3 of the Misrepresentation Act (Northern Ireland) 1967 is that the term shall have been a fair and reasonable one to be included having regard to the circumstances which were, or ought reasonably to have been, known to or in the contemplation of the parties when the contract was made.

(2) In determining for the purposes of section 6 or 7 above whether a contract term satisfies the requirement of reasonableness, regard shall be had in particular to the matters specified in Schedule 2 to this Act ; but this subsection does not prevent the court or arbitrator from holding, in accordance with any rule of law, that a term which purports to exclude or restrict any relevant liability is not a term of the contract.

(3) In relation to a notice (not being a notice having contractual effect), the requirement of reasonableness under this Act is that it should be fair and reasonable to allow reliance on it, having regard to all the circumstances obtaining when the liability arose or (but for the notice) would have arisen.

(4) Where by reference to a contract term or notice a person seeks to restrict liability to a specified sum of money, and the question arises (under this or any other Act) whether the term or notice satisfies the requirement of reasonableness, regard shall be had in particular (but without prejudice to subsection (2) above in the case of contract terms) to—

    (*a*) the resources which he could expect to be available to him for the purpose of meeting the liability should it arise ; and

    (*b*) how far it was open to him to cover himself by insurance.

(5) It is for those claiming that a contract term or notice satisfies the requirement of reasonableness to show that it does.

12.—(1) A party to a contract " deals as consumer " in relation to another party if—

    (*a*) he neither makes the contract in the course of a business nor holds himself out as doing so ; and

    (*b*) the other party does make the contract in the course of a business ; and

(c) in the case of a contract governed by the law of sale of goods or hire-purchase, or by section 7 of this Act, the goods passing under or in pursuance of the contract are of a type ordinarily supplied for private use or consumption.

PART I

(2) But on a sale by auction or by competitive tender the buyer is not in any circumstances to be regarded as dealing as consumer.

(3) Subject to this, it is for those claiming that a party does not deal as consumer to show that he does not.

13.—(1) To the extent that this Part of this Act prevents the exclusion or restriction of any liability it also prevents—

Varieties of exemption clause.

(a) making the liability or its enforcement subject to restrictive or onerous conditions ;

(b) excluding or restricting any right or remedy in respect of the liability, or subjecting a person to any prejudice in consequence of his pursuing any such right or remedy ;

(c) excluding or restricting rules of evidence or procedure ;

and (to that extent) sections 2 and 5 to 7 also prevent excluding or restricting liability by reference to terms and notices which exclude or restrict the relevant obligation or duty.

(2) But an agreement in writing to submit present or future differences to arbitration is not to be treated under this Part of this Act as excluding or restricting any liability.

14. In this Part of this Act—

Interpretation of Part I.

" business " includes a profession and the activities of any government department or local or public authority ;

" goods " has the same meaning as in the Sale of Goods Act 1893 ;

56 & 57 Vict. c. 71.

" hire-purchase agreement " has the same meaning as in the Consumer Credit Act 1974 ;

1974 c. 39.

" negligence " has the meaning given by section 1(1) ;

" notice " includes an announcement, whether or not in writing, and any other communication or pretended communication ; and

" personal injury " includes any disease and any impairment of physical or mental condition.

PART II

AMENDMENT OF LAW FOR SCOTLAND

Scope of
Part II.

15.—(1) This Part of this Act applies only to contracts, is subject to Part III of this Act and does not affect the validity of any discharge or indemnity given by a person in consideration of the receipt by him of compensation in settlement of any claim which he has.

(2) Subject to subsection (3) below, sections 16 to 18 of this Act apply to any contract only to the extent that the contract—

(a) relates to the transfer of the ownership or possession of goods from one person to another (with or without work having been done on them) ;

(b) constitutes a contract of service or apprenticeship ;

(c) relates to services of whatever kind, including (without prejudice to the foregoing generality) carriage, deposit and pledge, care and custody, mandate, agency, loan and services relating to the use of land ;

(d) relates to the liability of an occupier of land to persons entering upon or using that land ;

(e) relates to a grant of any right or permission to enter upon or use land not amounting to an estate or interest in the land.

(3) Notwithstanding anything in subsection (2) above, sections 16 to 18—

(a) do not apply to any contract to the extent that the contract—

(i) is a contract of insurance (including a contract to pay an annuity on human life) ;

(ii) relates to the formation, constitution or dissolution of any body corporate or unincorporated association or partnership ;

(b) apply to—

a contract of marine salvage or towage ;

a charter party of a ship or hovercraft ;

a contract for the carriage of goods by ship or hovercraft ; or,

a contract to which subsection (4) below relates,

only to the extent that—

(i) both parties deal or hold themselves out as dealing in the course of a business (and then only in so far as the contract purports to exclude or restrict liability for breach of duty in respect of death or personal injury) ; or

(ii) the contract is a consumer contract (and then only in favour of the consumer).

(4) This subsection relates to a contract in pursuance of which goods are carried by ship or hovercraft and which either—

(a) specifies ship or hovercraft as the means of carriage over part of the journey to be covered ; or

(b) makes no provision as to the means of carriage and does not exclude ship or hovercraft as that means,

in so far as the contract operates for and in relation to the carriage of the goods by that means.

16.—(1) Where a term of a contract purports to exclude or restrict liability for breach of duty arising in the course of any business or from the occupation of any premises used for business purposes of the occupier, that term— Liability for breach of duty.

(a) shall be void in any case where such exclusion or restriction is in respect of death or personal injury ;

(b) shall, in any other case, have no effect if it was not fair and reasonable to incorporate the term in the contract.

(2) Subsection (1)(a) above does not affect the validity of any discharge and indemnity given by a person, on or in connection with an award to him of compensation for pneumoconiosis attributable to employment in the coal industry, in respect of any further claim arising from his contracting that disease.

(3) Where under subsection (1) above a term of a contract is void or has no effect, the fact that a person agreed to, or was aware of, the term shall not of itself be sufficient evidence that he knowingly and voluntarily assumed any risk.

17.—(1) Any term of a contract which is a consumer contract or a standard form contract shall have no effect for the purpose of enabling a party to the contract— Control of unreasonable exemptions in consumer or standard form contracts.

(a) who is in breach of a contractual obligation, to exclude or restrict any liability of his to the consumer or customer in respect of the breach ;

(b) in respect of a contractual obligation, to render no performance, or to render a performance substantially different from that which the consumer or customer reasonably expected from the contract ;

if it was not fair and reasonable to incorporate the term in the contract.

(2) In this section " customer " means a party to a standard form contract who deals on the basis of written standard terms of business of the other party to the contract who himself deals in the course of a business.

PART II
Unreasonable
indemnity
clauses in
consumer
contracts.

18.—(1) Any term of a contract which is a consumer contract shall have no effect for the purpose of making the consumer indemnify another person (whether a party to the contract or not) in respect of liability which that other person may incur as a result of breach of duty or breach of contract, if it was not fair and reasonable to incorporate the term in the contract.

(2) In this section " liability " means liability arising in the course of any business or from the occupation of any premises used for business purposes of the occupier.

" Guarantee "
of consumer
goods.

19.—(1) This section applies to a guarantee—

(a) in relation to goods which are of a type ordinarily supplied for private use or consumption ; and

(b) which is not a guarantee given by one party to the other party to a contract under or in pursuance of which the ownership or possession of the goods to which the guarantee relates is transferred.

(2) A term of a guarantee to which this section applies shall be void in so far as it purports to exclude or restrict liability for loss or damage (including death or personal injury)—

(a) arising from the goods proving defective while—

(i) in use otherwise than exclusively for the purposes of a business ; or

(ii) in the possession of a person for such use ; and

(b) resulting from the breach of duty of a person concerned in the manufacture or distribution of the goods.

(3) For the purposes of this section, any document is a guarantee if it contains or purports to contain some promise or assurance (however worded or presented) that defects will be made good by complete or partial replacement, or by repair, monetary compensation or otherwise.

Obligations
implied by
law in sale
and hire-
purchase
contracts.
56 & 57
Vict. c. 71.
1973 c. 13.

20.—(1) Any term of a contract which purports to exclude or restrict liability for breach of the obligations arising from—

(a) section 12 of the Sale of Goods Act 1893 (seller's implied undertakings as to title etc.) ;

(b) section 8 of the Supply of Goods (Implied Terms) Act 1973 (implied terms as to title in hire-purchase agreements),

shall be void.

(2) Any term of a contract which purports to exclude or restrict liability for breach of the obligations arising from—

(a) section 13, 14 or 15 of the said Act of 1893 (seller's implied undertakings as to conformity of goods with description or sample, or as to their quality or fitness for a particular purpose);

(b) section 9, 10 or 11 of the said Act of 1973 (the corresponding provisions in relation to hire-purchase),

shall—

(i) in the case of a consumer contract, be void against the consumer;

(ii) in any other case, have no effect if it was not fair and reasonable to incorporate the term in the contract.

21.—(1) Any term of a contract to which this section applies purporting to exclude or restrict liability for breach of an obligation—

(a) such as is referred to in subsection (3)(a) below—

(i) in the case of a consumer contract, shall be void against the consumer, and

(ii) in any other case, shall have no effect if it was not fair and reasonable to incorporate the term in the contract;

(b) such as is referred to in subsection (3)(b) below, shall have no effect if it was not fair and reasonable to incorporate the term in the contract.

Obligations implied by law in other contracts for the supply of goods.

(2) This section applies to any contract to the extent that it relates to any such matter as is referred to in section 15(2)(a) of this Act, but does not apply to—

(a) a contract of sale of goods or a hire-purchase agreement; or

(b) a charterparty of a ship or hovercraft unless it is a consumer contract (and then only in favour of the consumer).

(3) An obligation referred to in this subsection is an obligation incurred under a contract in the course of a business and arising by implication of law from the nature of the contract which relates—

(a) to the correspondence of goods with description or sample, or to the quality or fitness of goods for any particular purpose; or

(b) to any right to transfer ownership or possession of goods, or to the enjoyment of quiet possession of goods.

(4) Nothing in this section applies to the supply of goods on a redemption of trading stamps within the Trading Stamps Act 1964.

1964 c. 71.

PART II
Consequence
of breach.

22. For the avoidance of doubt, where any provision of this Part of this Act requires that the incorporation of a term in a contract must be fair and reasonable for that term to have effect—

  (a) if that requirement is satisfied, the term may be given effect to notwithstanding that the contract has been terminated in consequence of breach of that contract ;

  (b) for the term to be given effect to, that requirement must be satisfied even where a party who is entitled to rescind the contract elects not to rescind it.

Evasion by
means of
secondary
contract.

23. Any term of any contract shall be void which purports to exclude or restrict, or has the effect of excluding or restricting—

  (a) the exercise, by a party to any other contract, of any right or remedy which arises in respect of that other contract in consequence of breach of duty, or of obligation, liability for which could not by virtue of the provisions of this Part of this Act be excluded or restricted by a term of that other contract ;

  (b) the application of the provisions of this Part of this Act in respect of that or any other contract.

The
" reasonable-
ness " test.

24.—(1) In determining for the purposes of this Part of this Act whether it was fair and reasonable to incorporate a term in a contract, regard shall be had only to the circumstances which were, or ought reasonably to have been, known to or in the contemplation of the parties to the contract at the time the contract was made.

(2) In determining for the purposes of section 20 or 21 of this Act whether it was fair and reasonable to incorporate a term in a contract, regard shall be had in particular to the matters specified in Schedule 2 to this Act ; but this sub-section shall not prevent a court or arbiter from holding, in accordance with any rule of law, that a term which purports to exclude or restrict any relevant liability is not a term of the contract.

(3) Where a term in a contract purports to restrict liability to a specified sum of money, and the question arises for the purposes of this Part of this Act whether it was fair and reasonable to incorporate the term in the contract, then, without prejudice to subsection (2) above, regard shall be had in particular to—

  (a) the resources which the party seeking to rely on that term could expect to be available to him for the purpose of meeting the liability should it arise ;

(*b*) how far it was open to that party to cover himself by insurance.

(4) The onus of proving that it was fair and reasonable to incorporate a term in a contract shall lie on the party so contending.

25.—(1) In this Part of this Act—

" breach of duty " means the breach—

(*a*) of any obligation, arising from the express or implied terms of a contract, to take reasonable care or exercise reasonable skill in the performance of the contract ;

(*b*) of any common law duty to take reasonable care or exercise reasonable skill ;

(*c*) of the duty of reasonable care imposed by section 2(1) of the Occupiers' Liability (Scotland) 1960 c. 30. Act 1960 ;

" business " includes a profession and the activities of any government department or local or public authority ;

" consumer " has the meaning assigned to that expression in the definition in this section of " consumer contract " ;

" consumer contract " means a contract (not being a contract of sale by auction or competitive tender) in which—

(*a*) one party to the contract deals, and the other party to the contract (" the consumer ") does not deal or hold himself out as dealing, in the course of a business, and

(*b*) in the case of a contract such as is mentioned in section 15(2)(*a*) of this Act, the goods are of a type ordinarily supplied for private use or consumption ;

and for the purposes of this Part of this Act the onus of proving that a contract is not to be regarded as a consumer contract shall lie on the party so contending ;

" goods " has the same meaning as in the Sale of Goods 56 & 57 Act 1893 ; Vict. c. 71.

" hire-purchase agreement " has the same meaning as in section 189(1) of the Consumer Credit Act 1974 ; 1974 c. 39.

" personal injury " includes any disease and any impairment of physical or mental condition.

(2) In relation to any breach of duty or obligation, it is immaterial for any purpose of this Part of this Act whether the act or omission giving rise to that breach was inadvertent or

PART II   intentional, or whether liability for it arises directly or vicariously.

(3) In this Part of this Act, any reference to excluding or restricting any liability includes—

- (a) making the liability or its enforcement subject to any restrictive or onerous conditions ;
- (b) excluding or restricting any right or remedy in respect of the liability, or subjecting a person to any prejudice in consequence of his pursuing any such right or remedy ;
- (c) excluding or restricting any rule of evidence or procedure ;
- (d) excluding or restricting any liability by reference to a notice having contractual effect,

but does not include an agreement to submit any question to arbitration.

(4) In subsection (3)(d) above " notice " includes an announcement, whether or not in writing, and any other communication or pretended communication.

(5) In sections 15 and 16 and 19 to 21 of this Act, any reference to excluding or restricting liability for breach of an obligation or duty shall include a reference to excluding or restricting the obligation or duty itself.

PART III

PROVISIONS APPLYING TO WHOLE OF UNITED KINGDOM

Miscellaneous

International supply contracts.

26.—(1) The limits imposed by this Act on the extent to which a person may exclude or restrict liability by reference to a contract term do not apply to liability arising under such a contract as is described in subsection (3) below.

(2) The terms of such a contract are not subject to any requirement of reasonableness under section 3 or 4: and nothing in Part II of this Act shall require the incorporation of the terms of such a contract to be fair and reasonable for them to have effect.

(3) Subject to subsection (4), that description of contract is one whose characteristics are the following—

- (a) either it is a contract of sale of goods or it is one under or in pursuance of which the possession or ownership of goods passes ; and

(b) it is made by parties whose places of business (or, if Part III they have none, habitual residences) are in the territories of different States (the Channel Islands and the Isle of Man being treated for this purpose as different States from the United Kingdom).

(4) A contract falls within subsection (3) above only if either—

(a) the goods in question are, at the time of the conclusion of the contract, in the course of carriage, or will be carried, from the territory of one State to the territory of another ; or

(b) the acts constituting the offer and acceptance have been done in the territories of different States ; or

(c) the contract provides for the goods to be delivered to the territory of a State other than that within whose territory those acts were done.

27.—(1) Where the proper law of a contract is the law of any Choice of part of the United Kingdom only by choice of the parties (and law clauses. apart from that choice would be the law of some country outside the United Kingdom) sections 2 to 7 and 16 to 21 of this Act do not operate as part of the proper law.

(2) This Act has effect notwithstanding any contract term which applies or purports to apply the law of some country outside the United Kingdom, where (either or both)—

(a) the term appears to the court, or arbitrator or arbiter to have been imposed wholly or mainly for the purpose of enabling the party imposing it to evade the operation of this Act ; or

(b) in the making of the contract one of the parties dealt as consumer, and he was then habitually resident in the United Kingdom, and the essential steps necessary for the making of the contract were taken there, whether by him or by others on his behalf.

(3) In the application of subsection (2) above to Scotland, for paragraph (b) there shall be substituted—

" (b) the contract is a consumer contract as defined in Part II of this Act, and the consumer at the date when the contract was made was habitually resident in the United Kingdom, and the essential steps necessary for the making of the contract were taken there, whether by him or by others on his behalf.".

28.—(1) This section applies to a contract for carriage by Temporary sea of a passenger or of a passenger and his luggage where provision the provisions of the Athens Convention (with or without modi- for sea carriage of fication) do not have, in relation to the contract, the force of passengers. law in the United Kingdom.

PART III
(2) In a case where—

(a) the contract is not made in the United Kingdom, and

(b) neither the place of departure nor the place of destination under it is in the United Kingdom,

a person is not precluded by this Act from excluding or restricting liability for loss or damage, being loss or damage for which the provisions of the Convention would, if they had the force of law in relation to the contract, impose liability on him.

(3) In any other case, a person is not precluded by this Act from excluding or restricting liability for that loss or damage—

(a) in so far as the exclusion or restriction would have been effective in that case had the provisions of the Convention had the force of law in relation to the contract ; or

(b) in such circumstances and to such extent as may be prescribed, by reference to a prescribed term of the contract.

(4) For the purposes of subsection (3)(a), the values which shall be taken to be the official values in the United Kingdom of the amounts (expressed in gold francs) by reference to which liability under the provisions of the Convention is limited shall be such amounts in sterling as the Secretary of State may from time to time by order made by statutory instrument specify.

(5) In this section,—

(a) the references to excluding or restricting liability include doing any of those things in relation to the liability which are mentioned in section 13 or section 25(3) and (5) ; and

(b) " the Athens Convention " means the Athens Convention relating to the Carriage of Passengers and their Luggage by Sea, 1974 ; and

(c) " prescribed " means prescribed by the Secretary of State by regulations made by statutory instrument ;

and a statutory instrument containing the regulations shall be subject to annulment in pursuance of a resolution of either House of Parliament.

Saving for other relevant legislation.

29.—(1) Nothing in this Act removes or restricts the effect of, or prevents reliance upon, any contractual provision which—

(a) is authorised or required by the express terms or necessary implication of an enactment ; or

(*b*) being made with a view to compliance with an inter- PART III
national agreement to which the United Kingdom is a
party, does not operate more restrictively than is con-
templated by the agreement.

(2) A contract term is to be taken—

　(*a*) for the purposes of Part I of this Act, as satisfying the
requirement of reasonableness ; and

　(*b*) for those of Part II, to have been fair and reasonable to
incorporate,

if it is incorporated or approved by, or incorporated pursuant to
a decision or ruling of, a competent authority acting in the
exercise of any statutory jurisdiction or function and is not a
term in a contract to which the competent authority is itself
a party.

(3) In this section—

　" competent authority " means any court, arbitrator or
arbiter, government department or public authority ;

　" enactment " means any legislation (including subordinate
legislation) of the United Kingdom or Northern Ireland
and any instrument having effect by virtue of such
legislation ; and

　" statutory " means conferred by an enactment.

30.—(1) In section 3 of the Consumer Protection Act 1961 Obligations
(provisions against marketing goods which do not comply with under
safety requirements), after subsection (1) there is inserted— Consumer
Protection

　" (1A) Any term of an agreement which purports to ex- Acts.
clude or restrict, or has the effect of excluding or restricting, 1961 c. 40.
any obligation imposed by or by virtue of that section, or
any liability for breach of such an obligation, shall be void.".

(2) The same amendment is made in section 3 of the Consumer 1965 c. 14
Protection Act (Northern Ireland) 1965. (N.I.).

General

31.—(1) This Act comes into force on 1st February 1978. Commencement;
(2) Nothing in this Act applies to contracts made before the amendments;
date on which it comes into force ; but subject to this, it applies repeals.
to liability for any loss or damage which is suffered on or after
that date.

(3) The enactments specified in Schedule 3 to this Act are
amended as there shown.

(4) The enactments specified in Schedule 4 to this Act are
repealed to the extent specified in column 3 of that Schedule.

PART III
Citation and
extent.

32.—(1) This Act may be cited as the Unfair Contract Terms Act 1977.

(2) Part I of this Act extends to England and Wales and to Northern Ireland ; but it does not extend to Scotland.

(3) Part II of this Act extends to Scotland only.

(4) This Part of this Act extends to the whole of the United Kingdom.

SCHEDULES

SCHEDULE 1

SCOPE OF SECTIONS 2 TO 4 AND 7

1. Sections 2 to 4 of this Act do not extend to—

 (a) any contract of insurance (including a contract to pay an annuity on human life) ;

 (b) any contract so far as it relates to the creation or transfer of an interest in land, or to the termination of such an interest, whether by extinction, merger, surrender, forfeiture or otherwise ;

 (c) any contract so far as it relates to the creation or transfer of a right or interest in any patent, trade mark, copyright, registered design, technical or commercial information or other intellectual property, or relates to the termination of any such right or interest ;

 (d) any contract so far as it relates—

    (i) to the formation or dissolution of a company (which means any body corporate or unincorporated association and includes a partnership), or

    (ii) to its constitution or the rights or obligations of its corporators or members ;

 (e) any contract so far as it relates to the creation or transfer of securities or of any right or interest in securities.

2. Section 2(1) extends to—

 (a) any contract of marine salvage or towage ;

 (b) any charterparty of a ship or hovercraft ; and

 (c) any contract for the carriage of goods by ship or hovercraft ;

but subject to this sections 2 to 4 and 7 do not extend to any such contract except in favour of a person dealing as consumer.

3. Where goods are carried by ship or hovercraft in pursuance of a contract which either—

 (a) specifies that as the means of carriage over part of the journey to be covered, or

 (b) makes no provision as to the means of carriage and does not exclude that means,

then sections 2(2), 3 and 4 do not, except in favour of a person dealing as consumer, extend to the contract as it operates for and in relation to the carriage of the goods by that means.

4. Section 2(1) and (2) do not extend to a contract of employment, except in favour of the employee.

5. Section 2(1) does not affect the validity of any discharge and indemnity given by a person, on or in connection with an award to him of compensation for pneumoconiosis attributable to employment in the coal industry, in respect of any further claim arising from his contracting that disease.

Sections 11(2)
and 24(2).

SCHEDULE 2

" Guidelines " for Application of Reasonableness Test

The matters to which regard is to be had in particular for the purposes of sections 6(3), 7(3) and (4), 20 and 21 are any of the following which appear to be relevant—

    (*a*) the strength of the bargaining positions of the parties relative to each other, taking into account (among other things) alternative means by which the customer's requirements could have been met ;

    (*b*) whether the customer received an inducement to agree to the term, or in accepting it had an opportunity of entering into a similar contract with other persons, but without having to accept a similar term ;

    (*c*) whether the customer knew or ought reasonably to have known of the existence and extent of the term (having regard, among other things, to any custom of the trade and any previous course of dealing between the parties) ;

    (*d*) where the term excludes or restricts any relevant liability if some condition is not complied with, whether it was reasonable at the time of the contract to expect that compliance with that condition would be practicable ;

    (*e*) whether the goods were manufactured, processed or adapted to the special order of the customer.

Section 31(3).

SCHEDULE 3

Amendment of Enactments

56 & 57 Vict.
c. 71.

In the Sale of Goods Act 1893—

    (*a*) in section 55(1), for the words " the following provisions of this section " substitute " the provisions of the Unfair Contract Terms Act 1977 " ;

    (*b*) in section 62(1), in the definition of " business ", for " local authority or statutory undertaker " substitute " or local or public authority ".

1973 c. 13.
1974 c. 39.

In the Supply of Goods (Implied Terms) Act 1973 (as originally enacted and as substituted by the Consumer Credit Act 1974)—

    (*a*) in section 14(1) for the words from " conditional sale " to the end substitute " a conditional sale agreement where the buyer deals as consumer within Part I of the Unfair Contract Terms Act 1977 or, in Scotland, the agreement is a consumer contract within Part II of that Act " ;

    (*b*) in section 15(1), in the definition of " business ", for " local authority or statutory undertaker " substitute " or local or public authority ".

SCHEDULE 4

REPEALS

Chapter	Short title	Extent of repeal
56 & 57 Vict. c. 71.	Sale of Goods Act 1893.	In section 55, subsections (3) to (11). Section 55A. Section 61(6). In section 62(1) the definition of " contract for the international sale of goods ".
1962 c. 46.	Transport Act 1962.	Section 43(7).
1967 c. 45.	Uniform Laws on International Sales Act 1967.	In section 1(4), the words " 55 and 55A ".
1972 c. 33.	Carriage by Railway Act 1972.	In section 1(1), the words from " and shall have " onwards.
1973 c. 13.	Supply of Goods (Implied Terms) Act 1973.	Section 5(1). Section 6. In section 7(1), the words from " contract for the international sale of goods " onwards. In section 12, subsections (2) to (9). Section 13. In section 15(1), the definition of " consumer sale ".

The repeals in sections 12 and 15 of the Supply of Goods (Implied Terms) Act 1973 shall have effect in relation to those sections as originally enacted and as substituted by the Consumer Credit Act 1974. 1974 c. 39.

PRINTED IN ENGLAND BY BERNARD M. THIMONT
Controller of Her Majesty's Stationery Office and Queen's Printer of Acts of Parliament

LONDON: PUBLISHED BY HER MAJESTY'S STATIONERY OFFICE
45p net

(389862)   ISBN 0 10 545077 4

Sale of Goods Act 1979

CHAPTER 54

ARRANGEMENT OF SECTIONS

PART I

CONTRACTS TO WHICH ACT APPLIES

PART II

FORMATION OF THE CONTRACT

Contract of sale

Formalities of contract

Subject matter of contract

The price

Conditions and warranties

A

ELIZABETH II

Sale of Goods Act 1979

1979 CHAPTER 54

An Act to consolidate the law relating to the sale of goods.   [6th December 1979]

BE IT ENACTED by the Queen's most Excellent Majesty, by and with the advice and consent of the Lords Spiritual and Temporal, and Commons, in this present Parliament assembled, and by the authority of the same, as follows:—

PART I

CONTRACTS TO WHICH ACT APPLIES

1.—(1) This Act applies to contracts of sale of goods made on or after (but not to those made before) 1 January 1894.   Contracts to which Act applies.

(2) In relation to contracts made on certain dates, this Act applies subject to the modification of certain of its sections as mentioned in Schedule 1 below.

(3) Any such modification is indicated in the section concerned by a reference to Schedule 1 below.

(4) Accordingly, where a section does not contain such a reference, this Act applies in relation to the contract concerned without such modification of the section.

PART II

FORMATION OF THE CONTRACT

Contract of sale

2.—(1) A contract of sale of goods is a contract by which the seller transfers or agrees to transfer the property in goods to the buyer for a money consideration, called the price.   Contract of sale.

A 2

(2) There may be a contract of sale between one part owner and another.

(3) A contract of sale may be absolute or conditional.

(4) Where under a contract of sale the property in the goods is transferred from the seller to the buyer the contract is called a sale.

(5) Where under a contract of sale the transfer of the property in the goods is to take place at a future time or subject to some condition later to be fulfilled the contract is called an agreement to sell.

(6) An agreement to sell becomes a sale when the time elapses or the conditions are fulfilled subject to which the property in the goods is to be transferred.

Capacity to buy and sell.   **3.**—(1) Capacity to buy and sell is regulated by the general law concerning capacity to contract and to transfer and acquire property.

(2) Where necessaries are sold and delivered to a minor or to a person who by reason of mental incapacity or drunkenness is incompetent to contract, he must pay a reasonable price for them.

(3) In subsection (2) above " necessaries " means goods suitable to the condition in life of the minor or other person concerned and to his actual requirements at the time of the sale and delivery.

Formalities of contract

How contract of sale is made.   **4.**—(1) Subject to this and any other Act, a contract of sale may be made in writing (either with or without seal), or by word of mouth, or partly in writing and partly by word of mouth, or may be implied from the conduct of the parties.

(2) Nothing in this section affects the law relating to corporations.

Subject matter of contract

Existing or future goods.   **5.**—(1) The goods which form the subject of a contract of sale may be either existing goods, owned or possessed by the seller, or goods to be manufactured or acquired by him after the making of the contract of sale, in this Act called future goods.

(2) There may be a contract for the sale of goods the acquisition of which by the seller depends on a contingency which may or may not happen.

(3) Where by a contract of sale the seller purports to effect a present sale of future goods, the contract operates as an agreement to sell the goods.

6. Where there is a contract for the sale of specific goods, and the goods without the knowledge of the seller have perished at the time when the contract is made, the contract is void.   Goods which have perished.

7. Where there is an agreement to sell specific goods and subsequently the goods, without any fault on the part of the seller or buyer, perish before the risk passes to the buyer, the agreement is avoided.   Goods perishing before sale but after agreement to sell.

The price

8.—(1) The price in a contract of sale may be fixed by the contract, or may be left to be fixed in a manner agreed by the contract, or may be determined by the course of dealing between the parties.   Ascertainment of price.

(2) Where the price is not determined as mentioned in subsection (1) above the buyer must pay a reasonable price.

(3) What is a reasonable price is a question of fact dependent on the circumstances of each particular case.

9.—(1) Where there is an agreement to sell goods on the terms that the price is to be fixed by the valuation of a third party, and he cannot or does not make the valuation, the agreement is avoided ; but if the goods or any part of them have been delivered to and appropriated by the buyer he must pay a reasonable price for them.   Agreement to sell at valuation.

(2) Where the third party is prevented from making the valuation by the fault of the seller or buyer, the party not at fault may maintain an action for damages against the party at fault.

Conditions and warranties

10.—(1) Unless a different intention appears from the terms of the contract, stipulations as to time of payment are not of the essence of a contract of sale.   Stipulations about time.

(2) Whether any other stipulation as to time is or is not of the essence of the contract depends on the terms of the contract.

(3) In a contract of sale " month " prima facie means calendar month.

A 3

PART II
When
condition to
be treated as
warranty.

11.—(1) Subsections (2) to (4) and (7) below do not apply to Scotland and subsection (5) below applies only to Scotland.

(2) Where a contract of sale is subject to a condition to be fulfilled by the seller, the buyer may waive the condition, or may elect to treat the breach of the condition as a breach of warranty and not as a ground for treating the contract as repudiated.

(3) Whether a stipulation in a contract of sale is a condition, the breach of which may give rise to a right to treat the contract as repudiated, or a warranty, the breach of which may give rise to a claim for damages but not to a right to reject the goods and treat the contract as repudiated, depends in each case on the construction of the contract ; and a stipulation may be a condition, though called a warranty in the contract.

(4) Where a contract of sale is not severable and the buyer has accepted the goods or part of them, the breach of a condition to be fulfilled by the seller can only be treated as a breach of warranty, and not as a ground for rejecting the goods and treating the contract as repudiated, unless there is an express or implied term of the contract to that effect.

(5) In Scotland, failure by the seller to perform any material part of a contract of sale is a breach of contract, which entitles the buyer either within a reasonable time after delivery to reject the goods and treat the contract as repudiated, or to retain the goods and treat the failure to perform such material part as a breach which may give rise to a claim for compensation or damages.

(6) Nothing in this section affects a condition or warranty whose fulfilment is excused by law by reason of impossibility or otherwise.

(7) Paragraph 2 of Schedule 1 below applies in relation to a contract made before 22 April 1967 or (in the application of this Act to Northern Ireland) 28 July 1967.

Implied
terms about
title, etc.

12.—(1) In a contract of sale, other than one to which subsection (3) below applies, there is an implied condition on the part of the seller that in the case of a sale he has a right to sell the goods, and in the case of an agreement to sell he will have such a right at the time when the property is to pass.

(2) In a contract of sale, other than one to which subsection (3) below applies, there is also an implied warranty that—

    (a) the goods are free, and will remain free until the time when the property is to pass, from any charge or encumbrance not disclosed or known to the buyer before the contract is made, and

(b) the buyer will enjoy quiet possession of the goods except so far as it may be disturbed by the owner or other person entitled to the benefit of any charge or encumbrance so disclosed or known.

(3) This subsection applies to a contract of sale in the case of which there appears from the contract or is to be inferred from its circumstances an intention that the seller should transfer only such title as he or a third person may have.

(4) In a contract to which subsection (3) above applies there is an implied warranty that all charges or encumbrances known to the seller and not known to the buyer have been disclosed to the buyer before the contract is made.

(5) In a contract to which subsection (3) above applies there is also an implied warranty that none of the following will disturb the buyer's quiet possession of the goods, namely—

(a) the seller ;

(b) in a case where the parties to the contract intend that the seller should transfer only such title as a third person may have, that person ;

(c) anyone claiming through or under the seller or that third person otherwise than under a charge or encumbrance disclosed or known to the buyer before the contract is made.

(6) Paragraph 3 of Schedule 1 below applies in relation to a contract made before 18 May 1973.

13.—(1) Where there is a contract for the sale of goods by description, there is an implied condition that the goods will correspond with the description.

Sale by description.

(2) If the sale is by sample as well as by description it is not sufficient that the bulk of the goods corresponds with the sample if the goods do not also correspond with the description.

(3) A sale of goods is not prevented from being a sale by description by reason only that, being exposed for sale or hire, they are selected by the buyer.

(4) Paragraph 4 of Schedule 1 below applies in relation to a contract made before 18 May 1973.

14.—(1) Except as provided by this section and section 15 below and subject to any other enactment, there is no implied condition or warranty about the quality or fitness for any particular purpose of goods supplied under a contract of sale.

Implied terms about quality or fitness.

(2) Where the seller sells goods in the course of a business, there is an implied condition that the goods supplied under the

contract are of merchantable quality, except that there is no such condition—

> (a) as regards defects specifically drawn to the buyer's attention before the contract is made ; or
>
> (b) if the buyer examines the goods before the contract is made, as regards defects which that examination ought to reveal.

(3) Where the seller sells goods in the course of a business and the buyer, expressly or by implication, makes known—

> (a) to the seller, or
>
> (b) where the purchase price or part of it is payable by instalments and the goods were previously sold by a credit-broker to the seller, to that credit-broker,

any particular purpose for which the goods are being bought, there is an implied condition that the goods supplied under the contract are reasonably fit for that purpose, whether or not that is a purpose for which such goods are commonly supplied, except where the circumstances show that the buyer does not rely, or that it is unreasonable for him to rely, on the skill or judgment of the seller or credit-broker.

(4) An implied condition or warranty about quality or fitness for a particular purpose may be annexed to a contract of sale by usage.

(5) The preceding provisions of this section apply to a sale by a person who in the course of a business is acting as agent for another as they apply to a sale by a principal in the course of a business, except where that other is not selling in the course of a business and either the buyer knows that fact or reasonable steps are taken to bring it to the notice of the buyer before the contract is made.

(6) Goods of any kind are of merchantable quality within the meaning of subsection (2) above if they are as fit for the purpose or purposes for which goods of that kind are commonly bought as it is reasonable to expect having regard to any description applied to them, the price (if relevant) and all the other relevant circumstances.

(7) Paragraph 5 of Schedule 1 below applies in relation to a contract made on or after 18 May 1973 and before the appointed day, and paragraph 6 in relation to one made before 18 May 1973.

(8) In subsection (7) above and paragraph 5 of Schedule 1 below references to the appointed day are to the day appointed for the purposes of those provisions by an order of the Secretary of State made by statutory instrument.

Sale by sample

15.—(1) A contract of sale is a contract for sale by sample Sale by where there is an express or implied term to that effect in the sample. contract.

(2) In the case of a contract for sale by sample there is an implied condition—

   (*a*) that the bulk will correspond with the sample in quality ;

   (*b*) that the buyer will have a reasonable opportunity of comparing the bulk with the sample ;

   (*c*) that the goods will be free from any defect, rendering them unmerchantable, which would not be apparent on reasonable examination of the sample.

(3) In subsection (2)(*c*) above " unmerchantable " is to be construed in accordance with section 14(6) above.

(4) Paragraph 7 of Schedule 1 below applies in relation to a contract made before 18 May 1973.

PART III

EFFECTS OF THE CONTRACT

Transfer of property as between seller and buyer

16. Where there is a contract for the sale of unascertained Goods goods no property in the goods is transferred to the buyer unless must be and until the goods are ascertained. ascertained.

17.—(1) Where there is a contract for the sale of specific or Property ascertained goods the property in them is transferred to the passes when buyer at such time as the parties to the contract intend it to be intended to pass. transferred.

(2) For the purpose of ascertaining the intention of the parties regard shall be had to the terms of the contract, the conduct of the parties and the circumstances of the case.

18. Unless a different intention appears, the following are Rules for rules for ascertaining the intention of the parties as to the time ascertaining at which the property in the goods is to pass to the buyer. intention.

   Rule 1.—Where there is an unconditional contract for the sale of specific goods in a deliverable state the property in the goods passes to the buyer when the contract is made, and it is immaterial whether the time of payment or the time of delivery, or both, be postponed.

   Rule 2.—Where there is a contract for the sale of specific goods and the seller is bound to do something to the goods for the purpose of putting them into a deliverable state, the property does not pass until the thing is done and the buyer has notice that it has been done.

Rule 3.—Where there is a contract for the sale of specific goods in a deliverable state but the seller is bound to weigh, measure, test, or do some other act or thing with reference to the goods for the purpose of ascertaining the price, the property does not pass until the act or thing is done and the buyer has notice that it has been done.

Rule 4.—When goods are delivered to the buyer on approval or on sale or return or other similar terms the property in the goods passes to the buyer : —

(a) when he signifies his approval or acceptance to the seller or does any other act adopting the transaction ;

(b) if he does not signify his approval or acceptance to the seller but retains the goods without giving notice of rejection, then, if a time has been fixed for the return of the goods, on the expiration of that time, and, if no time has been fixed, on the expiration of a reasonable time.

Rule 5.—(1) Where there is a contract for the sale of unascertained or future goods by description, and goods of that description and in a deliverable state are unconditionally appropriated to the contract, either by the seller with the assent of the buyer or by the buyer with the assent of the seller, the property in the goods then passes to the buyer ; and the assent may be express or implied, and may be given either before or after the appropriation is made.

(2) Where, in pursuance of the contract, the seller delivers the goods to the buyer or to a carrier or other bailee or custodier (whether named by the buyer or not) for the purpose of transmission to the buyer, and does not reserve the right of disposal, he is to be taken to have unconditionally appropriated the goods to the contract.

Reservation of right of disposal.

19.—(1) Where there is a contract for the sale of specific goods or where goods are subsequently appropriated to the contract, the seller may, by the terms of the contract or appropriation, reserve the right of disposal of the goods until certain conditions are fulfilled ; and in such a case, notwithstanding the delivery of the goods to the buyer, or to a carrier or other bailee or custodier for the purpose of transmission to the buyer, the property in the goods does not pass to the buyer until the conditions imposed by the seller are fulfilled.

(2) Where goods are shipped, and by the bill of lading the goods are deliverable to the order of the seller or his agent, the seller is prima facie to be taken to reserve the right of disposal.

(3) Where the seller of goods draws on the buyer for the price, and transmits the bill of exchange and bill of lading to the buyer together to secure acceptance or payment of the bill of exchange, the buyer is bound to return the bill of lading if he does not honour the bill of exchange, and if he wrongfully retains the bill of lading the property in the goods does not pass to him.

PART III

20.—(1) Unless otherwise agreed, the goods remain at the seller's risk until the property in them is transferred to the buyer, but when the property in them is transferred to the buyer the goods are at the buyer's risk whether delivery has been made or not.

Risk prima facie passes with property.

(2) But where delivery has been delayed through the fault of either buyer or seller the goods are at the risk of the party at fault as regards any loss which might not have occurred but for such fault.

(3) Nothing in this section affects the duties or liabilities of either seller or buyer as a bailee or custodier of the goods of the other party.

Transfer of title

21.—(1) Subject to this Act, where goods are sold by a person who is not their owner, and who does not sell them under the authority or with the consent of the owner, the buyer acquires no better title to the goods than the seller had, unless the owner of the goods is by his conduct precluded from denying the seller's authority to sell.

Sale by person not the owner.

(2) Nothing in this Act affects—

(a) the provisions of the Factors Acts or any enactment enabling the apparent owner of goods to dispose of them as if he were their true owner ;

(b) the validity of any contract of sale under any special common law or statutory power of sale or under the order of a court of competent jurisdiction.

22.—(1) Where goods are sold in market overt, according to the usage of the market, the buyer acquires a good title to the goods, provided he buys them in good faith and without notice of any defect or want of title on the part of the seller.

Market overt.

(2) This section does not apply to Scotland.

(3) Paragraph 8 of Schedule 1 below applies in relation to a contract under which goods were sold before 1 January 1968 or (in the application of this Act to Northern Ireland) 29 August 1967.

PART III
Sale under
voidable title.

23. When the seller of goods has a voidable title to them, but his title has not been avoided at the time of the sale, the buyer acquires a good title to the goods, provided he buys them in good faith and without notice of the seller's defect of title.

Seller in
possession
after sale.

24. Where a person having sold goods continues or is in possession of the goods, or of the documents of title to the goods, the delivery or transfer by that person, or by a mercantile agent acting for him, of the goods or documents of title under any sale, pledge, or other disposition thereof, to any person receiving the same in good faith and without notice of the previous sale, has the same effect as if the person making the delivery or transfer were expressly authorised by the owner of the goods to make the same.

Buyer in
possession
after sale.

25.—(1) Where a person having bought or agreed to buy goods obtains, with the consent of the seller, possession of the goods or the documents of title to the goods, the delivery or transfer by that person, or by a mercantile agent acting for him, of the goods or documents of title, under any sale, pledge, or other disposition thereof, to any person receiving the same in good faith and without notice of any lien or other right of the original seller in respect of the goods, has the same effect as if the person making the delivery or transfer were a mercantile agent in possession of the goods or documents of title with the consent of the owner.

(2) For the purposes of subsection (1) above—

    (*a*) the buyer under a conditional sale agreement is to be taken not to be a person who has bought or agreed to buy goods, and

    (*b*) " conditional sale agreement " means an agreement for the sale of goods which is a consumer credit agreement within the meaning of the Consumer Credit Act 1974 under which the purchase price or part of it is payable by instalments, and the property in the goods is to remain in the seller (notwithstanding that the buyer is to be in possession of the goods) until such conditions as to the payment of instalments or otherwise as may be specified in the agreement are fulfilled.

1974 c. 39.

(3) Paragraph 9 of Schedule 1 below applies in relation to a contract under which a person buys or agrees to buy goods and which is made before the appointed day.

(4) In subsection (3) above and paragraph 9 of Schedule 1 below references to the appointed day are to the day appointed for the purposes of those provisions by an order of the Secretary of State made by statutory instrument.

26. In sections 24 and 25 above " mercantile agent " means a mercantile agent having in the customary course of his business as such agent authority either—

   (*a*) to sell goods, or

   (*b*) to consign goods for the purpose of sale, or

   (*c*) to buy goods, or

   (*d*) to raise money on the security of goods.

PART III
Supplementary to
sections
24 and 25.

PART IV

PERFORMANCE OF THE CONTRACT

27. It is the duty of the seller to deliver the goods, and of the buyer to accept and pay for them, in accordance with the terms of the contract of sale.

Duties of seller and buyer.

28. Unless otherwise agreed, delivery of the goods and payment of the price are concurrent conditions, that is to say, the seller must be ready and willing to give possession of the goods to the buyer in exchange for the price and the buyer must be ready and willing to pay the price in exchange for possession of the goods.

Payment and delivery are concurrent conditions,

29.—(1) Whether it is for the buyer to take possession of the goods or for the seller to send them to the buyer is a question depending in each case on the contract, express or implied, between the parties.

Rules about delivery.

(2) Apart from any such contract, express or implied, the place of delivery is the seller's place of business if he has one, and if not, his residence ; except that, if the contract is for the sale of specific goods, which to the knowledge of the parties when the contract is made are in some other place, then that place is the place of delivery.

(3) Where under the contract of sale the seller is bound to send the goods to the buyer, but no time for sending them is fixed, the seller is bound to send them within a reasonable time.

(4) Where the goods at the time of sale are in the possession of a third person, there is no delivery by seller to buyer unless and until the third person acknowledges to the buyer that he holds the goods on his behalf ; but nothing in this section affects the operation of the issue or transfer of any document of title to goods.

(5) Demand or tender of delivery may be treated as ineffectual unless made at a reasonable hour ; and what is a reasonable hour is a question of fact.

PART IV

(6) Unless otherwise agreed, the expenses of and incidental to putting the goods into a deliverable state must be borne by the seller.

Delivery of wrong quantity.

30.—(1) Where the seller delivers to the buyer a quantity of goods less than he contracted to sell, the buyer may reject them, but if the buyer accepts the goods so delivered he must pay for them at the contract rate.

(2) Where the seller delivers to the buyer a quantity of goods larger than he contracted to sell, the buyer may accept the goods included in the contract and reject the rest, or he may reject the whole.

(3) Where the seller delivers to the buyer a quantity of goods larger than he contracted to sell and the buyer accepts the whole of the goods so delivered he must pay for them at the contract rate.

(4) Where the seller delivers to the buyer the goods he contracted to sell mixed with goods of a different description not included in the contract, the buyer may accept the goods which are in accordance with the contract and reject the rest, or he may reject the whole.

(5) This section is subject to any usage of trade, special agreement, or course of dealing between the parties.

Instalment deliveries.

31.—(1) Unless otherwise agreed, the buyer of goods is not bound to accept delivery of them by instalments.

(2) Where there is a contract for the sale of goods to be delivered by stated instalments, which are to be separately paid for, and the seller makes defective deliveries in respect of one or more instalments, or the buyer neglects or refuses to take delivery of or pay for one or more instalments, it is a question in each case depending on the terms of the contract and the circumstances of the case whether the breach of contract is a repudiation of the whole contract or whether it is a severable breach giving rise to a claim for compensation but not to a right to treat the whole contract as repudiated

Delivery to carrier.

32.—(1) Where, in pursuance of a contract of sale, the seller is authorised or required to send the goods to the buyer, delivery of the goods to a carrier (whether named by the buyer or not) for the purpose of transmission to the buyer is prima facie deemed to be a delivery of the goods to the buyer.

(2) Unless otherwise authorised by the buyer, the seller must make such contract with the carrier on behalf of the buyer as may be reasonable having regard to the nature of the goods and the other circumstances of the case ; and if the seller omits to do

so, and the goods are lost or damaged in course of transit, the buyer may decline to treat the delivery to the carrier as a delivery to himself or may hold the seller responsible in damages.

(3) Unless otherwise agreed, where goods are sent by the seller to the buyer by a route involving sea transit, under circumstances in which it is usual to insure, the seller must give such notice to the buyer as may enable him to insure them during their sea transit ; and if the seller fails to do so, the goods are at his risk during such sea transit.

33. Where the seller of goods agrees to deliver them at his own risk at a place other than that where they are when sold, the buyer must nevertheless (unless otherwise agreed) take any risk of deterioration in the goods necessarily incident to the course of transit.

Risk where goods are delivered at distant place.

34.—(1) Where goods are delivered to the buyer, and he has not previously examined them, he is not deemed to have accepted them until he has had a reasonable opportunity of examining them for the purpose of ascertaining whether they are in conformity with the contract.

Buyer's right of examining the goods.

(2) Unless otherwise agreed, when the seller tenders delivery of goods to the buyer, he is bound on request to afford the buyer a reasonable opportunity of examining the goods for the purpose of ascertaining whether they are in conformity with the contract.

35.—(1) The buyer is deemed to have accepted the goods when he intimates to the seller that he has accepted them, or (except where section 34 above otherwise provides) when the goods have been delivered to him and he does any act in relation to them which is inconsistent with the ownership of the seller, or when after the lapse of a reasonable time he retains the goods without intimating to the seller that he has rejected them.

Acceptance.

(2) Paragraph 10 of Schedule 1 below applies in relation to a contract made before 22 April 1967 or (in the application of this Act to Northern Ireland) 28 July 1967.

36. Unless otherwise agreed, where goods are delivered to the buyer, and he refuses to accept them, having the right to do so, he is not bound to return them to the seller, but it is sufficient if he intimates to the seller that he refuses to accept them.

Buyer not bound to return rejected goods.

37.—(1) When the seller is ready and willing to deliver the goods, and requests the buyer to take delivery, and the buyer does not within a reasonable time after such request take delivery of the goods, he is liable to the seller for any loss occasioned by his neglect or refusal to take delivery, and also for a reasonable charge for the care and custody of the goods.

Buyer's liability for not taking delivery of goods.

Part IV
(2) Nothing in this section affects the rights of the seller where the neglect or refusal of the buyer to take delivery amounts to a repudiation of the contract.

Part V

Rights of Unpaid Seller Against the Goods

Preliminary

Unpaid seller defined.
38.—(1) The seller of goods is an unpaid seller within the meaning of this Act—

(*a*) when the whole of the price has not been paid or tendered ;

(*b*) when a bill of exchange or other negotiable instrument has been received as conditional payment, and the condition on which it was received has not been fulfilled by reason of the dishonour of the instrument or otherwise.

(2) In this Part of this Act " seller " includes any person who is in the position of a seller, as, for instance, an agent of the seller to whom the bill of lading has been indorsed, or a consignor or agent who has himself paid (or is directly responsible for) the price.

Unpaid seller's rights.
39.—(1) Subject to this and any other Act, notwithstanding that the property in the goods may have passed to the buyer, the unpaid seller of goods, as such, has by implication of law—

(*a*) a lien on the goods or right to retain them for the price while he is in possession of them ;

(*b*) in case of the insolvency of the buyer, a right of stopping the goods in transit after he has parted with the possession of them ;

(*c*) a right of re-sale as limited by this Act.

(2) Where the property in goods has not passed to the buyer, the unpaid seller has (in addition to his other remedies) a right of withholding delivery similar to and co-extensive with his rights of lien or retention and stoppage in transit where the property has passed to the buyer.

Attachment by seller in Scotland.
40. In Scotland a seller of goods may attach them while in his own hands or possession by arrestment or poinding ; and such arrestment or poinding shall have the same operation and effect in a competition or otherwise as an arrestment or poinding by a third party.

Unpaid seller's lien

41.—(1) Subject to this Act, the unpaid seller of goods who is Seller's lien. in possession of them is entitled to retain possession of them until payment or tender of the price in the following cases: —

- (a) where the goods have been sold without any stipulation as to credit;
- (b) where the goods have been sold on credit but the term of credit has expired;
- (c) where the buyer becomes insolvent.

(2) The seller may exercise his lien or right of retention notwithstanding that he is in possession of the goods as agent or bailee or custodier for the buyer.

42. Where an unpaid seller has made part delivery of the Part delivery. goods, he may exercise his lien or right of retention on the remainder, unless such part delivery has been made under such circumstances as to show an agreement to waive the lien or right of retention.

43.—(1) The unpaid seller of goods loses his lien or right of Termination retention in respect of them— of lien.

- (a) when he delivers the goods to a carrier or other bailee or custodier for the purpose of transmission to the buyer without reserving the right of disposal of the goods;
- (b) when the buyer or his agent lawfully obtains possession of the goods;
- (c) by waiver of the lien or right of retention.

(2) An unpaid seller of goods who has a lien or right of retention in respect of them does not lose his lien or right of retention by reason only that he has obtained judgment or decree for the price of the goods.

Stoppage in transit

44. Subject to this Act, when the buyer of goods becomes Right of insolvent the unpaid seller who has parted with the possession stoppage of the goods has the right of stopping them in transit, that is in transit. to say, he may resume possession of the goods as long as they are in course of transit, and may retain them until payment or tender of the price.

45.—(1) Goods are deemed to be in course of transit from Duration the time when they are delivered to a carrier or other bailee or of transit. custodier for the purpose of transmission to the buyer, until the buyer or his agent in that behalf takes delivery of them from the carrier or other bailee or custodier.

PART V   (2) If the buyer or his agent in that behalf obtains delivery of the goods before their arrival at the appointed destination, the transit is at an end.

(3) If, after the arrival of the goods at the appointed destination, the carrier or other bailee or custodier acknowledges to the buyer or his agent that he holds the goods on his behalf and continues in possession of them as bailee or custodier for the buyer or his agent, the transit is at an end, and it is immaterial that a further destination for the goods may have been indicated by the buyer.

(4) If the goods are rejected by the buyer, and the carrier or other bailee or custodier continues in possession of them, the transit is not deemed to be at an end, even if the seller has refused to receive them back.

(5) When goods are delivered to a ship chartered by the buyer it is a question depending on the circumstances of the particular case whether they are in the possession of the master as a carrier or as agent for the buyer.

(6) Where the carrier or other bailee or custodier wrongfully refuses to deliver the goods to the buyer or his agent in that behalf, the transit is deemed to be at an end.

(7) Where part delivery of the goods has been made to the buyer or his agent in that behalf, the remainder of the goods may be stopped in transit, unless such part delivery has been made under such circumstances as to show an agreement to give up possession of the whole of the goods.

How stoppage in transit is effected.   **46.**—(1) The unpaid seller may exercise his right of stoppage in transit either by taking actual possession of the goods or by giving notice of his claim to the carrier or other bailee or custodier in whose possession the goods are.

(2) The notice may be given either to the person in actual possession of the goods or to his principal.

(3) If given to the principal, the notice is ineffective unless given at such time and under such circumstances that the principal, by the exercise of reasonable diligence, may communicate it to his servant or agent in time to prevent a delivery to the buyer.

(4) When notice of stoppage in transit is given by the seller to the carrier or other bailee or custodier in possession of the goods, he must re-deliver the goods to, or according to the directions of, the seller ; and the expenses of the re-delivery must be borne by the seller.

Re-sale etc. by buyer

47.—(1) Subject to this Act, the unpaid seller's right of lien or retention or stoppage in transit is not affected by any sale or other disposition of the goods which the buyer may have made, unless the seller has assented to it.

(2) Where a document of title to goods has been lawfully transferred to any person as buyer or owner of the goods, and that person transfers the document to a person who takes it in good faith and for valuable consideration, then—

(a) if the last-mentioned transfer was by way of sale the unpaid seller's right of lien or retention or stoppage in transit is defeated ; and

(b) if the last-mentioned transfer was made by way of pledge or other disposition for value, the unpaid seller's right of lien or retention or stoppage in transit can only be exercised subject to the rights of the transferee.

Rescission : and re-sale by seller

48.—(1) Subject to this section, a contract of sale is not rescinded by the mere exercise by an unpaid seller of his right of lien or retention or stoppage in transit.

(2) Where an unpaid seller who has exercised his right of lien or retention or stoppage in transit re-sells the goods, the buyer acquires a good title to them as against the original buyer.

(3) Where the goods are of a perishable nature, or where the unpaid seller gives notice to the buyer of his intention to re-sell, and the buyer does not within a reasonable time pay or tender the price, the unpaid seller may re-sell the goods and recover from the original buyer damages for any loss occasioned by his breach of contract.

(4) Where the seller expressly reserves the right of re-sale in case the buyer should make default, and on the buyer making default re-sells the goods, the original contract of sale is rescinded but without prejudice to any claim the seller may have for damages.

PART VI

ACTIONS FOR BREACH OF THE CONTRACT

Seller's remedies

49.—(1) Where, under a contract of sale, the property in the goods has passed to the buyer and he wrongfully neglects or refuses to pay for the goods according to the terms of the contract, the seller may maintain an action against him for the price of the goods.

PART VI   (2) Where, under a contract of sale, the price is payable on a day certain irrespective of delivery and the buyer wrongfully neglects or refuses to pay such price, the seller may maintain an action for the price, although the property in the goods has not passed and the goods have not been appropriated to the contract.

(3) Nothing in this section prejudices the right of the seller in Scotland to recover interest on the price from the date of tender of the goods, or from the date on which the price was payable, as the case may be.

Damages for non-acceptance.

50.—(1) Where the buyer wrongfully neglects or refuses to accept and pay for the goods, the seller may maintain an action against him for damages for non-acceptance.

(2) The measure of damages is the estimated loss directly and naturally resulting, in the ordinary course of events, from the buyer's breach of contract.

(3) Where there is an available market for the goods in question the measure of damages is prima facie to be ascertained by the difference between the contract price and the market or current price at the time or times when the goods ought to have been accepted or (if no time was fixed for acceptance) at the time of the refusal to accept.

Buyer's remedies

Damages for non-delivery.

51.—(1) Where the seller wrongfully neglects or refuses to deliver the goods to the buyer, the buyer may maintain an action against the seller for damages for non-delivery.

(2) The measure of damages is the estimated loss directly and naturally resulting, in the ordinary course of events, from the seller's breach of contract.

(3) Where there is an available market for the goods in question the measure of damages is prima facie to be ascertained by the difference between the contract price and the market or current price of the goods at the time or times when they ought to have been delivered or (if no time was fixed) at the time of the refusal to deliver.

Specific performance.

52.—(1) In any action for breach of contract to deliver specific or ascertained goods the court may, if it thinks fit, on the plaintiff's application, by its judgment or decree direct that the contract shall be performed specifically, without giving the defendant the option of retaining the goods on payment of damages.

(2) The plaintiff's application may be made at any time before judgment or decree.

(3) The judgment or decree may be unconditional, or on such   PART VI
terms and conditions as to damages, payment of the price and
otherwise as seem just to the court.

(4) The provisions of this section shall be deemed to be
supplementary to, and not in derogation of, the right of specific
implement in Scotland.

53.—(1) Where there is a breach of warranty by the seller, Remedy for
or where the buyer elects (or is compelled) to treat any breach breach of
of a condition on the part of the seller as a breach of warranty, warranty.
the buyer is not by reason only of such breach of warranty
entitled to reject the goods ; but he may—

- (*a*) set up against the seller the breach of warranty in
       diminution or extinction of the price, or
- (*b*) maintain an action against the seller for damages for
       the breach of warranty.

(2) The measure of damages for breach of warranty is the
estimated loss directly and naturally resulting, in the ordinary
course of events, from the breach of warranty.

(3) In the case of breach of warranty of quality such loss is
prima facie the difference between the value of the goods at
the time of delivery to the buyer and the value they would
have had if they had fulfilled the warranty.

(4) The fact that the buyer has set up the breach of warranty
in diminution or extinction of the price does not prevent him
from maintaining an action for the same breach of warranty
if he has suffered further damage.

(5) Nothing in this section prejudices or affects the buyer's
right of rejection in Scotland as declared by this Act.

Interest, etc.

54. Nothing in this Act affects the right of the buyer or the Interest, etc.
seller to recover interest or special damages in any case where
by law interest or special damages may be recoverable, or to
recover money paid where the consideration for the payment
of it has failed.

PART VII

SUPPLEMENTARY

55.—(1) Where a right, duty or liability would arise under Exclusion
a contract of sale of goods by implication of law, it may (sub- of implied
ject to the Unfair Contract Terms Act 1977) be negatived or terms.
varied by express agreement, or by the course of dealing 1977 c. 50.
between the parties, or by such usage as binds both parties to
the contract.

PART VII   (2) An express condition or warranty does not negative a condition or warranty implied by this Act unless inconsistent with it.

(3) Paragraph 11 of Schedule 1 below applies in relation to a contract made on or after 18 May 1973 and before 1 February 1978, and paragraph 12 in relation to one made before 18 May 1973.

Conflict
of laws.

56. Paragraph 13 of Schedule 1 below applies in relation to a contract made on or after 18 May 1973 and before 1 February 1978, so as to make provision about conflict of laws in relation to such a contract.

Auction sales.

57.—(1) Where goods are put up for sale by auction in lots, each lot is prima facie deemed to be the subject of a separate contract of sale.

(2) A sale by auction is complete when the auctioneer announces its completion by the fall of the hammer, or in other customary manner ; and until the announcement is made any bidder may retract his bid.

(3) A sale by auction may be notified to be subject to a reserve or upset price, and a right to bid may also be reserved expressly by or on behalf of the seller.

(4) Where a sale by auction is not notified to be subject to a right to bid by or on behalf of the seller, it is not lawful for the seller to bid himself or to employ any person to bid at the sale, or for the auctioneer knowingly to take any bid from the seller or any such person.

(5) A sale contravening subsection (4) above may be treated as fraudulent by the buyer.

(6) Where, in respect of a sale by auction, a right to bid is expressly reserved (but not otherwise) the seller or any one person on his behalf may bid at the auction.

Payment into
court in
Scotland.

58. In Scotland where a buyer has elected to accept goods which he might have rejected, and to treat a breach of contract as only giving rise to a claim for damages, he may, in an action by the seller for the price, be required, in the discretion of the court before which the action depends, to consign or pay into court the price of the goods, or part of the price, or to give other reasonable security for its due payment.

Reasonable
time a
question
of fact.

59. Where a reference is made in this Act to a reasonable time the question what is a reasonable time is a question of fact.

60. Where a right, duty or liability is declared by this Act, it may (unless otherwise provided by this Act) be enforced by action.

61.—(1) In this Act, unless the context or subject matter otherwise requires,—

" action " includes counterclaim and set-off, and in Scotland condescendence and claim and compensation ;

" business " includes a profession and the activities of any government department (including a Northern Ireland department) or local or public authority ;

" buyer " means a person who buys or agrees to buy goods ;

" contract of sale " includes an agreement to sell as well as a sale ;

" credit-broker " means a person acting in the course of a business of credit brokerage carried on by him, that is a business of effecting introductions of individuals desiring to obtain credit—

   (a) to persons carrying on any business so far as it relates to the provision of credit, or

   (b) to other persons engaged in credit brokerage ;

" defendant " includes in Scotland defender, respondent, and claimant in a multiplepoinding ;

" delivery " means voluntary transfer of possession from one person to another ;

" document of title to goods " has the same meaning as it has in the Factors Acts ;

" Factors Acts " means the Factors Act 1889, the Factors (Scotland) Act 1890, and any enactment amending or substituted for the same ;

" fault " means wrongful act or default ;

" future goods " means goods to be manufactured or acquired by the seller after the making of the contract of sale ;

" goods " includes all personal chattels other than things in action and money, and in Scotland all corporeal moveables except money ; and in particular " goods " includes emblements, industrial growing crops, and things attached to or forming part of the land which are agreed to be severed before sale or under the contract of sale ;

" plaintiff " includes pursuer, complainer, claimant in a multiplepoinding and defendant or defender counter-claiming ;

" property " means the general property in goods, and not merely a special property ;

" quality ", in relation to goods, includes their state or condition ;

" sale " includes a bargain and sale as well as a sale and delivery ;

" seller " means a person who sells or agrees to sell goods ;

" specific goods " means goods identified and agreed on at the time a contract of sale is made ;

" warranty " (as regards England and Wales and Northern Ireland) means an agreeement with reference to goods which are the subject of a contract of sale, but collateral to the main purpose of such contract, the breach of which gives rise to a claim for damages, but not to a right to reject the goods and treat the contract as repudiated.

(2) As regards Scotland a breach of warranty shall be deemed to be a failure to perform a material part of the contract.

(3) A thing is deemed to be done in good faith within the meaning of this Act when it is in fact done honestly, whether it is done negligently or not.

(4) A person is deemed to be insolvent within the meaning of this Act if he has either ceased to pay his debts in the ordinary course of business or he cannot pay his debts as they become due, whether he has committed an act of bankruptcy or not, and whether he has become a notour bankrupt or not.

(5) Goods are in a deliverable state within the meaning of this Act when they are in such a state that the buyer would under the contract be bound to take delivery of them.

(6) As regards the definition of " business " in subsection (1) above, paragraph 14 of Schedule 1 below applies in relation to a contract made on or after 18 May 1973 and before 1 February 1978, and paragraph 15 in relation to one made before 18 May 1973.

Savings: rules of law etc.   **62.**—(1) The rules in bankruptcy relating to contracts of sale apply to those contracts, notwithstanding anything in this Act.

(2) The rules of the common law, including the law merchant, except in so far as they are inconsistent with the provisions of this Act, and in particular the rules relating to the law of principal and agent and the effect of fraud, misrepresentation, duress or coercion, mistake, or other invalidating cause, apply to contracts for the sale of goods.

(3) Nothing in this Act or the Sale of Goods Act 1893 affects the enactments relating to bills of sale, or any enactment relating to the sale of goods which is not expressly repealed or amended by this Act or that.   PART VII

  1893 c. 71.

(4) The provisions of this Act about contracts of sale do not apply to a transaction in the form of a contract of sale which is intended to operate by way of mortgage, pledge, charge, or other security.

(5) Nothing in this Act prejudices or affects the landlord's right of hypothec or sequestration for rent in Scotland.

63.—(1) Without prejudice to section 17 of the Interpretation Act 1978 (repeal and re-enactment), the enactments mentioned in Schedule 2 below have effect subject to the amendments there specified (being amendments consequential on this Act).   Consequential amendments, repeals and savings. 1978 c. 30.

(2) The enactments mentioned in Schedule 3 below are repealed to the extent specified in column 3, but subject to the savings in Schedule 4 below.

(3) The savings in Schedule 4 below have effect.

64.—(1) This Act may be cited as the Sale of Goods Act 1979.   Short title and commencement.

(2) This Act comes into force on 1 January 1980.

SCHEDULES

Section 1.

SCHEDULE 1

MODIFICATION OF ACT FOR CERTAIN CONTRACTS

Preliminary

1.—(1) This Schedule modifies this Act as it applies to contracts of sale of goods made on certain dates.

(2) In this Schedule references to sections are to those of this Act and references to contracts are to contracts of sale of goods.

(3) Nothing in this Schedule affects a contract made before 1 January 1894.

Section 11 : *condition treated as warranty*

2. In relation to a contract made before 22 April 1967 or (in the application of this Act to Northern Ireland) 28 July 1967, in section 11(4) after " or part of them," insert " or where the contract is for specific goods, the property in which has passed to the buyer,".

Section 12 : *implied terms about title etc.*

3. In relation to a contract made before 18 May 1973 substitute the following for section 12 : —

Implied
terms about
title, etc.

12. In a contract of sale, unless the circumstances of the contract are such as to show a different intention, there is—

(a) an implied condition on the part of the seller that in the case of a sale he has a right to sell the goods, and in the case of an agreement to sell he will have such a right at the time when the property is to pass ;

(b) an implied warranty that the buyer will have and enjoy quiet possession of the goods ;

(c) an implied warranty that the goods will be free from any charge or encumbrance in favour of any third party, not declared or known to the buyer before or at the time when the contract is made.

Section 13: *sale by description*

4. In relation to a contract made before 18 May 1973, omit section 13(3).

Section 14: *quality or fitness (i)*

5. In relation to a contract made on or after 18 May 1973 and before the appointed day, substitute the following for section 14 : —

Implied terms about quality or fitness.

SCH. 1

14.—(1) Except as provided by this section and section 15 below and subject to any other enactment, there is no implied condition or warranty about the quality or fitness for any particular purpose of goods supplied under a contract of sale.

(2) Where the seller sells goods in the course of a business, there is an implied condition that the goods supplied under the contract are of merchantable quality, except that there is no such condition—

(a) as regards defects specifically drawn to the buyer's attention before the contract is made ; or

(b) if the buyer examines the goods before the contract is made, as regards defects which that examination ought to reveal.

(3) Where the seller sells goods in the course of a business and the buyer, expressly or by implication, makes known to the seller any particular purpose for which the goods are being bought, there is an implied condition that the goods supplied under the contract are reasonably fit for that purpose, whether or not that is a purpose for which such goods are commonly supplied, except where the circumstances show that the buyer does not rely, or that it is unreasonable for him to rely, on the seller's skill or judgment.

(4) An implied condition or warranty about quality or fitness for a particular purpose may be annexed to a contract of sale by usage.

(5) The preceding provisions of this section apply to a sale by a person who in the course of a business is acting as agent for another as they apply to a sale by a principal in the course of a business, except where that other is not selling in the course of a business and either the buyer knows that fact or reasonable steps are taken to bring it to the notice of the buyer before the contract is made.

(6) Goods of any kind are of merchantable quality within the meaning of subsection (2) above if they are as fit for the purpose or purposes for which goods of that kind are commonly bought as it is reasonable to expect having regard to any description applied to them, the price (if relevant) and all the other relevant circumstances.

(7) In the application of subsection (3) above to an agreement for the sale of goods under which the purchase price or part of it is payable by instalments any reference to the seller includes a reference to the person by whom any antecedent negotiations are conducted ; and section 58(3) and (5) of the Hire-Purchase Act 1965, section 54(3) and (5) of the Hire-Purchase (Scotland) Act 1965 and section 65(3) and (5) of the Hire-Purchase Act (Northern Ireland) 1966 (meaning of antecedent negotiations and

1965 c. 66.
1965 c. 67.
1966 c. 42.
(N.I.).

related expressions) apply in relation to this subsection as in relation to each of those Acts, but as if a reference to any such agreement were included in the references in subsection (3) of each of those sections to the agreements there mentioned.

Section 14: *quality or fitness (ii)*

6. In relation to a contract made before 18 May 1973 substitute the following for section 14: —

Implied terms about quality or fitness.

14.—(1) Subject to this and any other Act, there is no implied condition or warranty about the quality or fitness for any particular purpose of goods supplied under a contract of sale.

(2) Where the buyer, expressly or by implication, makes known to the seller the particular purpose for which the goods are required, so as to show that the buyer relies on the seller's skill or judgment, and the goods are of a description which it is in the course of the seller's business to supply (whether he is the manufacturer or not), there is an implied condition that the goods will be reasonably fit for such purpose, except that in the case of a contract for the sale of a specified article under its patent or other trade name there is no implied condition as to its fitness for any particular purpose.

(3) Where goods are bought by description from a seller who deals in goods of that description (whether he is the manufacturer or not), there is an implied condition that the goods will be of merchantable quality ; but if the buyer has examined the goods, there is no implied condition as regards defects which such examination ought to have revealed.

(4) An implied condition or warranty about quality or fitness for a particular purpose may be annexed by the usage of trade.

(5) An express condition or warranty does not negative a condition or warranty implied by this Act unless inconsistent with it.

Section 15: *sale by sample*

7. In relation to a contract made before 18 May 1973, omit section 15(3).

Section 22: *market overt*

8. In relation to a contract under which goods were sold before 1 January 1968 or (in the application of this Act to Northern Ireland) 29 August 1967, add the following paragraph at the end of section 22(1): —

" Nothing in this subsection affects the law relating to the sale of horses."

Section 25: *buyer in possession*

9. In relation to a contract under which a person buys or agrees to buy goods and which is made before the appointed day, omit section 25(2).

Section 35: *acceptance*

10. In relation to a contract made before 22 April 1967 or (in the application of this Act to Northern Ireland) 28 July 1967, in section 35(1) omit " (except where section 34 above otherwise provides) ".

Section 55: *exclusion of implied terms* (*i*)

11. In relation to a contract made on or after 18 May 1973 and before 1 February 1978 substitute the following for section 55 : —

Exclusion of implied terms.

55.—(1) Where a right, duty or liability would arise under a contract of sale of goods by implication of law, it may be negatived or varied by express agreement, or by the course of dealing between the parties, or by such usage as binds both parties to the contract, but the preceding provision has effect subject to the following provisions of this section.

(2) An express condition or warranty does not negative a condition or warranty implied by this Act unless inconsistent with it.

(3) In the case of a contract of sale of goods, any term of that or any other contract exempting from all or any of the provisions of section 12 above is void.

(4) In the case of a contract of sale of goods, any term of that or any other contract exempting from all or any of the provisions of section 13, 14 or 15 above is void in the case of a consumer sale and is, in any other case, not enforceable to the extent that it is shown that it would not be fair or reasonable to allow reliance on the term.

(5) In determining for the purposes of subsection (4) above whether or not reliance on any such term would be fair or reasonable regard shall be had to all the circumstances of the case and in particular to the following matters—

(*a*) the strength of the bargaining positions of the seller and buyer relative to each other, taking into account, among other things, the availability of suitable alternative products and sources of supply ;

(*b*) whether the buyer received an inducement to agree to the term or in accepting it had an opportunity of buying the goods or suitable alternatives without it from any source of supply ;

(c) whether the buyer knew or ought reasonably to
have known of the existence and extent of the
term (having regard, among other things, to any
custom of the trade and any previous course of
dealing between the parties) ;

(d) where the term exempts from all or any of the
provisions of section 13, 14 or 15 above if some
condition is not complied with, whether it was
reasonable at the time of the contract to expect
that compliance with that condition would be
practicable ;

(e) whether the goods were manufactured,
processed, or adapted to the special order of the
buyer.

(6) Subsection (5) above does not prevent the court
from holding, in accordance with any rule of law, that a
term which purports to exclude or restrict any of the
provisions of section 13, 14 or 15 above is not a term of
the contract.

(7) In this section " consumer sale " means a sale of
goods (other than a sale by auction or by competitive
tender) by a seller in the course of a business where the
goods—

(a) are of a type ordinarily bought for private use or
consumption ; and

(b) are sold to a person who does not buy or hold
himself out as buying them in the course of a
business.

(8) The onus of proving that a sale falls to be treated
for the purposes of this section as not being a consumer
sale lies on the party so contending.

(9) Any reference in this section to a term exempting
from all or any of the provisions of any section of this
Act is a reference to a term which purports to exclude
or restrict, or has the effect of excluding or restricting,
the operation of all or any of the provisions of that
section, or the exercise of a right conferred by any provision of that section, or any liability of the seller for
breach of a condition or warranty implied by any provision of that section.

(10) It is hereby declared that any reference in this
section to a term of a contract includes a reference to a
term which although not contained in a contract is
incorporated in the contract by another term of the
contract.

(11) Nothing in this section prevents the parties to a
contract for the international sale of goods from negativing or varying any right, duty or liability which would
otherwise arise by implication of law under sections 12
to 15 above.

(12) In subsection (11) above " contract for the international sale of goods " means a contract of sale of goods made by parties whose places of business (or, if they have none, habitual residences) are in the territories of different States (the Channel Islands and the Isle of Man being treated for this purpose as different States from the United Kingdom) and in the case of which one of the following conditions is satisfied : —

(a) the contract involves the sale of goods which are at the time of the conclusion of the contract in the course of carriage or will be carried from the territory of one State to the territory of another ; or

(b) the acts constituting the offer and acceptance have been effected in the territories of different States ; or

(c) delivery of the goods is to be made in the territory of a State other than that within whose territory the acts constituting the offer and the acceptance have been effected.

Section 55: exclusion of implied terms (ii)

12. In relation to a contract made before 18 May 1973 substitute the following for section 55 : —

Exclusion of implied terms.

55. Where a right, duty or liability would arise under a contract of sale by implication of law, it may be negatived or varied by express agreement, or by the course of dealing between the parties, or by such usage as binds both parties to the contract.

Section 56: conflict of laws

13.—(1) In relation to a contract made on or after 18 May 1973 and before 1 February 1978 substitute for section 56 the section set out in sub-paragraph (3) below.

(2) In relation to a contract made otherwise than as mentioned in sub-paragraph (1) above, ignore section 56 and this paragraph.

(3) The section mentioned in sub-paragraph (1) above is as follows : —

Conflict of laws.

56.—(1) Where the proper law of a contract for the sale of goods would, apart from a term that it should be the law of some other country or a term to the like effect, be the law of any part of the United Kingdom, or where any such contract contains a term which purports to substitute, or has the effect of substituting, provisions of the law of some other country for all or any of the provisions of sections 12 to 15 and 55 above, those sections shall, notwithstanding that term but subject to subsection (2) below, apply to the contract.

(2) Nothing in subsection (1) above prevents the parties to a contract for the international sale of goods from negativing or varying any right, duty or liability which would otherwise arise by implication of law under sections 12 to 15 above.

(3) In subsection (2) above " contract for the international sale of goods " means a contract of sale of goods made by parties whose places of business (or, if they have none, habitual residences) are in the territories of different States (the Channel Islands and the Isle of Man being treated for this purpose as different States from the United Kingdom) and in the case of which one of the following conditions is satisfied : —

(*a*) the contract involves the sale of goods which are at the time of the conclusion of the contract in the course of carriage or will be carried from the territory of one State to the territory of another ; or

(*b*) the acts constituting the offer and acceptance have been effected in the territories of different States ; or

(*c*) delivery of the goods is to be made in the territory of a State other than that within whose territory the acts constituting the offer and the acceptance have been effected.

Section 61(1): *definition of " business " (i)*

14. In relation to a contract made on or after 18 May 1973 and before 1 February 1978, in the definition of " business " in section 61(1) for " or local or public authority " substitute " , local authority or statutory undertaker ".

Section 61(1): *definition of " business " (ii)*

15. In relation to a contract made before 18 May 1973 omit the definition of " business " in section 61(1).

SCHEDULE 2

CONSEQUENTIAL AMENDMENTS

War Risks Insurance Act 1939 (2 & 3 Geo. 6 c.57)

1. In section 15(1)(*e*) of the War Risks Insurance Act 1939 for " section sixty-two of the Sale of Goods Act 1893 " substitute " section 61 of the Sale of Goods Act 1979 ".

Law Reform (Frustrated Contracts) Act 1943 (6 & 7 Geo. 6 c. 40)

2. In section 2(5)(*c*) of the Law Reform (Frustrated Contracts) Act 1943 for " section seven of the Sale of Goods Act 1893 " substitute " section 7 of the Sale of Goods Act 1979 ".

Frustrated Contracts Act (Northern Ireland) 1947 (c.2)

3. In section 2(5)(*c*) of the Frustrated Contracts Act (Northern Ireland) 1947 for " section seven of the Sale of Goods Act 1893 " substitute " section 7 of the Sale of Goods Act 1979 ".

Hire-Purchase Act 1964 (c. 53)

4. In section 27(5) of the Hire-Purchase Act 1964 (as originally enacted and as substituted by Schedule 4 to the Consumer Credit Act 1974)— 1974 c. 39.
   (*a*) in paragraph (*a*) for " section 21 of the Sale of Goods Act 1893 " substitute " section 21 of the Sale of Goods Act 1979 " ;
   (*b*) in paragraph (*b*) for " section 62(1) of the said Act of 1893 " substitute " section 61(1) of the said Act of 1979 ".

Hire-Purchase Act 1965 (c. 66)

5. In section 20 of the Hire-Purchase Act 1965—
   (*a*) in subsection (1) for " Section 11(1)(*c*) of the Sale of Goods Act 1893 " substitute " Section 11(4) of the Sale of Goods Act 1979 " ;
   (*b*) in subsection (3) for " sections 12 to 15 of the Sale of Goods Act 1893 " substitute " sections 12 to 15 of the Sale of Goods Act 1979 ".

6. In section 54 of the Hire-Purchase Act 1965 for " section 25(2) of the Sale of Goods Act 1893 " substitute " section 25(1) of the Sale of Goods Act 1979 ".

7. In section 58(1) of the Hire-Purchase Act 1965 for " the Sale of Goods Act 1893 " substitute " the Sale of Goods Act 1979 ".

Hire-Purchase (Scotland) Act 1965 (c. 67)

8. In section 20 of the Hire-Purchase (Scotland) Act 1965 for " 1893 " substitute " 1979 ".

9. In section 50 of the Hire-Purchase (Scotland) Act 1965 for " section 25(2) of the Sale of Goods Act 1893 " substitute " section 25(1) of the Sale of Goods Act 1979 ".

10. In section 54(1) of the Hire-Purchase (Scotland) Act 1965 for " the Sale of Goods Act 1893 " substitute " the Sale of Goods Act 1979 ".

Hire-Purchase Act (Northern Ireland) 1966 (c. 42)

11. In section 20 of the Hire-Purchase Act (Northern Ireland) 1966—
   (*a*) in subsection (1) for " Section 11(1)(*c*) of the Sale of Goods Act 1893 " substitute " Section 11(4) of the Sale of Goods Act 1979 " ;
   (*b*) in subsection (3) for " 1893 " substitute " 1979 ".

12. In section 54 of the Hire-Purchase Act (Northern Ireland) 1966 for " section 25(2) of the Sale of Goods Act 1893 " substitute " section 25(1) of the Sale of Goods Act 1979 ".

13. In section 62(5) of the Hire-Purchase Act (Northern Ireland) 1966 (as originally enacted and as substituted by Schedule 4 to the Consumer Credit Act 1974)—

(a) in paragraph (a) for " 1893 " substitute " 1979 " ;

(b) in paragraph (b) for " section 62(1) of the said Act of 1893 " substitute " section 61(1) of the said Act of 1979 ".

14. In section 65(1) of the Hire-Purchase Act (Northern Ireland) 1966 for " the Sale of Goods Act 1893 " substitute " the Sale of Goods Act 1979 ".

Uniform Laws on International Sales Act 1967 (c. 45)

15. For section 1(4) of the Uniform Laws on International Sales Act 1967 substitute the following: —

" (4) In determining the extent of the application of the Uniform Law on Sales by virtue of Article 4 thereof (choice of parties)—

(a) in relation to a contract made before 18 May 1973, no provision of the law of any part of the United Kingdom shall be regarded as a mandatory provision within the meaning of that Article ;

(b) in relation to a contract made on or after 18 May 1973 and before 1 February 1978, no provision of that law shall be so regarded except sections 12 to 15, 55 and 56 of the Sale of Goods Act 1979 ;

(c) in relation to a contract made on or after 1 February 1978, no provision of that law shall be so regarded except sections 12 to 15 of the Sale of Goods Act 1979 ".

Supply of Goods (Implied Terms) Act 1973 (c. 13)

16. In section 14(1) of the Supply of Goods (Implied Terms) Act 1973 (as originally enacted and as substituted by Schedule 4 to the Consumer Credit Act 1974) for " Section 11(1)(c) of the principal Act " substitute " Section 11(4) of the Sale of Goods Act 1979 ".

17. For the definition of " consumer sale " in section 15(1) of the Supply of Goods (Implied Terms) Act 1973 substitute —

" consumer sale " has the same meaning as in section 55 of the Sale of Goods Act 1979 (as set out in paragraph 11 of Schedule 1 to that Act).

Consumer Credit Act 1974 (c.39)

18. In section 189(1) of the Consumer Credit Act 1974, in the definition of " goods ", for " section 62(1) of the Sale of Goods Act 1893 " substitute " section 61(1) of the Sale of Goods Act 1979 ".

Unfair Contract Terms Act 1977 (c. 50)

19. In section 6 of the Unfair Contract Terms Act 1977—

(a) in subsection (1)(a) for " section 12 of the Sale of Goods Act 1893 " substitute " section 12 of the Sale of Goods Act 1979 " ;

(*b*) in subsection (2)(*a*) for " section 13, 14 or 15 of the 1893 Act " substitute " section 13, 14 or 15 of the 1979 Act ".

20. In section 14 of the Unfair Contract Terms Act 1977, in the definition of " goods ", for " the Sale of Goods Act 1893 " substitute " the Sale of Goods Act 1979 ".

21. In section 20(1)(*a*) and (2)(*a*) of the Unfair Contract Terms Act 1977 for " 1893 " substitute (in each case) " 1979 ".

22. In section 25(1) of the Unfair Contract Terms Act 1977, in the definition of " goods ", for " the Sale of Goods Act 1893 " substitute " the Sale of Goods Act 1979 ".

SCHEDULE 3

Section 63

REPEALS

Chapter	Short title	Extent of repeal
56 & 57 Vict. c. 71.	Sale of Goods Act 1893.	The whole Act except section 26.
1967 c. 7.	Misrepresentation Act 1967.	Section 4. In section 6(3) the words ", except section 4(2),".
1967 c. 14 (N.I.)	Misrepresentation Act (Northern Ireland) 1967.	Section 4.
1973 c. 13.	Supply of Goods (Implied Terms) Act 1973.	Sections 1 to 7. Section 18(2).
1974 c. 39.	Consumer Credit Act 1974.	In Schedule 4, paragraphs 3 and 4.
1977 c. 50.	Unfair Contract Terms Act 1977.	In Schedule 3, the entries relating to the Sale of Goods Act 1893.

SCHEDULE 4

Section 63.

SAVINGS

Preliminary

1. In this Schedule references to the 1893 Act are to the Sale of Goods Act 1893. 1893 c. 71.

Orders

2. An order under section 14(8) or 25(4) above may make provision that it is to have effect only as provided by the order (being provision corresponding to that which could, apart from this Act, have been made by an order under section 192(4) of the Consumer Credit Act 1974 bringing into operation an amendment 1974 c. 39. or repeal making a change corresponding to that made by the order under section 14(8) or 25(4) above).

SCH. 4

Offences

3. Where an offence was committed in relation to goods before 1 January 1969 or (in the application of this Act to Northern Ireland) 1 August 1969, the effect of a conviction in respect of the offence is not affected by the repeal by this Act of section 24 of the 1893 Act.

1893 Act, section 26

4. The repeal by this Act of provisions of the 1893 Act does not extend to the following provisions of that Act in so far as they are needed to give effect to or interpret section 26 of that Act, namely, the definitions of " goods " and " property " in section 62(1), section 62(2) and section 63 (which was repealed subject to savings by the Statute Law Revision Act 1908).

1908 c. 49.

Things done before 1 January 1894

5. The repeal by this Act of section 60 of and the Schedule to the 1893 Act (which effected repeals and which were themselves repealed subject to savings by the Statute Law Revision Act 1908) does not affect those savings, and accordingly does not affect things done or acquired before 1 January 1894.

6. In so far as the 1893 Act applied (immediately before the operation of the repeals made by this Act) to contracts made before 1 January 1894 (when the 1893 Act came into operation), the 1893 Act shall continue so to apply notwithstanding this Act.

PRINTED IN ENGLAND BY BERNARD M. THIMONT
Controller of Her Majesty's Stationery Office and Queen's Printer of Acts of Parliament

LONDON: PUBLISHED BY HER MAJESTY'S STATIONERY OFFICE

£1·50 net

ISBN 0 10 545479 6

INDEX

INDEX